Land and Spirit
in Native America

Recent titles in
Native America: Yesterday and Today
Bruce E. Johansen, Series Editor

Lethal Encounters: Englishmen and Indians in Colonial Virginia
Alfred A. Cave

George Washington's War on Native America
Barbara Alice Mann

The Native Peoples of North America: A History
Two Volumes
Bruce E. Johansen

Daughters of Mother Earth: The Wisdom of Native American Women
Barbara Alice Mann, editor

Iroquois on Fire: A Voice from the Mohawk Nation
Douglas M. George-Kanentiio

Native America, Discovered and Conquered: Thomas Jefferson,
Lewis & Clark, and Manifest Destiny
Robert J. Miller

The Praeger Handbook on Contemporary Issues in Native America
Volume 1: Linguistic, Ethnic, and Economic Revival
Volume 2: Legal, Cultural, and Environmental Revival
Bruce E. Johansen

The Tainted Gift: The Disease Method of Frontier Expansion
Barbara Alice Mann

Frontier Newspapers and the Coverage of the Plains Indian Wars
Hugh J. Reilly

Land and Spirit in Native America

∾

Joy Porter

NATIVE AMERICA: YESTERDAY AND TODAY
Bruce E. Johansen, Series Editor

 PRAEGER

AN IMPRINT OF ABC-CLIO, LLC
Santa Barbara, California • Denver, Colorado • Oxford, England

Library of Congress Cataloging-in-Publication Data

Porter, Joy, 1967–
    Land and spirit in native america / Joy Porter.
        p. cm. — (Native America: yesterday and today)
    Includes bibliographical references and index.
        ISBN 978–0–313–35606–3 (hardcopy : alk. paper) — ISBN 978–0–313–35607–0 (ebook)
1. Indians of North America—Religion. 2. Indian philosophy—North America. 3. Indigenous peoples—Ecology—North America. 4. Traditional ecological knowledge—North America. I. Title.
E98.R3P66   2012
299.7—dc23   2012010979

ISBN: 978–0–313–35606–3
EISBN: 978–0–313–35607–0

16 15 14 13 12   1 2 3 4 5

This book is also available on the World Wide Web as an eBook.
Visit www.abc-clio.com for details.

Praeger
An Imprint of ABC-CLIO, LLC

ABC-CLIO, LLC
130 Cremona Drive, P.O. Box 1911
Santa Barbara, California 93116-1911

This book is printed on acid-free paper (∞)

Manufactured in the United States of America

For John Fadden,
Six Nations Indian Museum,
Onchiota, New York

and for Leonard Peltier,
Hello in there, hello.

and in respectful remembrance of the loss to the FBI and to their families
of Agents Jack Coler and Ronald Williams;
and of the loss to his family and people of Joe Killsright Stuntz;
each of whom died at Pine Ridge, June 26, 1975.

Contents

Acknowledgments

❦

A number of debts were incurred in the writing of this book. The first and largest is to the series editor who suggested I produce it, the distinguished author of over 20 books on Indian and environmental themes Bruce E. Johansen, Jacob J. Isaacson Research Professor of Communication and Native American Studies at the University of Nebraska at Omaha. While he is in no way responsible for any shortcomings found within this volume, it was in large part inspired by his work, particularly *The Dirty Dozen: Toxic Chemicals and the Earth's Future* (2003) and *Ecocide of Native America: Environmental Destruction of Indian Lands and Peoples* (1995), co-authored with Donald A. Grinde.

The artwork in this volume by educator, illustrator, and painter John Fadden would not have appeared without the help of the artist Dave Kanietakeran Fadden of the Wolf Clan of the Mohawk Community of Akwesasne. For this he has my abiding gratitude. Thank you also to the editor of this book at Praeger, Kim Kennedy White.

Thank you to the attendees at the "Art Across Frontiers" symposium organized by Dr. Stephanie Lethwaite at the University of Nottingham, April 2011, under the auspices of the TERRA Foundation for American Art. Particular thanks are due to Grace Hampton, Professor of Art, Art Education, and Integrative Arts at Penn State, Pennsylvania and to Elizabeth Hutchinson, Assistant Professor of Art History, Barnard College/Columbia University.

Thank you also to James Luna of the La Jolla Reservation, Northern San Diego County, California and to Martha Anne Parker of Naples, New York.

Thanks are due to Professor James Kari of the Alaska Native Language Center at the University of Alaska Fairbanks and to Professor Alan Borass of Kenai

Peninsula College, Alaska. Thank you to Professor of Anthropology Ray Hames of the University of Nebraska; to Brian Wynne, Professor of Science Studies at the Centre for the Study of the Environment at Lancaster University, U.K.; and to the Virginia-based independent election analyst Dr. Rhodes Cook. Thank you also to my dear friend and colleague Professor Lee Schweninger of the Department of English, University of North Carolina, Wilmington. Thank you also to the independent scholar and writer Valerie Kuletz and to Kenneth Roemer of the University of Texas at Arlington. Thank you also to the ex-aerospace engineer Phil Catchesides of Gower, Wales.

An appreciation of land and spirit is something that benefits from being passed down the generations, so here I thank my father who tells stories about the fairy tree that grew next to the family home and who taught me to plant acorns and notice stones in the once-great oak grove of Derry, Northern Ireland. Thanks also to my elder brother John Porter and his wife Anne Chun of Pigeon Lake, Toronto who were most kind hosts during some of the writing of this book.

My deepest thanks are to my husband Jan Simons of Gower, Wales, to the distinguished wildlife expert M. R. Porter, and to young Artur Porter-Simons who is forever seeing "bootifu sky."

Series Editor's Foreword

∽

In 2006, Joy Porter asked me to speak at the "American Indian Workshop," a humbly named but rather large annual gathering of Europeans, Asians, and Americans who have an interest in Native American Studies. She was coordinating the event for that year on her campus, the University of Wales at Swansea, U.K. She also framed the conference's theme: "Place in Native American History, Literature, and Culture."

At first, I was taken aback. "Place?" What did "place" have to do with "Native American History, Literature, and Culture"? I gave the title some thought and suddenly realized: "Just about everything." The title touched on one of Dr. Joy Porter's premier strengths: as a European, sometimes sees forests where the rest of us see trees.

Professor Porter's *Land and Spirit in Native America* touches on many of the themes from that conference as she focuses on some of the most important and fundamental questions within human experience—what is land, how does it differ from landscape, what is space, and what is place? All of this is couched in a context that compares and contrasts European and Native American perspectives with a contemporary cast invoking environmental crisis. Her narrative leads to a discussion of what is unique about Indian environmentalism, and what it has to offer everyone.

Language is important to this inquiry. Beware the nineteenth-century diminishment of Native American political economies as "tribes," rather than nations or confederacies; English (and United States) real estate law allows usurpation for "highest and best use," usually for "settled" industrial or agricultural uses, over traditional, loose-knit Native American land tenure. Bear in mind that many native nations and groups of nations had settlements for hundreds or thousands of years before diseases, alcohol, invading armies, and other maladies reduced their populations by as much as 90 percent. In the linguistics of place, if we are honest, we will acknowledge that the immigrants were the nomads.

Part of conquest by language involves the appropriation of names. The sacred Mount Tacquoma, for example (one of many), was renamed for a British mariner (Rainier), as its name was anglicized and applied to a city (Tacoma). Dakota, Lakota, and Nakota, native peoples of the U.S. Northern Plains, became the names of states, while the immigrants called the people "Sioux," a truncated old French word for "snake," or "enemy." The map of North America abounds with such name appropriations.

Dr. Porter's book presents a study of contrasting perceptions, including a fascinating critique of Western religion vis a vis native spiritual beliefs. She traces the anthropocentrism at the heart of Christian beliefs back to the Bible and to the Old Testament idea that God granted humankind dominion over the earth and its creatures. The Old Testament makes humans superior, as the only creatures made in the European God's image. The Christian God then instructs man to "Be fruitful, and multiply, and replenish the earth, and subdue it: and have dominion over the fish of the sea, and over the fowl of the air, and over every living thing that moveth upon the earth" (Genesis, 1:28, King James Version).

Native American spiritual beliefs, those not yet mixed with Christianity, on the other hand, are not human-centered, but expressive of a great mystery, and a relationship with the Earth and its creatures that is less hierarchical. This duality also appears in attitudes toward the natural world. Before it was tamed in national parks as a tourist experience, "wilderness" was a forbidding place to the immigrants, home of "savages," a word that shorn of connotation, means, in old French, people who lived in the woods. In contrast, as Luther Standing Bear wrote, "We did not think of the great open plains, the beautiful rolling hills, and winding streams with tangled growth, as 'wild'. Only to the white man was nature a wilderness and only to him was the land 'infested' with 'wild' animals and 'savage' people. To us it was tame. Earth was bountiful..."[1]

As America industrialized, Porter writes, "wilderness in the dominant, non-Indian culture, became bound up with nostalgia for a mythic and supposedly regenerative frontier past. Instead of seeming untamably wild, deserted and frightening it now appeared inexpressibly beautiful, indeed as the precious sanctuary for Americans now increasingly brow-beaten by the woes of burgeoning city life. Once seen as the no-man's lands where Satan had free play, they were now recontextualized as the opposite, as holy sites, places offering special access to the transcendent and the divine. Wild places came to be seen as the sanctuary of the American individual." The Sierra Club was born as a hiking association. It has suffered factional splits between people who wish to maintain that focus and those who advocate a broader ecological view.

Dr. Porter describes how, to put America's "natural" cathedrals on tourist maps, Native peoples were aggressively dispossessed and their treaty rights ignored. The National Park Service picked up policies of removal and Indian cultural erosion that had begun in the previous decades by the American army. After 1850, the most conventionally beautiful and sacred parts of what had been known as "Indian country," including Yosemite, Yellowstone, Mt. Rainier, Crater Lake, Mesa Verde, Olympic, Grand Canyon, Glacier, and Rocky Mountain, had all been designated "wilderness" and their Indian peoples displaced.[2] The result was a human-centered "wilderness."

The rationalism of science tended to perpetuate a human-centered worldview, although the science of ecology has, recently, evolved a view of humanity as part of a natural web, much closer to Native American ideas. Porter warns that the "environmental-justice movement" is still rather anthropogenic, however. "The environmental justice movement again puts humans at the center of environmental discourse, redefining the environment since the late twentieth century as 'the place you work, the place you live, the place you play'. Some mainstream environmentalists argue that this replicates the same thinking that caused environmental despoliation in the first place." With tens of thousands of animal species in danger of extinction, many due to human actions (logging, ranching, mining, over-fishing, etc.), environmentalism as a solely human story is sorely incomplete.

Today, malign human influence envelops the Earth. Witness global warming and chemical toxicity, among other problems. Porter asserts that "as ecological problems dangerously accelerate, we are witnessing yet another mainstream shift whose ultimate features are as yet undecided. The hope is that our twenty-first century understanding of nature, of wilderness, of land will be informed by indigenous thinking and that we will have the courage to re-assess ideas and approaches that were previously taken for granted." The most acute analysis of environmental change must, argues Porter, take a broad view: "Environmental woes cannot be separated analytically from capitalism and in particular from the fact that an increasingly small number of people now control American wealth." Native America and its views can and will be used to influence a system at its roots.

Bruce E. Johansen

Introduction

Curiously, at a time of global climatic threat when indigenous peoples the world over are facing unprecedented attacks on their land and cultures, it has become fashionable for otherwise benign analysts to belittle hunter-gatherers of the past and with them the whole notion of indigenous ecological awareness in any era. It seems now that nothing is more ludicrous than the idea that indigenous populations of the past had any better ideas about relating to the earth's finite resources than dominant non-Indian cultures do today. By extension contemporary indigenous populations, when they are considered at all, are deemed to have little involvement in or possible contribution to make to the most pressing concerns of our age: climate change and man's accelerating despoliation of the earth. Perhaps this is a symptom of the current precedence of baby-boomer scholars who find themselves today in a position to disparage the once-fashionable ideas and stereotypes perpetuated by the mainstream during their own youth. It may also be a symptom of a new dawn for non-indigenous science and for certain types of scientistic thinking. We live, after all, at a time when science is set to dominate research, publishing, and scholarship as never before.

To illustrate, let us briefly consider the recent book *The Better Angels of Our Nature: The Decline of Violence in History and Its Causes* by the acclaimed Harvard evolutionary psychologist-turned-historian Steven Pinker.[1] Pinker's is a large but amusing and jauntily readable book, reminiscent with its comforting take on certain baby-boomer mores and values of another bestselling American baby-boomer tome, Robert Putnam's *Bowling Alone*. There is little need to revisit the wider criticisms of Pinker's Whiggish peon to progress, liberal humanism, and highly selective aspects of Western Enlightenment here, especially since the

British political philosopher John Gray has already done such a perhaps unnecessarily forceful job in *Prospect* magazine, but it is useful to add to them by looking closely at the book's simplistic and totalizing misrepresentation of indigenous people.[2]

Better Angels seeks to shock us with the news that we live in an unprecedented era of comparative peace between states, a peace the book claims has been brought about by "the civilising process." Few indigenous peoples will be surprised by this since they know that Europe's settler states (in Latin America, Australia, South America, and the United States) enjoy a peaceful prosperity now that is based on the violent annihilation of their "non-state" ancestors in the past. Such was the nature of Western "civilizing" but its specifics are not something Pinker's book chooses to grapple with. This is perhaps because the numbers of deaths through colonization are heavily contested and because the nature of colonial violence is myriad and complex. For example, progressive starvation imposed through deliberate destruction of the animals, flora, and fauna needed for subsistence or denial through forced migration of access to that means of subsistence is violent. Pinker ignores this complexity and instead, in order to prove that world-wide violence has been declining since the development of settled agriculture some 10,000 years ago, adjusts the statistics he selects on the past to a twentieth-century base and defines violence solely as sudden and violent death. He is probably right that violence so selectively defined has decreased, but wrong to downplay colonialism's impact and to imply that native and/or tribal peoples are confined to the early "stages" of human development.

Overall, Pinker's book resurrects a nonindigenous debate that was perhaps most current in the eighteenth century, the question of whether "primitive" peoples were or were not "noble savages." They were not then, of course, nor are they now. Regrettably, Pinker once again wrongly links Jean-Jacques Rousseau's complex corpus to the noble savage phrase and ambiguous myth.[3] He ignores Rousseau's arguments about the human animal and his comparatively recent alienation from the natural world—ideas and thought-experiments that are actually as generative and significant today as they ever were. Rousseau knew "Human nature does not go backwards, and one can never return to the times of innocence and equality when one has left them," but he sensed correctly that our need to create some sense of "post-natural" unity of the self was not a problem about to disappear.[4] To serve the thesis that violence has declined over time due to modernity—which Pinker defines as a globally positive "erosion of family, tribe, tradition and religion"—he conflates all hunter-gatherer and "non-state" societies wherever situated across time. Carefully selecting his sources and ignoring specific military, cultural, and colonizing contexts, he paints a salacious and incendiary picture of indigenous brutality, mixing data from the most unreliable sources in ethnography—nonindigenous captivity narratives. Those chosen describe capture in the Amazon in the 1930s and Australia in 1852. Pinker also quotes an Iñupiaq Inuit memory of indigenous sexual violence from 1965 that is pornographically extreme. Given the paucity of records on indigenous inter-tribal sexual violence, this record must have taken quite a bit of searching for, even if it may titillate some.[5] Few contemporary thinkers still agree with Konrad Lorenz's rosy mid-1960s picture of hunter-gatherer and simple horticulturalist conflict being limited and ritualized, so Pinker's recognition of the fact that indigenous people have always been as capable of violence as any other set of human beings in similar strategic and political contexts is hardly news.[6] Unfortunately, *Better Angels'* description of early indigenous cannibalism is as devoid of context and as historically superficial as much of the book's other references to tribal or indigenous peoples, many of which are also in the ethnographic present tense.[7] While all of the above is problematic, Pinker's is still an enormous and thought-provoking book. It is comforting to be reassured that the sacrifices of the past have been worthwhile and that the current long global peace may last in this nuclear age. Even so, the Chinese premier Zhou Enaia's comment about the impact of the 1968 French riots comes to mind. In terms of declaring a wholly new era, it is in fact probably "too soon to say."

Pinker's Panglossian[8] faith in "the civilising process" is at the heart of what is the latest in a long line of well-received books that spend time examining competing stereotypes of indigenous people but which tend to avoid engaging meaningfully with indigenous thinking itself either in philosophical, ecological, or cultural terms. Pinker's approach in this regard is part of an often-confused new orthodoxy that has been in place at least since 1991 following the publication of Kent Redford's "The Ecologically Noble Savage." Here Redford challenged romantic notions about indigenous peoples across time and made the seemingly innocuous statement that "[They] behaved as humans do now: they did whatever they had to do to feed themselves."[9] The remark and Redford's article caused uproar, in part because ideas about an inherent and essential blanket conservationist ethic within indigenous cultures across time are hard to separate from indigenous claims for social justice—social justice that ironically Redford's article had made a strong case for in the Amazonian context. Of course, the suggestion that native people have not and do not match externally (and sometimes internally) imposed stereotypes has always tended to shock and consequently to sell well—the best known recent examples being Shepherd Krech's 1999 book, *The Ecological Indian*, and Jared Diamond's 2003 *Collapse: How Societies Choose To Succeed or Fail*.

The debate about whether indigenous peoples have ever lived up to an external ecological stereotype continues, but it is possible to summarize the best thinking within it. This is especially useful for what follows in this book, so here I make clear at the outset what is generally agreed upon in terms of thinking about indigeneity, land, and spirit in America. Most thinkers recognize that indigenous peoples of the past were not universally conservationists in the Western sense although it is thought that most pre-contact native peoples harvested sustainably. It is also generally acknowledged that there may have been indigenous systems of "true" conservation that were destroyed by contact. "True" conservation in this context is thought of as conservation carried out deliberately with a "realistic" rather than ritualistic or spiritually based understanding of resource depletion. It is generally recognized that native peoples had, and in many cases continue to have, a unique ecological awareness and understanding of complex environmental interactions. This has been documented by traditional ecological knowledge (TEK) and by ethnoecology for decades. Furthermore, almost no one disputes that in the past Euro-Americans wreaked more ecological damage than Native Americans. From the above we can see that Pinker has not deeply engaged with what has been called the "ecologically noble savage debate." However, like a number of other commentators, he has dealt solely with what has been quantified, however contested the data, and ignored the spiritual and cultural.[10]

This is perhaps not surprising in Pinker's specific case since he could be described as an evangelical atheist. Thus in *Better Angels* he dismisses the Bible as a "wiki" and pays minimal attention to the role of West's religious heritage in fostering its supposed vanguard role in bringing about global peace.[11] In this rejection and/or avoidance of serious discussion of things spiritual he is representative of many serious thinkers. The academy, the collective entity that constitutes the community of scholars, is largely secular. This may or may not explain the great wealth of books that have been produced exploring American spirituality in the more distant past—in colonial, early national, and antebellum America, and the much smaller and less influential amount of scholarship produced about religion in America after 1870. Yet as Jon Butler, perhaps the foremost contemporary scholar of American religion, has explained, for some reason the intellectual interpretative mainstream finds religion in modern America a special challenge, deeming it "more anomalous than normal and more innocuous than powerful."[12] Yet like Butler, I feel that the spiritual life of Americans has always been important and that the new forms it has taken post-1870 matter greatly. Although increasingly privatized, American faith is a dinosaur, as H. L. Mencken put it, which refuses to die and is just too significant to ignore.[13] While some of the early American studies scholars such as Perry Miller and Kenneth Murdock recognized this as well as a few inspiring contemporary thinkers such as Susan L. Mizruchi, mostly religion has not received the attention it so clearly merits as a central category for understanding modern culture.[14] If comparatively few of the most lauded American history books have considered religion post-1870, even fewer have connected American forms of transcendent belief to environmental concerns. Instead, examination of such a connection has instead been more readily taken up by literary scholars, as John Gatta in his valuable 2004 book, *Making Nature Sacred: Literature, Religion and Environment in America from the Puritans to the Present*. Few scholars have looked in depth at the differing ways those sometimes called the first Americans—Native American Indians, and successive waves of colonists—have understood and related spiritually to American land. This lack, not least since 1870, is what this book seeks to address.

Such an analysis is important now as never before, since for us to successfully tackle the challenges resulting from climate change and unprecedented levels of global population, we need to understand the roots of our thinking about our fundamental resource and the most likely platform for all future life—land. We need to understand how values, beliefs, and ideas that transcend the rational have informed our approach to the environment and to understand how native and non-native ways have influenced each other on American soil. By taking the long view and by making native ideas about land and spirituality as central as those of certain settler generations, we have much to learn, not least a new awareness of how the life of spirit has always profoundly informed our approach to land and to each other as ethnic groups. It is hoped that by unpicking the threads that have led to the current environmental challenges within the United States, we may find the seeds for better thinking in the future—thinking that values rather than supplants Native America and that comprehends the conscious and unconscious spiritual underpinnings to our relationships with American land. The idea of learning lessons from history or of learning environmental lessons from any discrete set of peoples has now been so deeply problematized that it is almost intellectually unsustainable. Yet Indian history, literature, spirituality, and culture holds much that is too valuable to ignore, not least the native experience of what it means to live with profound environmental and spiritual loss. These kinds of loss are increasingly shared by us all.

It is not argued here that native thinking about American land is always and necessarily better than Euro-American thinking, rather it is suggested that a close examination of each is fruitful and important if we are to think anew about the most pressing issues of the future. The foremost challenges of the twenty-first century will be those of responding to the losses caused by environmental degradation and population pressure coupled with larger pressures stemming from new global patterns of wealth and resource distribution. Indigenous peoples have been coping with such pressures in acute form for generations. They have developed strategies for coping with environmental damage, cultural engulfment, and forced migration that have much to teach those of us who are only now beginning to feel the impact of the global step-change in our relationships to land, resources, and peoples that occurred post-Enlightenment. Indian peoples may be only around 1.7 percent of the current U.S. population (projected to be 2% in 2050 having grown a remarkable 18.4% from 2000 to 2010) but the significance of their philosophical, spiritual, and for want of a better word, ecological ideas, far outweighs their statistical presence.[15] The persistence of those ideas is in itself testimony to a set of peoples' unprecedented ability to survive while facing material, physical, spiritual, and cultural onslaught over generations.

There are well over 4.1 million Native American Indian peoples alive today, but their histories and their future should not be considered in isolation from a much larger number, that of the world's estimated 300 million indigenous people spread across more than 70 countries.[16] This broader indigenous context is instructive. Should we for a moment think that an indigenous identity necessarily equates to ecological virtue or that an indigenous spiritual understanding somehow transcends the usual gritty realities of contemporary politics, we need only consider for a moment the current furor surrounding one of the world's most powerful indigenous politicians, Bolivia's president Evo Morales. Elected to great fanfare in 2005, Morales, an Aymara Indian, promised to end centuries of racial discrimination against the indigenous. Once in power he spoke passionately in international contexts on behalf of what he calls Pachamama—"Mother Earth." Today his supporters are in uproar at his support of the building of a 185-mile road through the heart of the Isiboro-Sécure Indigenous Territory and National Park (Tipnis)—Amazonian rainforest teeming with biodiversity. Critics claim Morales is favoring the interests of one set of indigenous peoples against another, notably the Chiman, Yurucare, and Moxos peoples who live by farming, fishing, and hunting on the 12,000 sq km reserve. These groups claim to have not been consulted about the road and fear that it will open up their lands up to illegal logging and illegal cocoa-growing for cocaine. Recently, a number of the around one thousand individuals who were making a long-distance protest about the road by walking to La Paz were brutally attacked by government riot police. As so many voters have learned over time to their chagrin, a candidate's ethnic identity, racial affiliation, or gender is not *in itself* a fail-safe indicator of their future actions when in power.[17] For Bolivia and its socialist leader, squaring a circle that encompasses indigenous and environmental concerns, an economy dependent on the export of natural resources, and the influence of a powerful neighbor—Brazil—who is funding the building of the road is an almost impossible task. We would do well, therefore, when approaching the topic of land and spirit in America to remain vigilant of context in historical, cultural, and social terms, and of the complexities of power and its application.

There is a great deal more to native thinking about land and the appropriate spiritual and philosophical approach to it than the oft-repeated Iroquois edict that a people should think, plan, and act with an acute awareness of the impact "seven generations hence," yet the idea is pivotal. It encapsulates an awareness of community, of history, and of social morality shared by a number of Indian communities that has been compromised by forces external and internal to them intent on resource extraction and profit across a deep time frame. It is important to recognize that rather than having disappeared or been ossified in time, Indian peoples have shared the story of modernity with each of the other ethnic groups within America. If anything they been at the vanguard of environmental change, negotiating with the powerful and with global forces tied to capitalism in order to survive on and sustain American land both on and off reservations. In a real sense theirs is the story of the future, since all of us with a specific affinity to the land will increasingly have to fight analogous battles and make equally unpalatable choices about a nuclear future, about resource allocation, about spatial hierarchies of development, and about environmental preservation versus community development. In addressing these issues Indian peoples have proven themselves to be neither spiritual giants nor commercial pygmies intent on regression to a mythical pre-contact environmental idyll. Rather, their responses have been as varied as those of any set of communities when faced with comparable challenges. Yet it is argued here that knowledge of those responses and knowledge of their spiritual underpinnings is vital to allow us all to respond positively to the environmental challenges of the future. This is because a community's spiritual framework plays an important role in informing responses to environmental change, whether that framework is simply part of the social and historical matrix of a community or whether it directly and obviously informs decision making.

In one sense it is surprising that so few previous books have explored how Indians and Euro-Americans have related spiritually to land given that the most celebrated modern scholars have put much energy into warning the thinking man or woman about the dangers of ignoring the life of the spirit. Their calls that we return to pondering things spiritual have, if anything, grown stronger as the modern or what some prefer to think of as successive modernities have taken root. The French sociologist Émile Durkheim wrote in 1895 of "the essential role played by religion in social life" and in his work returned repeatedly to the relationship between religion and morality.[18] His contemporary Max Weber, betraying Christian influences in his language, fretted that modern intellectual culture had eaten from "the tree of knowledge" and had lost its access to meaning. Without the life of the spirit, he foresaw a profound "disenchantment of the world."[19] In *The Protestant Ethic and the Spirit of Capitalism* Weber expressed his fear that we moderns had removed from our lives the ingredients needed to live a replete and "satiated" life. Without access to what was sacred we could be nothing more, he said, than "specialists without spirit, sensualists without heart."[20]

Thus this book seeks to tap the recent thirst for analysis of space (not just events) and for analysis of the religious and spiritual (not just the political and social). It makes no claims to be all-encompassing—tribally, politically, or analytically—or to offer a synoptic overview of either theme, but it is interdisciplinary, incorporating Indian philosophy, history, art, and literature so as to give the reader a coherent and up-to-date look at those who have had most to say about the relationship between Indian peoples, land, and spirit across time. The book's overall emphases span from contact through the nineteenth and twentieth centuries to the discussion of future trends within Indian and non-Indian approaches. As happens perhaps too infrequently within American letters, this book does not shy away from discussion of how science, politics, theory, and scholarly analysis interact and/or fail to connect.

It is a book as much about Euro-America as it is about Native America, for in delineating what is unique about Indian approaches to American land, it necessarily explores the roots of our Euro-American understanding of man's relationship to the earth. These issues have taken on a new urgency of late as forms of environmentalism move intellectually, socially, and politically closer to the center stage, but it has always been the case that some of the best writers on ecological themes in the United States have also written on Indian themes. In fact, if there is one idea that binds most of us who have an interest in native issues together, it is not environmentalism per se, but the idea that land and the spiritual life of specific communities are indissolubly linked.[21] Thus this book stands firmly in opposition to the resounding dismissal of the spiritual and of nature advocated by commentators on climate change such as Director of the London School of Economics Anthony Giddens. In a confused paragraph in his recent largely commendable 2011 book, *The Politics of Climate Change*, he writes: "We must disavow any remaining forms of mystical reverence for nature, including the more limited versions which shift the centre of values away from human beings to the earth itself—tackling global warming has nothing to do with saving the earth, which will survive whatever we do. Living in harmony with the earth, respecting the earth, respecting nature—these ideas fall into the same category." For Giddens, respect for nature equates to a nostalgic and impossible quest to turn back time; instead he advocates "push[ing] the boundaries of the end of nature further."[22] This is a limited understanding both of nature and its material and spiritual enormity and, as knowledge of native peoples living with the reality of radioactive landscapes would make clear, of how earth can indeed fail to survive or be rendered in such a state as to preclude future birth and regeneration.

Giddens's fundamental point, that we can and should separate the earth from how we conceptualize man's future, is flawed and, more importantly, unlikely to help generate the kind of support for meaningful globally coordinated change his book calls for. The United States is a profoundly religious and spiritual nation, and it will by necessity be forced to play a determinant role in addressing climate change even if federal action in this regard has been limited to date. Currently the United States consumes a colossal 25 percent of global energy a year and pumps out 20 percent of the world's carbon emissions. Changing American behavior and garnering support for climate change governance is unlikely to be achieved without taking American relationships and understandings of land and spirit seriously. This becomes more obvious when we explore American political and religious relationships to climate change. A majority of American Republican voters are highly religious as defined by church attendance and, as a 2010 poll showed, only sixteen percent of Republican voters think climate change is real, caused by human activity, and dangerous, compared to over 50 percent of Democratic voters.[23] In sum, on a policy and intellectual level, we dismiss the life of the spirit and its links to our relationships to nature and the earth at our peril. It is also worth noting that the world's indigenous peoples and in turn their understandings of nature and man's relationship to it are a key constituent of what former World Bank economist Paul Collier dubs the bottom billion of the world's poor. These are the people who have been left out of the bonanza of prosperity enjoyed by the world's industrializing nations and who hold the key to any future plateau for global population levels and, arguably, for sustained world peace.[24]

This book's opening chapter gives the reader an orientating discussion of the roots of the main oppositions within Native American Indian and Euro-American thought about land and spirituality. It begins by defining each of the book's key terms and then using Yosemite as a touchstone, problematizes wilderness as an idea. Chapter two investigates the limitations of middle way thinking in books such as William Cronon's *Uncommon Ground*. So as to exemplify those limitations, it looks at the history and nature of Euro-American parks and gardening. It concludes by considering aspects of Native American Indian thinking in relation to land, exploring how this thinking relates to a series of contemporary scholarly debates. The book's third chapter ponders why Native American indigenous thinking about land and spirit has not received the attention it deserves. It traces the reasons back to the earliest settler expectations and preconceptions about the "New World" and to the loss within the West of a sense of enchantment and of a related sense of relationship to nature. The chapter concludes with a closer look at the idea of balance within indigenous hunting communities, at how animism is reflected in language, and at an instructive contemporary conflict between ecological activists and native peoples intent on asserting their sovereign right to hunt whale.

Chapter four looks at how the Indian imagination was initially thought about by European settlers. It explores the curious exchange that early European settlers imagined whereby Indian land and resources could be appropriated and Indians compensated with abstract European spiritual riches. It concludes with an examination of the Native American literary imagination today, arguing that profound sets of relationship to land, to nature, and to the idea of "home" persist in Indian country and continue meaningfully to develop. The book's fifth chapter is about Native American Indian art, land, and spirit. It makes language central to its analysis and explores how notions of authenticity have both limited and enabled Indian art across time. It argues that Indian art is enormous, capable both of encompassing relationships to the "authentic," the spiritual, and nature however defined and/or of transcending or ignoring them. Chapter six connects the nonindigenous, spiritually anthropocentric ideas explored in the book's first chapter to aspects of environmental justice in Native America. It explores the thinking that underpins the creation and expansion of National Sacrifice Areas on Indian lands as a result of the nuclear industry and spends time considering and contrasting a spectrum of scientific, native, and non-native relationships to nuclear power and toxic risk. It concludes by urging the reader to seek out the widest possible context when considering issues of environmental justice in Native America. It exemplifies this need by taking a close look at a recent *National Geographic* article that presented a series of Indian land projects as uncomplex examples of Indian environmentalism when in fact multiple larger determining political and resource issues were also at play.

Chapter seven again urges us to consider broader context, this time in terms of how the Indian presence on American land has been and is currently recorded and debated. It explores how Indians have vanished and reappeared across time, within debates over numbers at contact and via changes connected to U.S. census enumeration. The chapter concludes with discussion of future problems associated with blood quantum as a means of registering Indian identity and, rather grimly, of some of the main reasons how and why today's native peoples die. This book's final chapter asks us to think about the future. It considers why we are so resistant to making the major changes needed to address the implications of climate change and explores the remarkable persistence of outdated ideas about wilderness. It does this by analyzing the 2007 film of the life of the young outdoorsman Chris McCandless called *Into the Wild*, exploring the conflagration of thinking that created a superficially counter-cultural but in environmental terms, flawed film. This book ends with an evaluation of how a variety of contemporary voices are thinking about land and nature and its relationship to mankind. It closes with the hope that the diversity of indigenous thinking on land and spirit and the history of its reception in the past will begin to inform the debates that inevitably will dictate all our futures on what the Iroquois call Turtle Island.

As the above makes clear, this book is intent on crossing boundaries. It makes a deliberate attempt to bring Indian concerns and Indian thinking out of comparative intellectual isolation and into direct relationship with some of the things that matter most to everyone today—how to maintain life on earth, how to manage nuclear energy and toxic risk, and how to grow as a species through understanding ourselves and our history.

CHAPTER 1

❧

Approaches to Spirituality,
Tradition, Land, Wilderness, Nature,
Landscape, and Place

The idea of nature contains, though often unnoticed, an extraordinary amount of human history.

—Raymond Williams, *"Ideas of Nature,"* 1980.[1]

Unless we understand the history which produced us, we are determined by that history; we may be determined in any event, but the understanding gives us a chance.

— Yvor Winters, *Forms of Discovery: Critical and Historical Essays on the Forms of the Short Poem in English,* 1967.[2]

*A*t the start of an intellectual journey it is appropriate to begin at the beginning, in this case with the very terms used to describe land and spirit in America. Therefore this book begins with an initial consideration of what spirituality means, how the term differs from religion as it is commonly understood and how it might be defined. We consider what a spiritual tradition is and reasons why the term tradition is significant in the Native American context and important to retain. This chapter then addresses in outline some of the fundamental questions within human experience—what is land, what is wilderness, and what is place?

Having established some of the above and found a way through the larger points of contention, this chapter considers whether and how these foundational ideas relate to varieties of Indian thinking. It explores whether we can isolate ways in which Indian approaches differ from non-Indian ones. This leads inevitably to a discussion of what is unique about Indian environmentalism and to recognition of the irritating double bind that confronts Indian intellectuals and spokespeople when they speak and write their views on this globally important topic. Too often they find themselves confronting conflicting necessities, on the one hand the need to subvert the stereotypes tying all things Indian to "nature" in a simplistic, ahistorical, and racist fashion and on the other, the need to articulate the abiding centrality of land and spirit within Indian life. Navigating this historical and rhetorical catch twenty-two is essential work, not least lest future generations find themselves condemned to slowly learning things to do with land and spirit that many Indian communities have always known and which now more than ever need greater exposure. This is not to suggest that Indian thinking about any of the above is homogenous. To the contrary, Indian approaches to land, to nature, however defined, and to place are as varied as Indian societies always have been and remain.

Perhaps inevitably, as this chapter closes we will be forced to acknowledge that much about how approaches to land, landscape, and nature have been understood over time has primarily reflected the changing thinking of the dominant Euro-American society. One of its greatest shifts has been from seeing nature as [*connects to*] transcendent and sublime in the nineteenth century, to viewing it as recreational [*whites*] and consumable in the twentieth. As ecological problems dangerously accelerate [*reading*] in the twenty-first century, we are witnessing yet another mainstream shift whose ultimate features are as yet undecided. The hope is that our twenty-first century understanding of nature, of wilderness, and of land will be informed by indigenous thinking and that we all will have the courage to reassess ideas and approaches that were previously taken for granted.

ON SPIRITUALITY AND TRADITION

This book uses the larger term spirituality rather religion. It does so even though the term "spirituality" has suffered considerable intellectual attack. A number of theorists have derided it as being "fuzzy" and "a word that encompasses obscurity with a passion."[3] Yet spirituality is useful and rightly defended by many other thinkers because of its fluidity and the fact that it allows for discussion of a wide range of experiences that are rejected by many conservative religious traditions. In contrast to the word "religion," spirituality is a broader, more inclusive term to use when discussing Native American belief systems since it is more to do with a person's beliefs, values, and behavior than to do with a person's involvement in a religious tradition and institution. On top of all of this, in popular usage the term religion has suffered in relation to the larger term spirituality in the last 15 years or so. More of us, it would seem, are comfortable with the term spirituality and less happy to use a bounded term like religion.[4]

Certainly, when it comes to discussing Native American spirituality using the term religion has its inherent problems. The Western word "religion" sits uneasily with indigenous spiritual practices and traditions that number in the hundreds and have their own associated ritual systems and applications to everyday life. A number of indigenous communities actively discourage use of the term in conjunction with their beliefs because their spirituality constitutes a seamless part of their being in a way the term "religion" simply cannot encompass. The word comes from the Latin *religio*, which translates as "obligation" or "bond." The Oxford English Dictionary defines it as "the human recognition of super-human controlling power, and especially of a personal God or gods entitled to obedience or worship." Such a definition is more appropriate to theistic religions like Christianity, Judaism, and Islam than to indigenous American forms of spirituality which may include Shamanism (however defined) and often a fundamental orientation toward the natural world as well as respect for a pervasive, cosmic force or principle.[5] Even if we reduce the definition of religion to perhaps its most basic, the idea that it involves simply belief in a nonmaterial dimension, we still run into difficulties. This is because "religion" is unable to embrace the fundamental significance of place and of cultural community within indigenous spiritual traditions and, however carefully defined, it still suggests things indigenous spiritual traditions tend not to have, such as central didactic texts, prescribed theology and rituals as well as the urge to proselytize. Furthermore, there is a strong argument that only native language can express any form of native transcendent experience and that in any case, such experiences can only be understood via embeddedness and personal commitment to a specific native community.

Admittedly, some of these problematics are reflected in the dissatisfaction some of the foremost religious studies thinkers have expressed with the whole concept of religion. They argue that the term has limited value because it is indefinable and at heart, Western. For example, Nielsen et al. argue that "The notion that something called *religion* can be isolated, analysed or defined is primarily a Western conceit."[6] This is because dominant Western beliefs have tended to split off what is deemed sacred from everyday life. God to a greater or lesser extent is thought about as being separate from what he created, nature conceived as a realm that operates in its own sphere and one over which man fundamentally has been given dominion. Following the Enlightenment, this was heavily bolstered by Western science. Science sets itself the task of fully understanding nature and does so in part in the modern era, through fully separating itself from issues of belief, transcendence, or religion. It is worth recognizing, however, that this separation was less stark in the sixteenth and seventeenth centuries, when what was known in the West as natural philosophy had important interrelationships with Christian religion and theology.[7]

In comparison, the trajectory of much Native American thinking and development has been wholly different. Its various traditions tend to include the seen and unseen and build upon rather than segregate the sacred. As one of the foremost Indian thinkers of recent times Vine Deloria Jr. put it: "Indians developed as comprehensive analysis of the nature of the world as has Western science, but the goals have been very different. Western science is based on Roger Bacon's command to pry nature's secrets from her, by torture, if nothing else. The medicine men sought additional alliances with other entities and, according to some tribes, accumulated both spiritual powers and cumulative knowledge over several lifetimes."[8]

Using the term spirituality gets us free of some of these departures and issues if we use a definition of it at its most basic—as mental or material energy and if we see it as a word that allows us to get us beyond ideas we may have inherited from Western traditions about mind being separate from body and nature being separate from the sacred. That said, like the word religion, spirit is also a non-Indian word with a Latin stem, coming as it does from the Latin word for breath (thus God is said to have *in-spired* Adam, breathing the spirit of life into him). It is perhaps best to think of that breath, of spirituality as it will be used in the succeeding chapters, as a force or energy that is not bound by dimension. In the Native American Indian context it is also useful to bear in mind the themes anthropologists have deemed to be common to a great number of indigenous spiritualities. These include certain cosmological approaches, the idea of pervasive supernatural force, respect for dreams and visions, for song and dance, varying understandings of the afterlife, respect for ancestors, a sense of kinship with all things including the animate and inanimate and specific reverence for certain symbols and materials such as tobacco and medicine bundles.

Another term this book uses is "tradition." It is used even though, like the term spirituality, it too has been justifiably contested as being too broad to be meaningful. Readers will recognize that Native American Indian communities are at least as diverse as Euro-American ones and that any all-encompassing term or generalized set of perceived characteristics will inevitably be inadequate, but it is still important to speak of tradition in the sense that Raymond Williams wrote of it, as an active process within communities where ideas and beliefs (which may only require two generations to become "traditional") are nonetheless valuable, dynamic, enabling, and historically significant. It is important to at least try to get beyond the Western intellectual "tradition" of thinking about tradition (here I exclude a number of anthropologists) as something stultifying and liable to enforce cultural homogeneity, and as analogous if juxtaposed to progress, to other nineteenth-century dichotomies like nature/nurture, primitive/civilized, mind/body. This negative Western intellectual "tradition" includes Durkheim, Weber, Tönnies, and Marx, the last of whom went so far as to write of the tradition of all the dead generations weighing "like a nightmare on the brain of the living." This is an intellectual perspective on tradition that remains pervasive and persistent. Even more recent scholars such as Jürgen Habermas, who recognize that traditions are not static, see the continuity of tradition as coercive and deem change to be solely the outcome of rationality and reflectivity.[10] In contrast, a more productive way to think about tradition when it comes to a number of Native American Indian practices is to recognize what Arnold Krupat has dubbed a *both/and* modality of thought at work. Thus Indian communities and individuals are seen to be able to encompass what might appear at first to be mutually contradictory, able, for example, to combine elements of both Christianity and non-Christian indigenous tribal spirituality; able to respect what are thought of as nonrational, ancient traditions, and certain scientific approaches within the contemporary world. This indigenous, complementary way of thinking, of comprehending difference in terms of balance as opposed to in the Aristotelian, analytic, *either/or* mode of thought more familiar in the West is what makes "Indian tradition" so flexible, inclusive, and arguably, ultimately indestructible.[11] It will be this awareness, rather than the homogenizing, synoptic gloss that generally surrounds use of the term "tradition," that will be invoked in the chapters that follow.

LAND, LANDSCAPE, PLACE, WILDERNESS, NATURE

It is worth considering at the outset some very basic differences. Intellectually, Indian approaches to land or place tend to see it as space invested with meaning through lived experience and as something defined by its construction rather than its borders. In comparison, European and later Euro-American approaches to land have tended to view it through the lens of Christianity. Thus for early settler societies, American land beyond their settlements represented spiritual danger. The wilderness was a place of potential peril, a place where the Christian could become profoundly both physically and spiritually lost. After all, it was in the wilderness that Jesus found himself "be*wild*ered" and tempted by Satan.[12]

Interestingly, as Vine Deloria pointed out in his 1972 book *God Is Red*, the Christian idea of God is more or less humanlike (often meddlesome and vengeful), whereas in many native religions supreme authority is placed in a Great Spirit or Great Mystery who is not necessarily human-like; instead it symbolizes the life forces of nature. We might say that most Indian traditions map onto an egalitarian/kinship model in the ecological historian Donald Worster's terms, rather than an imperial tradition where knowledge of nature is used to exert power over it.[13] In comparison, Western anthropocentrism goes back as least as far as the Greek Stoics, but the anthropocentrism at the heart of Christian spirituality can be traced directly back to the Old Testament idea that God gave man dominion over the earth and its creatures.[14] The Old Testament puts man forward as the only creature made in God's image, making man superior to and separate from all others. God's instruction was: "Be fruitful, and multiply, and replenish the earth, and subdue it: and have dominion over the fish of the sea, and over the fowl of the air, and over every living thing that moveth upon the earth."[15] This makes the earth and its creatures significant primarily in terms of their usefulness or otherwise to man. The statement appears to be indifferent to those creatures or landscapes without such an inherent usefulness. This point was made very powerfully in 1968 by Lynn White in an influential essay called

"The Historical Roots of Our Ecologic Crisis" that triggered much new thinking in the then-nascent ecological movement. The Bible, of course, is open to interpretation and as Christian ecologists have been at pains to point out in response to White's criticisms, there is a long history of Christian husbandry or stewardship of the earth and its creatures, an ethic that maintains that mankind has a divinely ordained moral responsibility to care for God's earth. Another recent thread of thinking within ecumenical discourse concerned with environmental matters centers on emphasizing the idea of the whole household (*oikos*) of God. As a root metaphor this allows Christian thinkers to think and speak of the earth as God's home and to formulate an ethics of eco-justice, a term popularized by theological scholar Dieter Hessel.[16] Neither are Christian thinkers the only people who have taken issue with Lynn White's arguments. White argued that a direct link existed across centuries between Judaeo-Christianity and post-Baconian science and technology, a direct connection that for several notable scholars, is simply too much of a stretch.[17]

Deloria's point about the essential anthropocentrism of the Old Testament instruction remains valid nonetheless. It is also the case that Christian man's relationship to the earth is clearly utilitarian. A comparable utilitarianism can also be seen in early American political philosophy. In John Locke's thinking, in for example his 1690 *Second Treatise on Government*, we find a theory of property underpinning the legitimacy of democratic government. This was a set of ideas wildly popular throughout the eighteenth century and it included the idea that by *using* nature, a free man through his labor could legitimately transform what was worthless into property. The West, all that land beyond the confines of existing colonial settlement and with it all of its indigenous inhabitants, was therefore "worthless" until converted into property by questing Euro-Americans. Even Locke, however, placed some limitations on the uses to which nature might be put. An individual was not to take more than they could use and no man should appropriate more land than they could work. Even so, Locke established a bulwark of thinking in the United States that solidified connections between ideas of national freedom (as opposed to life under monarchy) and the use of nature primarily for man's benefit. A similar sort of anthropocentric utilitarian approach to nature would late be powerfully put forward by the first chief of the U.S. Forest Service Gifford Pinchot. Pinchot was a great friend of President Theodore Roosevelt who valued his advocacy of "conservation," which was as Pinchot put it, the sustainable use of resources so as to ensure "the greatest good for the greatest number." The idea was thought of as a middle way during the nineteenth century, a means of assuaging the demands on the one hand of the "timber barons" of the time intent upon maximizing profit and on the other, the demands of "preservationists" who saw in American land a vital spiritual and psychological resource that needed to be protected from exploitation and preserved as national treasure.

Gradually such preservationist thinking gained sway and settler thinking within the United States began to shift. By the early nineteenth century, wilderness had become less about danger and more about the opportunity to commune with God. A legacy of this way of thinking is that it is perhaps how most of us, whether religious or not, have been conditioned to think about wilderness today—that it is sacred and potentially transcendent space. Parts of the American landscape had by the early nineteenth century been deemed holy and were seen as potential portals to the ecstatic and the sublime. This was what "nature" meant, for example, to the philosopher Ralph Waldo Emerson (1802–1882) and to John Muir (1838–1914), the individual who used this rhetoric to spearhead the creation of the first American national parks. Muir had come to America from Scotland at age 11 and founded the Sierra Club in 1892. It was largely through Muir and the Sierra Club's efforts that Yosemite National Park gained its current boundaries. Like a number of visionary individuals whose efforts ultimately changed the world, much about Muir was more than a little strange. He was obsessive, thirsty even, for the beauty he perceived in the wild and intoxicated on a romantic, mystical level by the wonder of places like Yosemite. His identification with nature was startlingly passionate, as complete we might say, as Catherine's was for Heathcliff in the novel *Wuthering Heights* published just 20 years before Muir had what might be called his "wilderness conversion."[18] He wrote to a friend in 1870:

> I'm in the woods, woods woods, & they are in *me-ee-ee*. The King tree & me have sworn eternal love- sworn it without swearing & I've taken the sacrament with Douglass Squirrell drank Sequoia blood, & with its rosy purple drops I am writing this woody gospel letter. I never before knew the virtue of Sequoia juice. Seen with sunbeams in it, its color is the most royal of all royal purples. No wonder the Indians instinctively drink it for they know not what. I wish I was so drunk & Sequoical that I could preach the green brown woods to all the juiceless world, descending from this divine wilderness like a John the Baptist eating Douglas Squirrels & wild honey or wild anything, crying, Repent for the Kingdom of Sequoia is at hand.[19]

It is perhaps unfair to judge someone as they describe one of the most profound realizations of their life in a private letter to a friend, but a number of points with reference to this quotation by Muir call out for comment. Here, a son of a Methodist minister uses all the language of revealed religion to extol the ecstasy and sacramental wonder of his encounter with nature. It is as though he has found his faith in the woods; his King is now King Sequoia as opposed to Christ. He will not go on to found a church but his highly individual and solitary experience will spawn a movement nonetheless, one dedicated to the preservation of "wilderness."

The individual and personal nature of Muir's relationship to the woods stands in stark contrast to a number of Indian traditions and their relationship to the non-human world. Notably, Muir's experience is outside of community rather than within it and while the language is as passionate as that within a Gothic novel, he relates his experience just as a Christian prophet might, descending from the wild to spread the word of a new gospel. For Muir in the quotation above, Indian peoples are very far from his own consciousness. Like animals, they are "instinctive" rather than intelligent and, it seems, drink liquids without having a cogent reason to do so. His views about Indian people would later develop, but the larger point that the wilderness movement has tended to section off the Indian activities so that they are perceived as somehow not constitutive of what goes on in the "wild" still stands.[20]

INTO THE WILD: THE ORIGINS OF AN IDEA

We will return to Muir, but at this stage it is worth going back in time so as to better understand the shift he represents. Muir did not invent "wilderness," but his approach articulated a new American understanding of it. In the centuries previous, wilderness had been thought of as places of almost unnatural barrenness, places of desert, loneliness, and danger—wastelands where a man without his community might find himself subject to every sort of terror and where inevitably he would fall prey to abject despair. Moses wandered with his people in the wilderness for 40 years and they felt so bereft they almost set about worshipping a graven image. Christ was driven into the wilderness so that Satan might tempt him, and Adam and Eve were driven out of God's garden Eden into wilderness that only hard labor could transform.[21] According to Carolyn Merchant, it was this expulsion that spawned since the seventeenth century a "recovery project . . . to turn the earth itself into a vast cultivated garden." The United States in particular took to its heart the task of "reinventing Eden."[22] It was a reinvention that at points was acutely brutal and as the quotation from Vine Deloria earlier suggests, it demonstrated thinking with its roots in seventeenth-century Europe, thinking such as that of Francis Bacon (1561–1626), a lawyer and official in the closing years of Queen Elizabeth's reign. Bacon could justify severely "vexing" the earth to rectify the loss of innocence and agency caused by the Fall. He advocated dissecting nature just as scientists of the time were dissecting bodies, exploring her bowels and "recovering that right over nature which belongs to [the human race] by divine bequest" so as "to establish and extend the power and dominion of the human race itself over the entire universe." His dream was to witness the dawn of the dominance of a new way of thinking, a "new organon" that might prize apart "the secrets still locked in nature's bosom." Top-dressing his plea with overtly sexual language, he explicitly called for the utter subjugation and exploitation of the earth.[23]

In one sense, Bacon has been unjustly maligned by writers such as Merchant, since in truth, rather than adopt a mechanical view of nature like René

Descartes's, he believed in a constant ebb and flow of "vital sparks." Furthermore, the larger context to his ideas on nature and experiment are, in intention at least, steward-like and centered around the common good. In fact, advancing the betterment of all was why he advocated the scientific method of systematic study through experiment. Furthermore environmental degradation did not begin with the scientific revolution something Merchant at points comes close to recognizing. Yet Merchant's key argument still stands; Bacon, Descartes, and a number of the primary thinkers associated with the scientific revolution in the West produced work that was used to advance a project of fundamental and profound "vexation" of the earth and it invoked the larger biblical project of recovering through man's agency the paradise of a lost Eden. Without question, their language was riddled with the misogyny that characterized much about their time.

[we are not taught this]

European thinking therefore had at its roots notions of the wild as Other. Wilderness was held to be the home not of man primarily but of wild beasts (one source suggests it stems from the Old English *wilddēoren*, another, less convincingly, that it stems from wild deer, that is, wild-deer-ness). Correspondingly the men who were said to live there were deemed hardly to be men at all. According to medieval legend and art, the "wild man" (in German *wilder mann*) was halfway between beast and man, governed only by instinct, hairy, naked, and fundamentally ignorant of God and his teachings. According to Richard Bernheimer's *Wild Men in the Middle Ages: A Study in Art, Sentiment, and Demonology*:

[No interelation]

> Wildness meant more in the Middle Ages than the shrunken significance of the term would indicate today. The word implied everything that eluded Christian norms and the established framework of Christian society, referring to what was uncanny, unruly, raw, unpredictable, foreign, uncultured, and uncultivated. It included the unfamiliar as well as the unintelligible. Just as the wilderness is the background against which medieval society is delineated, so wildness in the widest sense is the background of God's lucid order of creation. Man in his unreconstructed state, faraway nations, and savage creatures at home thus came to share the same essential quality.[24]

The European notion of the wild owed most to the European imagination, and it was conjured especially ardently at times when Europeans felt the strongest need to exercise their imaginations. This was pithily explained in perhaps the best essay ever written on wildness, its meanings, and history published in 1972 by the theorist and historian Hayden White. White saw wildness as a fiction, a sign that mankind's imagination imbues with certain characteristics. The idea of wildness he said had moved across time from myth to fiction and back again to myth, but it had retained its essential characteristic as first and foremost a projection of our repressed desires and anxieties.[25] Like Berkeimer, he linked a European

emphasis on wildness since the fourteenth century, whether in the form of primitivism or in the idea of the Noble Savage, with periods of oppression and cruelty.
Attention paid to the wild, he suggested, was a recurring symptom of the need for
greater liberty in a Europe dealing with the realities of population density,
inequality, and scarcity. Always wildness represented what had been sacrificed
for society to function and grow. As White put it:

> It was the oppressed, exploited, alienated, or repressed part of humanity that
> kept on reappearing in the imagination of Western man—as the Wild Man, as
> the monster, and as the devil—to haunt or entice him thereafter. Sometimes
> this oppressed or repressed humanity appeared as a threat and a nightmare, at
> other times as a goal and a dream; sometimes as an abyss into which mankind
> might fall, and again as a summit to be scaled; but always as a criticism of what-
> ever security and peace of mind one group of men in society had purchased at
> the cost of the suffering of another.[26]

Or, one might say, an obsession with the wild in whatever form is and always has
been, a sign of our moral, spiritual, and cultural desire to reconcile our almost
limitless wish for comfort with our conflicting inherent wish to share.

THE CREATION OF AMERICAN WILDERNESS

As America industrialized, wilderness in the dominant, non-Indian culture
became bound up with nostalgia for a mythic and supposedly regenerative frontier past. Instead of seeming untameably wild, deserted, and frightening, the wild
now appeared inexpressibly beautiful; indeed it became prized as a precious
sanctuary for Americans increasingly brow-beaten by the woes of burgeoning city
life. Once seen as the no-man's land where Satan had free play, the same places
were now recontextualized as the opposite, as holy sites, places offering special
access to the transcendent and the divine. Wild places came to be seen as
the sanctuary of the American individual, as feminized spaces, but at the
same time as crucibles capable of forging the quintessence of manly virtue. They
were the appropriate backdrop both for Owen Wister's novels and for the rugged
exploits of the nation's darling, President Theodore Roosevelt. Equally significant,
landscape and nature came to be seen as recreational, as something to be bought
and consumed by the weary as a salve to the by now rapidly increasing physical
and psychological pressures of city life. Especially among elites, landscape was
seen as something that might be consumed, as part of the new idea of "recreation." However, it is important to keep in mind that this thinking had most
salience for the intellectual and social elite. It is perhaps still this way today.
The idea of land as pristine heritage had little currency for many of the workers
on America's various frontiers or for many Indian peoples on reservations. Too

often, their lives were limited by the broader context of bitterly hard work and racial exploitation. This in itself conceals an acute irony. After all, part of what had always informed Euro-American attitudes to their "new" territory was collective memory of how previous Europeans generations had themselves lost vital access to land. In medieval times royal control over forests was one of the most hated aspects of monarchy across Western Europe. The right to hunt was strictly monitored with infraction resulting in rigorous punishment. It was only with significant colonial expansion into North America in the seventeenth century that via emigration a proportion of Europe's poor were again able to access the fauna and flora necessary to subsistence. In turn the creation of American "wilderness" areas was sold to the American people in part as a democratization of access to land, but in another sense it was a recapitulation of an old European idea that the best of nature was rightfully appreciated by an elite. When Frederick Law Olmsted (1822–1903) set about "designing" Niagara Falls and Yosemite he justified their being set aside by arguing that failure to do so would be undemocratic. Without such government intervention, American sites of beauty would, he argued, end up just as parks were in Great Britain—the exclusive preserve of the rich. Americans needed its set-aside parks, its Yosemites and Niagaras, so that its scenery might improve the morals of its working classes and imbue them with possibilities for happiness. The demand for Niagara's water had reduced its flow to a trickle in the 1860s; but subsequently, Olmsted was able to garden and design both sites so that they could handle high visitor numbers and retain the image of wilderness that would ensure their preservation.

Idolization by the dominant society of aspects of the environment was in fact, as Kenneth R. Olwig has pointed out, nothing less than a form of narcissistic triumphalism given that the process of creating and enshrining "wilderness" happened at the same time as the removal and destruction of Native American communities.[27] To put America's "natural" cathedrals on tourist maps, Indian peoples had to be aggressively dispossessed and their treatied rights ignored. In an era characterized by immense Indian suffering, the Park Service carried on the process of removal and Indian cultural erosion that had been begun in the previous decades by the American army. After 1850, the most conventionally beautiful and sacred parts of what had been known as "Indian country," including Yosemite, Yellowstone, Mt. Rainier, Crater Lake, Mesa Verde, Olympic, Grand Canyon, Glacier, and Rocky Mountain, had all been designated "wilderness" and their Indian peoples removed.[28] The pages of print devoted to the idolizing of certain American environments all served the purpose of drawing attention away from actual processes of cultural displacement and resource extraction. To paraphrase Renato Rosaldo, in this process the active and morally responsible colonial agent got transformed into an innocent bystander. It was by no means a coincidence, as Rosaldo points out, that "[the] attitude of reverence toward the natural developed at the same time that North Americans intensified the destruction of their human and natural environment."[29] In sum, an idealized wilderness was a necessary accompaniment for the lone, white hero of frontier myth as he carried out the tricky work of making the sustained attempt to culturally and physically erase Indians appear somehow morally tolerable.

Niagara Falls was the first American site to be deemed a sublime portal to the heavens in this way; it was followed by Yosemite, deeded to California in 1864, and then Yellowstone was designated the first true national park in 1872. The veneration of landscape these designations represent was bolstered by elite thinking about the sublime in work by a host of writers including, Edmund Burke, Immanuel Kant, and William Gilpin.[30] It was a predominantly white, male elite—the group who had benefitted most from the exploitation of the American wild—who in general could be said to have been at the forefront of the movement to preserve wilderness. The class that contained the modernizers and industrializers were the very people most powerfully articulating an antimodern nostalgia for a supposedly pristine past. It is another example of the stream and counterstream within modernism so ably described by T. J. Jackson Lears in his seminal text, *No Place of Grace: Antimodernism and the Transformation of American Culture 1880–1920* (1981). It was a symptom of psychological and spiritual yearning, of a desire to recover the self. As Lears notes, "Antimodern dissent more often contained a vein of deep religious longing, an unfulfilled yearning to restore infinite meaning to an increasingly finite world."[31] The wilderness preservation movement contained within it a desire for atonement as part of the idea that areas could be cordoned off where man would be powerless and the long story of his impact on earth rubbed away.

The history above paints in comparatively broad brushstrokes, and it is important to remember that for Americans of all sorts, nature had its own contours specific to context. As it was across the world, nature was understood variously by different peoples in differing places; but nonetheless, the general pattern described above holds true for the United States. Ironically it was the very husbandry of wild spaces by indigenous peoples that had made those spaces appear especially park-like and attractive to Euro-Americans. Settler communities could not or would not recognize the efforts indigenous communities had made to keep landscapes looking so primally inviting to humans with their wide expanses suitable for game. In truth, the land settlers encountered and found so pleasingly like an optimal European proto-park was most often very carefully managed. Rather than "virgin land," to use George Bancroft's infamous term, it was indeed a park, a wildlife park belonging to someone else—America's indigenous inhabitants.[32] Euro-Americans found it difficult to perceive this because they clung to the idea that Indians simply did not use land. As William Cronon pointed out in *Changes in the Land* in 1983, the issue was the difference between individual ownership of land and collective sovereignty. Indian peoples generally did own things individually (the implements of their work, clothing, items used daily) but land was held collectively. Therefore when Euro-Americans encountered large tracts of it under intensive management for hunting and agriculture, it appeared to them to be not used at all. Since it was not fenced and it was not being used to farm domestic animals, it was only too easy for settler communities to believe the very thing that was most convenient for them to believe—that here was "empty" land, gifted to them by God, a veritable Eden rediscovered in a "New World." This conviction is and was remarkable for its persistence. As Francis Jennings has explained at length, early Puritan records in particular teem with formulas explaining away Indian use of their own lands. Lawyers like John Winthrop argued that Indians had neither national territory nor private property because they did not always live on land the whole year round. Legally he deemed most Indian land to be *vacuum domicilium* because Indians had not "subdued" it as the English might. Carefully managed Indian hunting lands were therefore "waste without inhabitant" or "traversed but not occupied" or "ranged rather than inhabited." Since Indian peoples could not produce written evidence of the sale or transfer of designated lands between themselves in a form the Euro-Americans understood, their possession of land was categorized as only a natural rather than civil right and, as such, was considered easy to usurp.[33]

An excellent example of Euro-American blindness to Indian use of land is how the landscape architect and conservationist Frederick Law Olmsted perceived Yosemite Valley when he first encountered it in 1864. He deemed it a "wild park" and because he felt it had been created just how man might like it *without* man's intervention. In fact glacial action and the work of indigenous peoples had created Yosemite's almost level floor, gentle pools, broad meadows deep with grass, wildflowers, azalea, great oak groves, pines, meandering riverbank lined with willows and colorful rocky outcrops. Yosemite teemed with bird life, grizzly, and all kinds of wildlife only because it had been kept so carefully kept for generations. Settlers named it Yosemite from a corruption of the Sierra Miwok word *Yo-ham'-i-te*, describing a band called *Ah-wah'-nee-ches* who had a large village south side of the Merced River. They were known as excellent hunters of grizzly bear, known as *Oo-hoo'-ma-te/O-ham'-i-te*, thus their name. Upon "discovery" Yosemite supported a large population—there were at least 36 sites in 1870. Some villages were lived in all year; some just from May to October; and some were geared exclusively for hunting and fishing. It is perhaps unsurprising that such a beautiful and abundant environment would have been home to a large population of humans over time. After all, Yosemite's isolation made it easy to defend and it teemed with edible, fish, reptiles, insects, game, water, and edible plants—especially acorn, which, when shelled and dried, was something of a staple. Subsistence living always means regular effort but at Yosemite indigenous living was not hard. There was plenty of time for a rich ceremonial life carried out in two large, semi-subterranean assembly houses of about 40 feet in diameter in the valley. Yosemite native peoples carried out extensive political and cultural activities including dances and musical instrument playing. They had a vast hinterland of stories as well as stories tied specifically to places in Yosemite. They played a game like lacrosse, gambled, and held a great annual mourning ceremony each September or October to connect with the dead. Each fall, they set fire to Yosemite's dry grass so as to keep its meadows open.[34]

like the video inclosed of controlled burns

"IT ALREADY HAS A NAME": YOSEMITE

A key voice from this generation of *Ah-wah'-nee-ches* at what is now known as Yosemite is that of Tenaya. He was a renowned leader in the largest and most important village in the valley and had a large ceremonial house beside a gigantic oak just below Yosemite Falls.[35] He is repeatedly on record reminding early settlers that the remarkable landscapes and geological features they were "discovering" at Yosemite did not need to be named by them since they already had names—names with deeply embedded and powerful cultural and spiritual significance. Yosemite Valley already had a name, Ahwahne, meaning it is thought, large open mouth (*awo*).[36] When, in the process of his people's displacement, it was suggested to Tenaya that a deep blue lake be named after him he said "It already has a name. We call it Py-we'-ack."[37]

how could they deny the culture + people were so clearly established

This propensity of settlers to see and perceive what they wanted to see, and to not perceive indigenous presence and their sacred practice fundamentally oriented around specific homelands, can be traced from the very earliest records of contact. Columbus felt such a sense of cultural and religious superiority that he wholly dismissed the linguistic abilities of the indigenous peoples he first encountered. Because they did not speak *his* language, he deemed them to have no conceptual language at all. He told the Spanish monarchs who were his employers that he would bring six Arawak natives to them "in order that they might learn to speak." In the same way, he dismissed the ability of native peoples to relate meaningfully to place and went around renaming and recontextualizing the islands and phenomenon he encountered so as to mark non-Indian possession of them. He even renamed all the indigenous people of the Americas with one single collective descriptor, Indian.[38] That great homogenizing term, dismissive as it was of so many diverse sovereign tribal peoples, would continue to irk native peoples for generations until it was deemed to have been reinscribed and made indigenous through use. The Pequot William Apess, who wrote one of the earliest native autobiographies, *A Son of the Forest* (1829), was one of the first to articulate in print the negative impact of settler nonperception of native diversity and of native names. He wrote, "I know of nothing so trying to a child as to be repeatedly called by an improper name." Given that the word Indian was not in the Bible, he concluded that it must have been "imported for the special purpose of degrading us."[39] The whole process, or we might say, settler compulsion, was satirized very successfully by the indigenous/Greek author Thomas King in his 1993 novel *Green Grass*. Here Green encourages us to laugh at the desire to hierarchize through naming by juxtaposing Christian and Native origin myths. His character Ahdamn, first son of the Christian God, lives with First Woman in a garden created by Thought Woman and, preposterously, he starts renaming

Indian

everything he encounters after preconceived images from American consumerism. He tells Elk he is in fact a microwave oven and Old Coyote he is a cheeseburger.[40]

The inability to perceive indigenous presence and the desire to rename what is new to the settler experience in one sense has never gone away. It is a "rechristening" process, a symptom of linguistic imperialism, that too many of us do not realize has happened. Despite park managers in Yosemite's cultural outreach efforts, for example, how many of us know the native names for the key geographical features of the nation's foremost nature park? For that matter, how many Americans know the Indian translation for any one of the host of Indian names they have retained and still routinely use—words, for example, such as *Chicago*, probably translatable as "wild onion place" and *Tucson*, "black mountain base"?[41] We forget that a name is rarely just a name; it signifies how a community perceives reality. In forgetting this process of rechristening and translation, we lose sight also of previous Indian understandings of place. Two of the best books to help us reconnect in this sense involve the anthropologist Keith Basso, who wrote *Wisdom Sits in Places: Landscape and Language among the Western Apache* in 1996 and produced with Steven Feld the edited collection, *Senses of Place* the same year.[42] Basso tells of how he began what seemed like a straightforward mapmaking project to mark the locations of physical features around Cibecue territory in Arizona and note the Western Apache place names. He discovered among the Apache a fundamental belief that place names were the direct quotes of the ancestors who first named the places and settled the land. Tied to the places are stories about specific events with specific cultural meanings such that place names are capable of having moral import for the person about whom the place-name comments. Place names are thus connected with "correct" behavior, language, metaphor, and history, and they are culturally dynamic and subject to responsive change. Basso made a plea that we see beyond three-dimensional ideas about place and instead *sense* place and be aware of how different peoples are alive to the world around them. Following Martin Heidegger, he focused on the concept of *dwelling*, where importance is assigned to the forms of consciousness with which individuals perceive and apprehend geographical space.[43]

While no single statement necessarily holds true for all indigenous peoples, here one is also reminded of Vine Deloria Jr.'s general statement in *God is Red* that "American Indians hold their lands—place—as having the highest possible meaning, and all their statements are made with this reference point in mind." In his experience with the Apache Basso learned to perceive landscape as storied, as akin to theater, as a locale that calls up "thoughts of fabled deeds and the singular cast of actors who there has played them out." This awareness of places is crucial to gaining wisdom—'igo=+ in Apache thinking, which Basso defines in Apache terms as "a heightened mental capacity that facilitates the avoidance of harmful events by detecting threatening circumstances when none are apparent." Thus place is revealed as key to wisdom, which is in itself a key to survival and based on three mental conditions, smoothness, resilience, and steadiness of mind. Basso asserts that, for many Native peoples, places, and place names are one means by which not only identity but also "portions of the past" are "brought into being." In this sense, Basso argues that place names quite literally embody an "eyewitness voice."[44] Thus place names and naming in general are seen to be heavy with the cultural and spiritual understanding necessary to indigenous survival. Names matter. To answer Shakespeare's Juliet's question, a rose by any other name does not smell as sweet. Renaming risks destroying the webs of meaning that support a community. Equally importantly, indigenous naming often allows for dynamism and ambiguity that is irksome in terms of non-Indian military and economic imperatives that call for static names and a one-to-one correspondence between the name and what is named (as in the name "High Peak").

In comparison, the record of settler "discovery" in the United States is most often one of ethnocentric tunnel vision. Admittedly, those who first set foot on indigenous lands had a sense of history but it was of a history calibrated almost exclusively in terms of Western nation-states and of individual and later racial narratives. For example, when in the fall of 1833 58 fur trappers and hunters "discovered" Yosemite, they were being watched by Ahwahneeche who had been secretly trailing them. Despite subsequently discovering this and despite all later evidence to the contrary, they persisted in perceiving Yosemite as pristine and devoid of human imprint.[45] Yet this sort of specific blindness and wondrously self-serving understanding of place was not unique to Euro-Americans. It was, as Mary Louise Pratt has shown, part of the overall history of what she calls "imperial meaning-making." Europeans "discovering" key natural wonders across the world were most often directed or in some cases physically carried by indigenous guides but still kept up the myth of theirs as "first sight." The story of "discovery" always discounted the long history of indigenous knowledge and possession of land. The myth of "discovery" and associated ideas about indigenous land being "empty," "pristine," or "virgin" were all part of what Pratt dubs "anti-conquest," the delicate sleight-of-hand that sought to accentuate the heroism, endurance, and providential good fortune of the venturing settler and to downplay his actual purpose—to secure and control land and resources. Renaming was and is, in the Kenyan author Ngũgĩ wa Thiong'o's terms, a cultural bomb whose effect is devastating. He writes:

> The effect of a cultural bomb is to annihilate a people's belief in their names, in their languages, in their environment, in their heritage of struggle, in their unity, in their capabilities and ultimately in themselves. It makes them see their past as one wasteland of non-achievement and it makes them want to identify with that which is furthest removed from themselves, for instance, with other people's languages rather than their own.[46]

Regrettably a historically underanalyzed understanding of this imperialist process also characterizes some of the best-known writing on place even today. Yi-Fu Tuan has done sterling work constructing a paradigm for the concept of "place" and created the term "topophilia" to suggest the link between persons and place or the physical environment. Yet he finds the reinscription of place through renaming symptomatic simply of the role of gesture in defining place, when in truth it signifies a great deal more. He writes: "Explorers conjure places out of the wilderness by simply naming peaks and rivers . . . Gestures, either alone or in association with speech and the making of things, create place. For example, when an explorer names a mountain he may at the same time put a cross on it: the ritual words for place-making are reinforced by ritual gesture." Tuan is right about place being intimately connected to symbols, language, propaganda, gesture, and culture in a general sense but there is a real danger in divorcing place, as he tends to, from the often bloody history of colonialism and from the specific relationships within discrete communities. This in turn is linked to other analytical choices in his approach such as his commitment to seeing nature and culture as being separate (albeit in tension) and to conceiving of culture as being unique to human.[47]

The stories about Yosemite's "discovery," and perhaps John Muir's own stories about his uncovering of Yosemite's beauty, should be seen in Pratt's words, as "strategies of representation whereby European bourgeois subjects seek to secure their innocence in the same moment as they assert European hegemony."[48] Muir's writing about his discovery of Yosemite's beauty, to the extent that it served to bring about the consolidation of Yosemite and its resources for non-Indian use and classified and categorized what was beautiful about it, was writing about land perceived through "imperial eyes." It is perhaps only now that landscapes such as Yosemite are slowly coming to be perceived in ways other than how Muir and others suggested. In time, as Yosemite's indigenous heritage becomes better known and better understood, Muir's aestheticizing may no longer remain the dominant gaze. We may begin to tear away the veil of names, classifications, and standardizations imposed on landscapes to fit bureaucratic imperatives linked ultimately to various stages of capitalism. Today, parks like Yosemite shock the public by embarking on a 10-year program of tree destruction to preserve iconic "wilderness" vistas, but such activity is simply a reminder that "wilderness" has always been a constructed notion, constructed in relation to the gaze of the nonindigenous tourist. Yosemite's current "Scenic Vista Management Plan" will see the cutting down of thousands of evergreen trees, some one hundred feet tall and thirty inches wide, so as to preserve a balance between oaks, grassy meadows, and conifer trees that was once maintained by Indian peoples and naturally occurring fire. The reason? To preserve a camera-ready version of "wilderness" that will keep tourists visiting the park. As a historical landscape architect at Yosemite recently explained, "Enjoyment means allowing people to connect with nature. But you have to be able to see it."[49]

It is because of this history that a number of our most eminent thinkers today advocate that we abandon wilderness thinking in favor of some form of "middle way" where the dualism at the heart of the idea of wilderness (thought of as pristine, historyless, and innocent) as opposed to non-wilderness (dismissed as contaminated, sullied, impure) is dispensed with. They argue that the very idea that there can or should be landscapes that remain unworked, or ever were unworked, is a fantasy specific to those who have not and do not expect to have to work the land to make a living. Wilderness in such an analysis is an urban idea, the corollary to a city-based life divorced from the seasons and from soil-based production. Wilderness suggests that man is outside of nature, outside of the natural. In this sense it is a profound rejection of the human self and a profoundly egotistical overestimation of man's potential relationship to the non-human world. For writers such as William Cronon in his ground-breaking 1996 book, *Uncommon Ground*, this is acutely dangerous because "The wilderness dualism tends to cast any use as *ab*-use, and thereby denies us a middle ground in which responsible use and non-use might attain some kind of balanced, sustainable relationship."[50] For Cronon and others "wilderness thinking" is in fact a key part of the contemporary period's ecological problem. The binary thinking involved in setting aside and preserving areas so that they might (impossibly) remain untouched by mankind allows us to ignore the great bulk of the world where awkward choices must be made to accommodate man's impact and the differing imperatives of capital, politics, race, and class. Thus Cronon quotes Wendell Berry and his contradictory-seeming statement that "The only thing we have to preserve nature with is culture; the only thing we have to preserve wildness with is domesticity."[51]

It is hard not to see the heavy hand of a certain Puritan form of sexual ethics at play in the binary thinking Cronon describes. Just as a "fallen" woman who has given herself up to be debauched was once thought of beyond redemption, "fallen" or non-pristine land is too often deemed to be not worth preserving. It is something of a zero-sum game. As Michael Pollan wrote in an essay discussing the ethics of equating nature with wilderness, "Thanks to exactly this kind of either/or thinking, Americans have done an admirable job of drawing lines around certain sacred areas (we did invent the wilderness area) and a terrible job of managing the rest of our land . . . Once a landscape is no longer 'virgin' it is typically written off as fallen, lost to nature, irredeemable. We hand it over to the jurisdiction of that other sacrosanct American ethic: laissez-faire economics." This means around 8 percent or less of American land today is preserved as wilderness and the rest is subject in some form or other to market forces.[52] As Thom Kuehls has pointed out, an added problem with the wilderness idea today is that wilderness areas tend to be thought of as bounded, finite, and regionally discrete, whereas environmental despoliation and with it associated issues to do with politics and economics are porous and global in nature. The wilderness idea in this sense can act as a barrier to the transnational strategies that are often required to tackle environmental stress.[53]

This urge to separate man from nature is something a number of Indian intellectuals wish to see abandoned and for similar reasons they wish for words like "landscape" to be dispensed with or at least for a broader recognition of the historical cultural baggage they carry as terms. In an essay entitled "Landscape, History, and the Pueblo Imagination," the Laguna writer Leslie Marmon Silko claims that the very definition of the term "landscape" embodies the kind of non-native separatist worldview described above. She writes:

> So long as the human consciousness remains *within* the hills, canyons, cliffs, and the plants, clouds, and sky, the term *landscape*, as it has entered the English language, is misleading. "A portion of territory the eye can comprehend in a single view" does not correctly describe the relationship between the human being and his or her surroundings. This assumes the viewer is somehow *outside* or *separate from* the territory he or she surveys.[54]

Silko bluntly asserts the inability of this linguistic definition to address Pueblo connections between "human consciousness" and spatial location. The term "landscape" thus represents the failure to "correctly describe" the relationship between humans and their physical surroundings. More explicitly, Silko has sought to wholly deconstruct the idea of sacred lands. "It is dangerous to designate some places sacred when we are all sacred," she explains. "Such compromises imply that there is a hierarchy of value, with some places and some living beings not as important as others. No part of the earth is expendable, the earth is a whole that cannot be fragmented."[55]

Given that such binaries are decried by key native and non-native figures alike, is the answer conceptually, to focus on some sort of "middle way"? It is to this idea and its limitations that we now turn.

CHAPTER 2

~

On Middle Way Thinking, Gardening, Parks, and Aspects of Indian Thinking about Land

The danger in the binary thinking surrounding wilderness as Cronon and others describe it is real and the ethnic cleansing involved in the creation of so many of the United States' national parks is to the United States' enduring shame, but I am probably not alone in feeling grateful to Muir and his ilk for, after a fashion at least, keeping certain sorts of capitalist and exploitative interests away from some of the United States' most conventionally beautiful sites.[1] After all, there *are* qualitative differences in land use in terms of sustainability and ecological damage and as Cronon's critics remind us, deconstructing "nature" is not an answer in itself to environmental problems.[2] Evidently, "wilderness" areas need now to be returned where possible to the descendants of those who once lived there, and there needs to be much greater recognition of the indigenous history of these places. However, this larger issue of Indian redress and restitution is so far not one that has garnered much attention from mainstream environmental writers and even less consideration is given to the counterfactual—what might have happened to the native peoples living on "wilderness" and that wilderness itself had Muir and his followers not agitated to preserve designated landscapes. While the value so many contemporary thinkers find in a generally ill-defined "middle way" between pure wilderness on one hand and debauched polluted landscapes on the other sounds and is comforting, reasonable, liberal, and fair, unfortunately it has little practical historical precedent in a country that for over a century has been at the forefront of industrial capitalism. Incidences where the conflict between capital and the environment have resulted in a middle way having been found are to be fostered and valued but are comparatively rare. Before we abandon wilderness, its protection, and the associated thorny and current issue of native redress for "wilderness" lands lost, it might be well to first cultivate more middle-way praxis, lest middle-way rhetoric is used to serve the interests of those who seek to limit native redress and expand the direct access by non-natives to areas of increasingly precious ecological wealth.

Overall, the contributors to Cronon's *Uncommon Ground* were much taken with "middleness," with the idea that some fair and relatively uncontested central way can be arrived at where both the intellectual difficulties surrounding terms such as "nature" and "wilderness" can be set aside along with the hideous legacy of cutthroat competition for resources that have characterized battles over land. Indeed, one of the volume's key contributors, Richard White, is well known for a book about middleness, his 1991 volume *The Middle Ground: Indians, Empires, and Republics in the Great Lakes Region 1650–1815*. Here White described an historical juncture after the American Revolution and the War of 1812 when "Indians ceased to have the power to force whites onto the middle ground." Thereafter, White argued, Indian peoples lost the agency to require intercultural interaction and were forced to live with an identity forced upon them externally by settler communities.[3] White's characterization of "middle ground" has been systemically critiqued by a number of scholars such as Cohen (2002) and Herman (1999) who decry the idea that any romantic "middle ground" existed that could have assuaged the basic hierarchies of colonial exchange. Justifiably, they warn against any history such as White's that can be said to sidestep the larger reality of conquest in the United States, which is characterized not by meetings in the middle but by asymmetrical relationships of power.

The *Uncommon Ground* idea of an ecological and environmental "middle way" is open to similar critique. After all, it seems unlikely that a posited "middle way" can somehow make structural and cultural inequalities of power disappear or circumvent the capitalist imperatives that have up until now underpinned environmental despoliation and indigenous displacement. The idea of a middle way presupposes that some kind of abstract state of fairness can be arrived at and enforced, but who is to be the judge of such "middleness"? It seems likely to remain those with most access to power, the same interest groups who have always sought a means whereby they can mask the theft of native land and resources. My fear is that "wilderness" will be evaluated and justified on a universal balance sheet invented by settlers and that "middle way" rhetoric will serve to evade the fact that "fairness" is likely to be unilaterally defined. Here it is worth recalling Stanley Diamond's admonition that imperialism is something that *always* strives to take the guise of mutuality, to appear as a joint enterprise, as a collaboration of cultures, because such a collaboration feeds into the old idea of Western cultural superiority and progress.[4] I am not suggesting that the motives of the *Uncommon Ground* contributors are anything but pure, but I am suggesting that "middle way" rhetoric is not in itself "pure," that is, it is unlikely to wholly refigure the balance of power between communities seeking on the one hand to preserve clean air, resources, and/or spiritually imbued landscapes and, on the other, to exploit those same resources for short-term gain. Those who recommend we find a "middle way" environmentally must begin to reckon with the very real concern that such hopes are close to the perfect colonial fantasy, a fantasy that has always sought to mask asymmetrical power relations using a rhetoric of mutuality and unforced exchange.

ON GARDENING AND PARKS

The only true voyage of discovery ... would be not to visit new landscapes, but to possess other eyes, to see the universe through the eyes of another, of a hundred others, to see the hundred universes that each of them sees.

—Marcel Proust, 'La Prisonnière', À la recherché du temps perdu (1913–27).[5]

For Cronon and others, the garden offers a solution to the problems inherent to any strict nature/culture divide. As a place of "middleness" that incorporates aspects of human endeavor and human presence it seems to hold a vision for the future. Alas, Cronon's faith in gardens as benign spaces ignores the heavy hand of class and colonialism at play within them historically. Within Western cultures hobby farms and gardens have existed in opposition to how the vast bulk of mankind has related to nature over time—that is, as a place of work. Gardens are nature mediated, places constructed through human effort to resemble a version of the natural most acceptable to man at that time. Many of them teem with carefully selected imports from around the globe, indicators of knowledge and plants colonial powers have extracted from peoples and lands they have dominated.[6] Gardens are essentially sites of human effort to construct a new version of reality. They are most usually, places where human desires are imposed. Thus Michael Pollen is driven to write about the inevitable challenge inherent in garden work, admitting: "The refusal of this land to conform to my ideas of it—even just to *sit still* for a while—frequently drives me crazy."[7]

The Caribbean writer Jamaica Kincaid's *My Garden (Book)* raises particularly interesting and thoroughly colonial questions in this regard. Kincaid recognizes that gardens, even those produced so as to create joy, are an exercise in power. In becoming a gardener, she admits she "joined the conquering class." "I have crossed a line," she acknowledges, "but at whose expense? I cannot begin to look, because what if it is someone I know?"[8] The good she finds in gardening lies with the way in which it brings humans literally in touch with elemental forces; but it is not an unalloyed good. Rather, the garden, like certain forms of art, is primarily a reflection of the gardener, his perceptive capabilities, and the extent to which the non-human has facilitated the execution of his dream.

In a real sense, praising gardens is difficult for a committed environmentalist since so much about the contemporary garden and specifically the contemporary lawn, in the middle class and North American context at least, is antithetical to nature. As Paul Robbins and Julie T. Sharp have shown masterfully in their 2003 study, "Producing and Consuming Chemicals: The Moral Economy of the American Lawn," late twentieth-century wealth has brought about an unprecedented spread in what they call a monocultural "lawn aesthetic" and with it serious environmental hazard from the burgeoning urban application of chemical fertilizers, pesticides, herbicides, and insecticides. They argue that while the total use of chemicals applied in argriculture has been decreasing because of land-use conversion, these gains are increasingly offset by the greater use of chemicals on home lawns, making lawns "a significant problem." Intriguingly and worryingly in an era of recycling and popular environmentalism, U.S. homeowners apply chemicals to their lawns even though they understand the negative environmental impacts of doing so. Why? Robbins and Sharp suggest it is because advertising and culture more generally signs the lawn representationally as part of consumers' identity. It is seen as a badge of middle-class status, as a symbol of collective consumption and as a way of participating in and strengthening the traditional nuclear family. Lawns allow for the conspicuous performance of class identity with agrochemicals playing a key part in gardening rituals that display the ability of the gardener to refrain from productive work. What's more, the lawn (and with it pesticides and chemical fertilizers) are sold to consumers as a means of restoring lost community, of restoring a lost link to nature, a lost sense of integrated family life, and a lost sense of work as meaningful and tangible. All this may seem very far from the experience you or I may have of gardening, but it speaks to a larger truth—that too often our conscious concerns about environmental hazards are overrun by largely unconscious desires mediated through advertising that ironically cause us to exacerbate—environmental hazard.[9]

As the quote from Marcel Proust which opens his chapter suggests, positive change can come as much from a new perspective as from new territory. If gardening as most Americans experience it is to have a positive actual and metaphorical influence in the twenty-first century, it needs to be seen with new awareness. Exotic foreign blooms need, perhaps, to be thought about in historical, ecological, and colonial context—"weeds" to be viewed as the best adapted species for the space they inhabit and garden landscapes to be thought of as distinctly part of rather than extraneous to wider land use patterns. In a more temporally synoptic sense, it is worth also bearing in mind the amount of conflict gardening has spawned because of its innate territoriality. There is much anthropological and archaeological evidence to suggest that mankind's adoption of agriculture led to a significant increase in war and aggression between communities. What has been planted cannot be easily left behind and is easily destroyed. Furthermore, the population boom associated in distant time with the onset of an agricultural way of life is thought to have triggered its own ongoing battles over resources.[10]

The idea of the garden is as fraught with historical complexity, biblical roots, and ugly memories as any other. "Garden" has always existed in juxtaposition with the other terms now out of fashion and prone to deconstruction—terms such as "wilderness" and "park." For Judeo-Christian peoples the Garden of Eden was the original park, a paradise—paradise being a word whose primary dictionary definition is that of an "enclosed park." In Eden mankind is said to have been born in a bucolic ideal, with a fertile orchard, a river, and animals grazing. "Garden" is a Germanic term, related to the English word "yard," both of which primarily mean "enclosed area." Thus from the foundational Western story, mankind in right relationship to the world lives in a garden in contrast to its opposite, a wilderness. Olwig explains: "The garden idea is potent because it has long been a vital symbol in Western culture of a moral society living in natural social and environmental harmony. Historically, the counterpositioning of the paradise garden park to the wilderness was a means of making a symbolic statement about the *nature* of *natural* national existence."[11] In essence, garden is good, and wilderness bad according to these oppositions as the previous chapter explored.

It is important to bear in mind that all gardens, like all parks and enclosed areas, are as much about who and what gets excluded as they are about who and what gets included. Furthermore, there is little that is a priori "natural" about the process of enclosure. Enclosure of land is stage one of a process of constructing an image or series of images that reflect the intention of the gardener. Consider Yosemite, the first nature reserve set aside by Congress, in this context. John Muir described the area and the neighboring smaller version Hetch Hetchy valley (later be the subject of so much controversy) as the perfect park landscape, "a spacious flowery lawn four or five miles long, surrounded by magnificent snowy mountains." It was for Muir, just like the Garden of Eden, a place with boundaries "drawn by the Lord."[12] From the first Yosemite was as much about constructing space as it was about preserving it. It provided an amplitude of picturesque theatrical scenes or *scenery* (a term first used in 1784) and it made for good landscape, a term originally used by Dutch artists (*landskip*) and later adapted by the English to describe a gently appealing view. To create and maintain an Eden-like image much had to be removed, including a whole (non-Indian) village whose buildings were eventually destroyed between 1959 and 1963 by the Park Service leaving only a church that dates from 1879. However, prior to this as explained, the original inhabitants of Yosemite-as-Eden had been much more brutally removed so as to create an environment that matched the non-Indian imagination.

Yosemite was set aside by Abraham Lincoln in 1864. It seemed so blissfully inviting as a park vista to elite non-Indian Americans because just twelve years earlier the original Miwok/Ahwahneechee inhabitants who had practiced the horticulture that helped make it so had been forcibly driven out or killed. According to Robert H. Keller and Michael F. Turek, the foremost scholars of the Indian relationship to the national park phenomena, it would be difficult for any park to have built a worse record overall when it comes to treatment of native peoples than Yosemite. Its record includes: "prior occupation with extensive horticulture by Indians, brutal military conquest of the land, a park created with no regard for past or present native claims; an Indian petition for redress of grievances; the ignoring of the petition by Congress; repeated efforts by park rangers to evict remnant villages, Park Service neglect of ethnographic interpretation; and belated NPS recognition that Yosemite was, and is, important to aboriginal people."[13] It is also essential to recognize that the native peoples in Yosemite Valley and California had survived a brutal legacy prior to Yosemite being set aside in 1864. Drastic population loss followed contact with American, Mexican, and Spanish settlers, and the 1849 gold rush and the giant influx of settler population accelerated an existing high death rate from Hispanic slavery and disease. The Mariposa Indian War that then ensued saw a litany of Indian abuses and brutal attacks on Indian peoples, a number of whom had been forced to work in gold mines or forced onto reservations.[14] In 1890 52 Ahwahneechee asked Congress for a million dollars in gold compensation for what their ancestors had suffered. The petition noted how non-Indians had misused Yosemite and its resources: "The valley is cut up completely by dusty, sandy roads, leading from the hotels of whites in every direction . . . All seem to come only to hunt money . . . This is not the way in which we treated this park when we had it . . . This valley was taken away from us [for] a pleasure ground . . . Yosemite is no longer a National Park, but merely a hay-farm and cattle range."[15] No one listened.

Of course, Yosemite is not unique in terms of national parks having a complex and contested relationship with indigenous peoples. As Keller and Turek's work reveals, a closer look at almost all of America's national parks reveals a history of Indian peoples fighting to regain sovereignty over lands designated "wilderness" and fighting to regain access to land they have recognized as sacred for generations. While "wilderness" sites are well known, the indigenous peoples who for generations have lived there or who have claim to those sites are generally not. For example, the Nez Percé in Yellowstone and at the Big Hole; the Sioux in the Badlands; the Havasupai, Hopi, and Zuni at the Grand Canyon; the Seminoles in the Everglades; Chippewas on Lake Superior; Paiutes at Pipe Spring; Quinault and Klallam at Olympic; Shoshone in Death Valley; Sheepeaters in Yellowstone; Papagos at Smokies; Navajo at Chaco Canyon and Rainbow Bridge; Blackfeet in Glacier; or Pueblos at the Petroglyph National Monument in Albuquerque. Many more could be written about—Big Bend, the Badlands, Grand Teton, Nez Percé, Great Smoky, Death Valley, Alaska, Hawaii.[16] Essentially, between 1864 and 1916 when the National Park Service was formed, the United States engaged in the forceful creation of wilderness areas enclosed as national parks with their original inhabitants forcefully removed either by coercion and/or treaty or other means. In this sense, park creation was a stage in the process of conquest. Over time Indian peoples have been removed from "wilderness" areas because their presence and activities have jarred with a dearly held non-Indian image of what pristine wilderness should look like.

Admittedly when the artist George Catlin made his voice among the very first to call for the creation of a "Nation's Park," he had also hoped to protect Plains Indians peoples as well as the larger game and landscape they were associated with. In *North American Indians* (1832) he wrote:

> And what a splendid contemplation too, when one (who has traveled these realms, and can duly appreciate them) imagines them as they might in future be seen (by some great protecting policy of government) preserved in their pristine beauty and wildness, in a magnificent park, where the world could see for ages to come, the native Indian in his classic attire, galloping his wild horse, with sinewy bow, and shield and lance, amid the fleeting herds of elks and buffaloes. What a beautiful and thrilling specimen for America to preserve and hold up to the view of her refined citizens and the world, in future ages! A Nations Park, containing man and beast, in all the wild and freshness of their nature's beauty![17]

But these were Indians frozen in aspic. They were not, in Catlin's idea, coeval with a developing America; rather, they were part of a vision of perfection that he felt represented the quintessence of the United States. The Park as he imagined it was not unlike a living diorama and Indian peoples were there as part of a snapshot scene—the West in all its pristine beauty and wildness. He wrote of them in the same way that he wrote about bison and other American fauna. National parks in this sense can be thought of as related to museums—both were triumphalist spaces where America represented itself to itself and to the wider world. The Indian role in this representation was always as a primitive, prior stage, now vanished. The museum movement and the national park movement were more or less coterminous. As elite representations, they were to deliver similar messages to future generations about American superiority and American Indian absence and/or savagery.

The original act of enclosure of national park lands has not lessened in impact over time in Native America. Acute conflicts have persisted into the twenty-first century between native groups and park administrations over issues to do with spiritual freedom, rights to water, the right to hunt, gather, and subsist, the right to sell beads and other Indian crafts, the right to seasonally occupy land as well as over outright claims to sovereignty over land itself. To its credit the National Park Service in 1987 officially committed in its Native American Relationships Management Policy to actively promote tribal cultures within parks. However, this has not necessarily made it easier for park administrators to balance the multiple conflicting interests in parks and such cultural empathy on its own cannot address fundamental claims to exclusive access and/or for land redress.

It was ever thus. Parks and the power politics of enclosure cannot be separated however far back one looks. It is thought that Eden was modelled on enclosed parks owned by Assyrian and Persian nobility. Scholars of the park idea have suggested that the word "Eden" derives from both the Hebrew epithet for delight and the Persian word *Edina* meaning field and park. If the book of Genesis was written or edited around the time of the Jewish exile to Babylon (597–538 BC), then it is likely that Jews during their deportation would have learned of Assyrian and Persian royal game parks.[18] These would have seemed to a people coping with desert, like heavenly spaces, flowing with water and every sort of amenable animal and plant. For Americans, however, the primary image of the park was European. Europe had undergone something of a park-making frenzy in the centuries prior to 1700, and those parks had also been all about hunting—about ensuring that game came and stayed in a designated area where royals and the nobility could hunt and be sure of a constant supply of animals. Thus many of these parks would have a pale, a steep bank with stakes, so that wild deer could jump into the park but not be able to escape from it. They were carefully managed so that game suitable for the hunt thrived and predators such as wolves were kept out. The ideal medieval park amplified its pleasure-making possibilities by having scenic, rolling landscapes that amplified the sounds of hunting, which added to the hunting nobility's general delight and thrill at carrying out the activity.

European parks were also a means whereby the rich and powerful could advertise their good taste and dominance over others. Their creation, just like the creation of American national parks much later, had required the driving off of hunter-gatherers. Parks reserved land such that the poor found themselves bereft of spaces to graze their own livestock, gather fuel, or glean subsistence. Peasants who dared to steal the English King's venison could be punished by castration, amputation, transportation to the colonies, or by hanging. Deer parks were attacked during the English Civil War (1642–1649) and, unsurprisingly, when Oliver Cromwell's "people's" government was basking in a new world following the execution of King Charles 1st at the end of the war, it offered up 93 parklands for sale to raise national revenue. A letter dated July 8, 1524 describing a large stretch of North American coastline to King Francis 1 promoted its virtues not primarily in terms of any supposed gold and spices but in terms of its potential as an excellent game park. It read, "There are animals in great numbers: stags, roebuck, lynxes, wolves, and other sorts" as well as "wild animals that are considerably more wild than in our land of Europe, on account of their being continually disturbed by the hunters," and a host of birds "suitable and convenient for all the delightful pleasures of the chase."[19]

Park-making today involves the same kinds of enforced exclusion as in the past, something that Thomas R. DeGregori, an economics professor at the

University of Houston, recently made clear in a wonderfully no-nonsense book, *The Environment, Our Natural Resources and Modern Technology*. DeGregori discusses shoot-to-kill policies for tribal Africans found hunting on African game parks, the thousands of tribal people evicted in India in the 1970s in order to create tiger parks, and the legal penalties applied today to tribal peoples who attempt to subsist on what were their homelands at Park Montagne 'Ambre in Madagascar, Ranomafana National Park, Madagascar, and the Manas Wildlife Sanctuary in India. He points out that the name the Tsonga gave to the rest camp in Kruger National Park, Skukuza, means "he who sweeps clean." It was so named by the tribesmen because they were forced to leave their villages so the Kruger "wilderness" could be created.[20] We can add to DeGregori's examples the abuse suffered by the Samburu people in Kenya after the land they had lived on for two decades was sold to two U.S.-based wildlife charities, the Nature Conservancy and the African Wildlife Foundation. The charities gifted the land to Kenya to create the Laikipia National Park. The Samburu then found themselves displaced by militias and their livestock impounded in November 2011. The NGO Survival International has now taken the Samburu case which includes allegations of an associated shooting, rape and intimidation to the UN. A further recent example of forceful indigenous displacement involves Botswana's Kalahari Bushmen who have been fighting since February 2002 to have wells unblocked and to regain access to their home, the Kalahari game reserve. Their eviction is linked by many to the fact that the Kalahari game reserve is in the middle of the world's richest diamond-producing region. Mining for diamonds will start in 2013, although now Gem Diamonds who bought the rights from De Beers, have promised to work with the Bushmen to ensure no further degradation of their communities.

To an extent, American national parks were conceived as democratic spaces in opposition to the parks of Europe. In practice, however, they replicated the same processes of exclusion but in the American case that exclusion was predominantly racial—it was Indian peoples rather than a peasant class who found themselves locked out of Eden. American preserves were thought of as sites of restoration and renewal for American people, available to all as an antidote to the hurried getting and spending of the nation's cities. President Roosevelt, who dedicated five national parks during his presidency, said explicitly in 1903 that America's parklands offered "essential democracy" compared to the walled exclusivity of European hunting parks.[21] John Muir for his part certainly saw national parks as salves for the nation. He wrote in 1901, "Thousands of tired, nerve-shaken, over-civilized people are beginning to find out that going to the mountains is going home ... that mountain parks and reservations are useful not only as fountains of timber and irrigating rivers, but as fountains of life."[22] Aside from their democratic and psychological value to the nation, national parks were also seen as a means of demonstrating a uniquely American sense of identity and beauty. Yosemite, for example, was shaped by the landscape designer Frederick

Law Olmsted because it had the potential to demonstrate spectacularly to the world a uniquely American identity. Here, after all, was a natural cathedral capable in its beauty of rivalling the most dramatic religious buildings in Europe dripping in gold. Olmsted saw Yosemite as a monument to American national identity in the same way as Thomas Crawford's Statue of Liberty (1886), Central Park in New York (1857), and the Capitol dome in Washington, DC (1866). America's national parks were seen as repositories of beauty unique among the sights in the world and the fact that such wonders were set aside and preserved by Americans was held up as evidence of the young nation's enlightened nature, democratic spirit, and cultural maturity. But this rhetoric, like the rhetoric of assimilation that accompanied it at the time, did not stretch to Indians. Even for John Muir, for whom Yosemite was "a people's park," those people did not include Indians. Although the parklands had been their home they were to forfeit the right to burn so as to manage the land or to gather and hunt so as to subsist.[23]

In *Uncommon Ground*, Cronon ends his critique of the concept of wilderness by suggesting that "Nature is a mirror onto which we project our own ideas and values; but it is also a material reality that sets limits [] on the possibilities of human ingenuity and storytelling."[24] This seems true when we look at the histories of national parks in the United States, but even if we confine our analysis to them still only superficially so. If parks do show our attempt to hold up a mirror to ourselves, to our own settler sense of paradise and Eden, then that mirror is cracked. National parks, like the land that surrounds them, cannot escape history or relationships of power. Neither will nature in the wider sense allow us to perceive it solely as we would like to. It controls *our* survival, something perhaps better recognized now due to a rise in catastrophic natural events than when Cronon produced his collection.

ASPECTS OF INDIAN THINKING

Indigenous approaches to space, place, land, and to the environment have tended to be and to remain wholly different from those of Euro-Americans. Most often, there is no sense of "the wild." Instead, be it desert, forest, or canyon, Indian peoples have simply registered a sense of home and, more often than not, have over time rejected the notion that there should be the designation "wild" at all. As the Sioux figure Luther Standing Bear put it, "We did not think of the great open plains, the beautiful rolling hills, and winding streams with tangled growth, as wild." Only to the white man was nature a wilderness and only to him was the land 'infested' with 'wild' animals and 'savage' people. To us it was tame. Earth was bountiful . . . "[25]

One of the best pieces of writing explaining these differences is by the Maori writer Linda Tuhiwai Smith (Ngāti Awa and Ngāti Porou) in her book *Decolonizing Methodologies: Research and Indigenous Peoples*, where she writes at length about different indigenous and nonindigenous conceptions of space and of how over time, "indigenous space has been colonized." Western notions of space are embedded in Western language, she explains, and as we have already discussed, are rooted in the exactitudes of Western mathematics and are concerned primarily with a process of compartmentalization. Indigenous communities do not share such an emphasis on differentiation for example between earth/cosmos, public/private space, city/country space.[26] Instead, for many indigenous communities and individuals, land is a basic source of identity. It is foundational to a sense of cultural belonging and central to the oral traditions that reflect the great diversity of Indian lifeways. As Luther Standing Bear put it in his 1933 book, Indians belong to America because of repeated birth and rebirth, because their bodies are "formed in the dust of their forefather's bones."[27] Many Indian oral traditions emphasize a fundamental sense, not of compartmentalization, but of interconnectedness and relationship between all things, between animals, land, peoples, and their languages. Often linked to this in a number of native cultures is a requirement to seek individual, communal, and environmental balance so as to ensure the survival of community within specific landscapes. Thus the self in Indian oral traditions has unlimited context: It benefits from a profound sense of kinship to all animate and inanimate forms of being and there is no split between the sacred and the secular or between humanity and the rest of creation. Place, self, and community are so intimately linked that loss of territory constitutes a deprivation of psychic strength.

The centrality of place to Indian lifeways is centrally reflected in the foundational stories of various groups and in the writing and reflections of the foremost Native American Indian writers. The primary purpose of American Indian origin stories, according to Clara Sue Kidwell and Alan Velie, is to give Indian people their sense of place in the world and establish human relationships with existing environments, those environments being physical manifestations of spirituality and the source of tribal memory. The rock formations, for example, scattered to the north of the Navajo reservation are the remains of the monsters slain by Child of Waters and Monster Slayer. The great monolith in Wyoming named by the National Park Service as Devil's Tower is where seven Kiowa sisters took refuge when their brother turned into a bear. The Black Hills in South Dakota were pushed up when the land was pounded during the great race between the two leggeds (the Lakota people, the birds, and the bears) and the four leggeds (all the other creatures).[28]

This same sense of the fundamental importance of place has been reiterated by many Native American contemporary writers, each of whom echo in their own way A. A. Hedge Coke's remark that "Place is important. Essential."[29] As the Acoma poet Simon Ortiz has put it, Native Americans are admired and respected for their insistence "on a concept of self that is absolutely tied to the interdependence of land and people." For many, land and language itself are indissolubly linked. Jeannette C. Armstrong points out how, according to her Okanagan ancestors, "language was given to us by the land we live within," a belief she connects to the N'silxchn concept of speaking as a profound and sacred responsibility.[30] Leslie Marmon Silko has stressed the same deep connection, praising the fact that "the interior process of the imagination" in the Paguate and Laguna context, "never deteriorated into Cartesian duality, cutting off the human from the natural world."[31] This same relationship to land and place or, specifically, Christianity's lack of a relationship to land is also key to Vine Deloria Jr.'s critique in *God is Red*, where he suggests that Western European peoples and their twentieth-century spiritual, economic, and ecological crises all stem from their biggest problem—a time-centered, rather than place-centered theology. Such a settler emphasis on events rather than places, on unfolding history rather than abiding relationship has in turn been linked to the fact that many non-native religions place an ultimate stress on some future world or "heaven," rather than focusing in a more psychologically beneficial fashion on the present. Deloria sums it up as follows:

> The vast majority of Indian tribal religions . . . have a sacred center at a particular place, be it a river, a mountain, a plateau, valley, or other natural feature. This center enables the people to look out along the four dimensions and locate their lands, to relate all historical events with the confines of this particular land, and to accept responsibility for it . . . Other religions also have a sense of sacred places. The Holy Land has historically been a battlefield of three world religions, each of which has particular sacred places it cherishes. But these places are appreciated primarily for their historical significance and do not provide the sense of permanency and rootedness that the Indian sacred places represent.[32]

Does this set of fundamental connections between such a number of Indian communities and land mean that Indian peoples have a special or better understanding of their link to American soil? Certainly there is a long history of Indian voices warning Euro-America of the dangers of continual exploitation of land. The most often cited is Chief Seal'th, a leader of the Duwamish, who in 1854 prepared to move his people across Puget Sound and away from the growing city of Seattle. There has been much debate about whether words were put into Chief Seal'th's mouth by his original translator, Dr. Henry Smith (1854), but these sorts of debate cannot erase the larger story—a long history of Indian spokespeople bemoaning the conceptual and practical differences in how native and non-native peoples relate to Indian land. Some of the strongest voices in this regard were Luther Standing Bear who watched the last years of settlement on the Great Plains; the Wampanoag sachem Massasoit; Tecumseh, leader of the pan-Indian alliance of 1805; Black Hawk in the 1830s; and in 1877 in particular, the Nez Perce leader Chief Joseph.

A long history of Indian concern for land and its use is one thing, but this does not mean Indian peoples deserve the kind of blanket identification with nature that non-native culture has imposed on them almost since discovery. A number of arguments within American history and anthropology have opened up the fault lines in thinking about these issues. One especially forceful debate has been over whether native peoples actually ever used the term "Mother Earth." On one side Sam Gill in *Mother Earth* (1987) has claimed they did not, while on the other Vine Deloria has documented the metaphor of earth as mother within indigenous traditions as far back as 1776. It is perhaps easier to document the personification of nature in female form within Western traditions. As Peter Coates points out in *Nature* (1998), a personified nature (natura) had become an object of piety, endowed with moral purpose and a meaning independent of mankind, as early as the fifth century in Greece. Sometimes the ancient Greeks explicitly personified that creative force as female.[33]

A bigger set of ongoing arguments has developed over whether Indians ever actually were ecologically minded at all. Calvin Martin in *Keepers of the Game: Indian-Animal Relationships and the Fur Trade* (1978) suggested such thinking is just another stereotype from the late 1960s. He argued that the Indian was, "Propped up for everything that was environmentally sound, the Indian was introduced to the American public as the great high priest of the Ecology Cult."[34] He also suggested that the rapid depopulation of beaver that accompanied the fur trade testifies to Indian culpability as market-oriented capitalists intent on species destruction. Too often this debate has deteriorated into a non-productive blame game as, for example, in Coates's discussion that opens "Were Native Americans really such innocents?" In truth such language masks the larger issue of colonial guilt, which regularly telescopes the Indian past across the centuries so as to highlight instances of demonstrable Indian culpability in species extinction. Most often, the provenance and authenticity of Seattle's 1854 pro-environment speech is questioned in these discussions so as to somehow suggest that this in itself weakens the overwhelming evidence across time of a reciprocal and spiritual approach to land and nature within the great bulk of Indian communities.[35] It was the film producer Ted Perry who put some of the environmentally aware phrases in Chief Seal'th's mouth. He has pointed out that in fact the truly pertinent question is why non-Indians are generally so ready to accept environmentalism when it comes from an Indian but so resistant to taking responsibility for their own actions with reference to the environment.[36]

Of course, the real evidence of positive Indian reciprocal relationships to the environment comes not just from spokespeople such as Seattle; it is littered throughout Indian cultures and spiritualities, as demonstrated by writers such as Christopher Vecsey and Robert W. Venables in *American Indian Environments*.[37] Other writers such as the Yamasee academic Donald Grinde and the prolific environmental and Indian studies scholar Bruce Johansen in

Ecocide of Native America: Environmental Destruction of Indian Lands and Peoples have provided powerful evidence of positive Indian relationships to the natural world over time, especially when it comes to issues of sustainability. They record examples of pre-contact Indian population control, of the conscious spacing of children and the use of plant contraceptives.[38] Thomas Jefferson commented of the Indians he encountered: "They have fewer children than we do . . . [and] have learned the practice of procuring abortion by the use of some vegetable."[39] Similarly, the Cherokee's oral history, for example, has stories in which animals worry about the land becoming too crowded with human beings. In sum, it hard to disagree with Johansen and Grinde's overall conclusions that "the written and oral histories of many Native American peoples indicate that their cultures evolved over thousands of years largely in symbiosis with the earth that sustained them. Often these customs were incorporated into religious rituals that held the earth to be the sustainer of all things and linked the welfare of the earth to the survival of people who lived upon it."[40]

In a real sense the most obvious evidence of a powerful and abiding ecological awareness among Indian communities comes from indigenous languages themselves. A community's language is a testimony to how that community comprehends the world. That language's inbuilt orientation, whether toward positive and sustainable participation with nature or away from it, speaks volumes. As Illinois scholar James Treat has pointed out, there is ample evidence of such participation with nature in languages such as *este-cate em opunvkv*, the Mystoke language. He explains, "The months of the year are named for important moments in the annual round of subsistence: seasonal observations and activities related to agricultural production, but also times for gathering the fruit of undomesticated plants. An older way of life is signified by *em vliketv* that define Myskoke kinship and by *opvnkv* performed at Myskoke ceremonial grounds: various clans and dances mostly named for animals, many of which provided sustenance to our hunter-gatherer ancestors. Even the phrase *este-cate em opunvkv*, literally 'red people, their talk,' uses sensory metaphors—visual and aural—to describe itself." Treat stresses that Myskoke is like many American Indian languages in the sense that it is action-oriented. It has a grammar that revolves around verbs. Thus it stresses actions rather than objects, connections rather than separations, an emphasis suited to fostering an awareness of reciprocity and exchange.[41]

As Grinde and Johansen have pointed out, the truly salient issue is not in fact how Indian peoples related to nature in the past but how they are to cope with environmental issues today, given that Indian lands are subject to some of the worst environmental threats within the United States from strip mining, radioactive fallout caused by uranium mining, and air and groundwater pollution caused by toxic industrial wastes. The current crisis in Indian country is about survival in the first instance as much as it is about the potential to preserve traditional Indian approaches to land and the life of the spirit in late capitalism.

A difficulty that persists is how to and whether to separate aspects of Indian history, belief, and practice from varieties of anti-modernism. A great deal within mainstream Indian thinking has always gelled with anti-modernism, and it has always had an attraction for anti-modernists within the ecology movement. One of the latest exceptional examples is the work of ex-advertising executive Jerry Mander who wrote *In the Absence of the Sacred* in 1991. Here he asks us to reassess what he calls our "technoutopic" ways, which he argues are in fact decreasing rather than increasing our quality of life and workloads while leading us inexorably toward environmental exhaustion. His ideas are backed up by various Indian writers, not least the editors of the Haudenosaunee (Iroquois') *Akwasasne Notes*, who argue "The way of life known as Western Civilization is on a death path on which their own culture has no viable answers."[42]

IN CONCLUSION

Much about the differences between Indian and non-Indian thinking isolated within this and other chapters has to do with a non-Indian limiting of perspective, to do with a non-Indian desire to categorize, demarcate, and separate. Inclusion of Indian perspectives would necessitate a fundamental expansion of thinking concerning space, place, or, for that matter, landscape and nature. This is because Indian approaches to space are large. They include among much else memory, story, and ancestral knowledge. It is a largeness that if we are to believe Luther Standing Bear writing in 1933 is formative to art, culture, individual self-knowledge, and in the broadest sense, to a fundamental understanding of America. Standing Bear understood his contemporaries' angst as a symptom of their distance from American land. The white man he said, "is too far removed from its formative processes. The roots of the tree of his life have not yet grasped the rock and soil [. . .] The man from Europe is still a foreigner and an alien." That is, for Standing Bear, white America had no place and therefore insufficient orientation to create beauty and art. He asked, "For who but the man indigenous to the soil could produce its song, story, and folk-tale; who but the man who loved the dust beneath his feet could shape it and put it into undying ceramic forms; who but he who loved the reeds that grew beside still waters, and the damp roots of shrub and tree, could save it from seasonal death, and with almost superhuman patience weave it into enduring objects of beauty-into timeless art!"[43]

Of course, Indian peoples are not alone in having this enabling and creatively spacious approach to land. Gaelic-speaking Irish, to give just one example for whom place might be said culturally to be almost everything, have their own term that builds story directly into place—*dinnsheanchas*, meaning "the lore of place." In contrast, for a number of thinkers writing in the Western tradition from the late 1950s, nature is less about this primary expansiveness, about this fundamental link between the spoken word and place, instead it is merely what we chose to represent it as and as such it is infinitely malleable and subjective. Thus C. S. Lewis could write, I suspect, vastly underestimating the discriminating powers both of ants and men: "If ants had a language they would, no doubt, call their ant-hill an artifact and describe the brick wall in its neighbourhood as a *natural* object. Nature in fact would be for them all that was not 'ant-made'. Just so, for us, *nature* is all that is not man-made; the natural state of anything is its state when not modified by man."[44] Marjorie Hope Nicolson was even more explicit, making how nature is represented brutally definitive. She wrote, "we see in nature what we have been taught to look for, we feel what we have been prepared to feel."[45]

Yet much is changing. For the first time, unique and discrete histories of specific animals, plants, rivers, and forests are being written. Such narratives and analyses make the category "nature" broader and richer and help us to conceive of man's cultural relationships to the non-human world in a more textured fashion.[46] While place is notoriously difficult to theorize and define (Lineu Castello in a recent wonderful book, *Rethinking the Meaning of Place*, compared it to "passion" whose definition is similarly damaged when put into words), it is something culturally resonant that we deeply fear the loss of.[47] Even as the twenty-first century world embraces inauthenticity and tolerates what has been called the Disneyfication and cloning of lived environments, we yearn to reconnect spirit, memory, story, and place. It is a yearning that was powerfully expressed by the anthropologist/philosopher David Abram in his 1996 book, *The Spell of the Sensuous: Perception and Language in a More-than-Human World*, where he writes:

> Once the stories are written down, the visible text becomes the primary mne-monic activator of spoken stories—the inked traces left by the pen as it traver-ses the page replacing the earthly tracks left by the animals, and by one's animal ancestors, as they moved across the land. The places themselves are no longer necessary to the remembrance of the stories, and often come to seem wholly incidental to the tales, the arbitrary backdrops for human events that might just as well have happened elsewhere. The transhuman, ecological deter-minants of the originally oral stories are no longer emphasized, and often are written out of the tales entirely. In this manner the stories and myths, as they lose their oral, performative character, forfeit as well their intimate links to the more-than-human earth. And the land itself, stripped of the particularizing sto-ries that once sprouted from every cave and streambed and cluster of trees, begins to lose its multiplicitous power. The human senses, intercepted by the written word, are no longer gripped and fascinated by the expressive shapes and sounds of particular places. The spirits fall silent. Gradually the felt pri-macy of *place* is forgotten, superseded by a new, abstract notion of "space" as a homogenous and placeless void.[48]

Other writers, such as the Columbia scholar William Leach, share some of these fears and the intensity with which the attack on place has intensified since the 1960s. For Leach, the post-1988 transformation of certain Indian reservations into "placeless" oases for gambling is a prime example of a larger set of processes leading to "the destruction of a sense of place and to the transformation of America into a country of exiles." If the preceding discussion of the key terms surrounding land and spirit in America has proven unsettling, it is only because these terms link so closely to our sense of security and well-being, that is, to our place in the world. Place, as Leach suggests, is at its best, "the collective outgrowth of our control over our own lives and destinies." It is to explaining our disenchantment with place over time and to Indian responses to that disenchantment that we now turn.

CHAPTER 3

≈

Spiritual Approaches to Life in America

The trees and the stars and the blue hills appear to us as symbols.

Aching with a meaning that can never be uttered in words.

— Rabindranath Tagore, *Sādhanā: The Realisation of Life*, 1913.[1]

The quotation above is from a different sort of indigenous Indian, not a Native American but a Bengali from a wealthy Brahmin family who went on to become the first Asian winner of the Nobel Prize for Literature in 1913. Tagore's was one of the first non-Western voices to bring a different consciousness of land, nature, and spirituality to prominence in the West, but today he is little read. This is in part because he became popular as a caricature of Indian mysticism and exoticism and deeper engagement with his work and actions invariably reveals a more complex and less readily marketable commitment to equality, reason, and civilization. He was, if his life's work can be summed up, against what he called "the insolence of might." He combined a political commitment to peoples' freedom from asymmetries of power with an acute awareness of the millennium-old spiritual legacy he inherited. He coupled all of this with a profound desire to see harmony between man's progress and the natural world that sustains him.[2] The lack of attention now paid to Tagore and to the difficult combination of spiritual, environmental, and political imperatives he invoked speaks to larger lacunae in contemporary thinking. Western discourse remains, it seems, particularly resistant to engaging meaningfully with key spokespeople from previously colonized nations when they demand we think in terms that include the conflation of these categories.

One suspects that for similar reasons recent theoretical thinking about space, place, and land has largely ignored Native American Indian approaches. Even when nature and religion are thought about by American scholars, Indian and for that matter African/African American thinking tends simply to get referenced rather than examined, as for example in Catherine L. Albanese's influential 2002 publication, *Reconsidering Nature Religion*. A big part of the problem is rooted in terms and what they signify. Since conceptually both "nature" and "religion" are alien to many native and African ways of thinking, it is perhaps unsurprising that they do not map easily onto Western analyses. Albanese finds this ironic, although it is in truth a symptom of inequality of power and of cultural incomprehension. She does at least recognize the problem, writing "Ironically, this religion of nature was never identified as such by native Indian peoples: in Indian cultural circles and communities there was no abstract 'nature' to which or whom to relate. To say this another way, both word and abstraction are Western European designations for referents named and understood differently among Native Americans and also among others."[3] Because the language of analysis, English, is saturated in signifiers and understanding that reflect non-Indian histories and values, it is difficult, but I would argue not impossible, to talk meaningfully and inclusively about Indian values, Indian understandings, and Indian relationships to land and the material world. In a real sense, this difficulty is the reason *why* we should strive to talk about Indian approaches to land and how they may differ from Western thinking.

The existence of these difficulties should not surprise us, since language has always been at the root of cultural incomprehension on American soil. A European and later Euro-American cultural inability to think beyond linguistic and conceptual boundaries severely limited how much they could comprehend about the "New" World they encountered. It is essential to keep in mind that the America Euro-Americans explored was new only to them. From an indigenous perspective, American soil was something communities had formed close relationships with for countless generations. Among the bulk of native communities there were great and enabling sets of consciousness, a heritage of oral traditions that were to prove consistently resistant to the onslaught of Euro-American cultural attack as the decades wore on. An example is the Laguna oral tradition that Leslie Marmon Silko draws on in her award-winning novels and other writing. In her 1977 work, *Ceremony*, the narrator begins by invoking an oral tradition that is not confined by a linear understanding of time; it speaks not just to a history of the past but to a Laguna consciousness that is ongoing. Thus *Ceremony*'s narrator begins by telling the reader that "Thought-Woman, the spider," created the world through thought and is thinking the story about to be told.[4] This was the sort of robust and alien conceptual landscape expressed through oral tradition that Europeans faced when they first arrived in the Americas, but they failed to comprehend the different, sophisticated ways of understanding existence they encountered or the languages and dialects that articulated them. As ground-breaking and abidingly pertinent books such as Robert F. Berkhofer Jr.'s *The White Man's Indian: Images of the American Indian From Columbus to the Present* (1979) remind us, Europeans were determined to find in the "New" World primarily what they feared and expected to find. Their experiences were guided and framed by sets of expectations that were discrete from their actual experience. They were led as much by their imaginations as by opportunity.

FANTASTIC VISITORS: RAPE, CANNIBALISM, AND WONDROUS LAND

European settlers in the Americas were determined to encounter what was to them exotic whether they found it or not. Back home, their countrymen were just as anxious to have their suspicions confirmed that the "New World" was truly fantastic, a repository of all that their society was not. They therefore repeated the most outrageous traveler's tales long after more sober reports from multiple sources had confirmed them to be untrue. Indigenous peoples, for their part, sooner or later found it best to placate this need in their new European "younger brothers" by repeatedly assuring them that just over the next horizon they would be sure to find the amazing wonders they lusted after. This we can only suspect, not only had the effect of concluding a tedious round of questioning, it also encouraged the aliens to move on. Thus the Arawak in the West Indies, the first people Columbus encountered, confirmed for him that yes, indeed, men with wondrous features did indeed exist but they were, alas, some distance hence. On the north coast of Cuba Columbus had better luck. He was told of "men with one eye, and others with dogs' noses, who ate men, and that when they took a man, they cut off his head and drank his blood and castrated him."[5] Better yet, in Haiti he learned of "people who had one eye in the forehead."[6] When Columbus did not find the fantastical, he consoled his readers with tales of Indian cannibalism, writing, "In these islands I have so far found no human monstrosities, as many expected, but on the contrary the whole population is very well formed . . . Thus I have found no monsters, nor had any report of any, except in an island "Carib," which is the second at the coming into the Indies, and which is inhabited by a people who are regarded in all the islands as very fierce and who eat human flesh."[7] Such a thirst for the fantastic was not simply a peculiarity of the Spanish. In *Sphaera Mundi* (1498) John of Holywood wrote of the New World's peoples as being "blue in colour with square heads."[8]

Columbus was told wondrous tales of an island full only of women by the indigenous peoples he met. Women, it is worth noting, and sex were a particular fascination for him and a majority of other early colonizers and commentators. Coming from an overpopulated, sexually repressive and, for the upper classes in particular, habitually overdressed Europe, encountering so much Native American nakedness was truly remarkable. Columbus repeatedly stressed Indian generosity, their supposed guileless and defenseless nature, and their nakedness. In his widely published 1493 letter he wrote: "The people of this island and of all the other islands which I have found and of which I have information, all go naked, men and women, as their mothers bore them, although some of the women cover a single place with the leaf of a plant or with a net of cotton which they make for the purpose. They have no iron or steel or weapons, nor are they fitted to use them."[10] Elsewhere Amerigo Vespucci, who gave the New World continents their new name, described his understanding of native women in his highly influential *Mundus Novus* (1504–1505). To Vespucci, indigenous Americans lived in what late-nineteenth-century ethnographers would call a "promiscuous horde,"[11] a lust-fueled sexual free-for-all so incestuously debauched it sat easily beside routine gorging on the flesh of fellow Indians. He wrote: "All of both sexes go about naked, covering no part of their bodies; and just as they spring from their mother's wombs they go until death." Indian women, "being very lustful, cause the private parts of their husbands to swell up to such a huge size that they appear deformed and disgusting; and this is accomplished by a certain device of theirs, the biting of certain poisonous animals. And in consequence of this many lose their organs which break through lack of attention, and they remain eunuchs." Indian sexual relationships it seemed were as devoid of structure as Vespucci perceived Indian political and cultural relationships to be: "They live together without king, without government, and each is his own master. They marry as many wives as they please; and son cohabits with mother, brother with sister, male cousin with female, and any man with the first woman he meets. They dissolve their marriages as often as they please, and observe no sort of law with respect to them." Sexual abandon seemed to go along with boundless appetites for other transgressions. Vespucci noted that "human flesh is a common article of diet with them. Nay be assured of this fact because the father has already been seen to eat children and wife, and I knew a man whom I also spoke to who was reputed to have eaten more than three hundred human bodies." Yet even cannibalism did not merit as much attention in Vespucci's narrative as did the sexual availability to Christians of native women and their looks, especially the shape of their breasts. Returning to a favorite theme, he wrote:

> The women as I have said go about naked and are very libidinous; yet they have bodies which are tolerably beautiful and cleanly. Nor are they so unsightly as one perchance might imagine; for, inasmuch as they are plump, their ugliness is the less apparent, which indeed is for the most part concealed by the excellence of their bodily structure. It was to us a matter of astonishment that none was to be seen among them who had a flabby breast, and those who had borne children were not to be distinguished from virgins by the shape and shrinking of the womb; and in the other parts of the body similar things were seen of which in the interest of modesty I make no mention. *When they had*

the opportunity of copulating with Christians, urged by excessive lust, they defiled and prostituted themselves.[12]

We can all recognize that the opportunity to copulate with a Christian is not something to be taken lightly even today, but from evidence elsewhere it seems likely that Vespucci was primarily justifying European Christian lust as opposed to recording the supposed rapaciousness of the Indian women Europeans encountered. Although it is not disputed, it is too infrequently acknowledged that rape, slavery, and the forcible extraction of value were what Columbus was about in what was for him a "New World." For Jack Forbes, the rape that was part of the earliest colonizers activities was part of a wider psychosocial condition endemic to Western culture, a disease he calls *wétiko* (cannibal) psychosis. Forbes is Powhatan-Delaware but takes the term from the Cree who use it to denote "an evil person or spirit who terrorizes other creatures by means of terrible evil acts, including cannibalism." The psychosis, he argues, "includes, or is closely inter-twined with, sexual abnormality and also a hatred for, and aggressive attitudes towards, women."[13]

As for cannibalism, we can be fairly sure that it existed in the Americas, but to what extent and to what extent it was ritualistic and part of established processes of limited war we cannot know. It is more useful to think of the descriptions by Columbus and other early commentators of native cannibalism as part of a long history within the West whereby flesh-eating was used as the ultimate signifier of difference, a means of differentiating reasonable humans from the wholly alien. As far back as Herodotus, the Greek fifth century "father of history," we have descriptions of lawless, desert-living flesh-eating savages. He wrote:

> These Scythian husbandmen then occupy the country eastward for three days' journey. Beyond this region the country is desert for a great distance; and beyond the desert Androphago dwell. The Androphagi have the most savage customs of all men; they pay no regard to justice, nor make use of any established law. They are nomads and wear a dress like a Scythian; they speak a peculiar language; and of these nations, are the only people that eat human flesh.[14]

Crucially, signifying inhumanity in others has always made it easier to treat those others in inhuman ways.

Interestingly, for Forbes and a number of recent writers who might be seen as thinking in his wake following publication in 1978 of *Columbus and Other Cannibals: The Wétiko Disease of Exploitation, Imperialism and Terrorism*, the real cannibals of this world have always resided in the West. Thus bell hooks writes of the Euro-American desire to incorporate and consume what is ethnic as "eating the other"; Dean MacCannell characterizes the postmodern present as neocannibalism and Deborah Root describes Western civilization as cannibal culture.[15] Root also finds it useful to invoke a native term, this time the Lakota idea *wasi'chu*, interpreted as describing Europeans as big-talkers and greedy fat-eaters.[16] Such books have been criticized for reinscribing an inverted form of the same binary thinking that characterized early descriptions of contact, but they nevertheless usefully serve to unsettle our understanding of what true cannibalism in all its forms might entail.[17] Rather than be appalled at descriptions of fifteenth-century native cannibalism, it might be more useful to see them primarily as part of a constellation of thinking and labeling that early colonizers carried with them that facilitated colonialism. Given how Europeans of the time thought and acted when it came to territorial expansion, it would have been surprising had they *not* described cannibalism along with much else that they wanted to find that was new, exploitable and/or fantastic, weird, and inherently transgressive. It is worth also noting that cannibalism as a marker of inappropriate human behavior can be seen in more than one way. Where it has existed outside the West there is much to suggest that it has done so historically within a nexus of relationship and ritual that tends ultimately toward a balance of sorts. For example, when the noted Polish anthropologist and proponent of participant observation Bronislaw Malinowski was in Melanesia he recalled:

> Cannibalism shocks us terribly. Yet I remember talking to an old cannibal who from missionary and administrator had heard news of the Great War then raging in Europe. What he was most curious to know was how we Europeans managed to eat such enormous quantities of flesh, as the casualties of a battle seemed to imply. When I told him indignantly that Europeans do not eat their slain foes, he looked at me with real horror and asked me what sort of barbarians we were to kill without any real object.[18]

[handwritten margin note: barbaric is a relative term with varying connotations]

CULTURAL INCOMPREHENSION, NATURE, AND THE WESTERN LOSS OF A SENSE OF ENCHANTMENT

The gaps between a number of traditional Indian approaches to the life of the spirit within the United States and those of the dominant society in the United States and throughout the West are wide. One gap in particular tends to get overlooked perhaps because it is so obvious. It concerns the amount of energy a number of non-Indian communities have put into the scientific understanding of religion—a conundrum most Indian communities have found little value in pursuing. The conundrum has important links to how nature has been and is still thought about in the West. Few dominant thinkers deny that religion or some sense of the spiritual has been and remains a fundamental means whereby mankind satisfies a central need—to make sense of personal experiences and of the wider world. However, the debate about exactly how spiritual drives relate to how individuals or communities live in specific environments is by no means resolved.

Non-Indian cultures have retained a fascination with the global persistence of religious or spiritual understanding because it has persisted even after science is
deemed to have provided explanations for all natural phenomenon, that is, after
Western science has supposedly explained away the natural causes stimulating
the fear that was once thought to lie at the root of all human spirituality.

One influential answer to the question of why religion/spirituality persists
in spite of Western science came in the mid–twentieth century from W.
McDougall (1950). He suggested that people found religion satisfying because it
appealed to three emotions: admiration, awe, and reverence. Prior to this
Sigmund Freud (1927) had dismissed religious belief as a negative phenomenon,
as both a symptom of man's need for a protective father and as a culturally conditioned ego defense mechanism. Freud, of course, firmly believed in the superiority of science over religion and was also a firm Darwinist. In comparison, his
foremost adversary, Carl Jung, saw religion more positively, as something that
mankind needs to express in order to be psychologically healthy. Jung saw the
pitiful violence wreaked by the First World War as evidence of mankind having
divorced itself from fundamental religious archetypes and having become dominated by materialism and the fearful consequences of science and technology.
He also pointed out that Christian thinking dangerously did not recognize mankind's dark side, what he called its "shadow," and thus instead of recognizing
mankind's darkness within, projected that darkness outward and demonized
others. Jung also was concerned that the Western concept of the Trinity lacked
a feminine element and argued that this linked religion perilously to aggression,
authority, and power.[19] While recognizing a number of critics of Jung's work
and registering its sometime lack of status within the academy, one of today's
foremost psychologists David Fontana sees him as key to a gradual Western move
toward a positive psychological relationship to nature. He notes:

> it is consistent with Jung's ideas to suppose he would argue that man's failure to
> recognize his own shadow is a main reason for his failure to understand and live
> in harmony with nature. Failure to recognize the destructive tendencies of his
> own shadow has led man to destroy and exploit nature for his own selfish ends,
> thus inadvertently putting himself at the mercy of natural forces to which he
> could with better sense accommodate himself.[20]

Admittedly, the above is a brutally truncated summation of aspects of Western
psychological thinking, but it does serve to highlight how non-Indian thinking
has over time struggled to reconcile the legacy of its religious thinking and how
it has been forced particularly of late, to reassess how science and all forms of
spirituality relate to how mankind approaches the non-human world. There is,
of course, much more to non-Indian thinking on the topic than is referenced
above, but the outline holds true. It remains the case that non-Indian thinking

has not made either speedy or especially fruitful progress over the last few centuries when it comes to either explaining the impulse to spirituality or mapping a new and positive set of relationships between mankind, his transcendent mind, and the natural world.

This is not to say that intellectually, at least, Western thinking has not begun to readdress on a fundamental level the Enlightenment project that coincided with the "discovery" of the "New World" and with it the onset of recurrent bouts of unprecedented despoliation of nature. The whole idea of progress took an intellectual body blow in 1944 when Adorno and Horkheimer published their *Dialectic of Enlightenment*. Here both Bacon's readiness to dominate nature and Marx and Engel's blithe assumption that controlling it would necessarily bring about general advancement were attacked. Adorno and Horkheimer's greatest lament was that capitalism and science had reduced what was most precious about life simply to what could be enumerated and divided up. As they put it "Number becomes the canon of the Enlightenment. The same equations dominate bourgeois justice and commodity exchange ... Myth turns into enlightenment and nature into mere objectivity."[21] These new material emphases were connected to an even greater spiritual loss, a loss, in the West and its orbit, of a sense of enchantment.

As Charles Taylor has explained at length, this surrender of the sense of an "enchanted world" and, with it, the sense of fullness it can bestow is no small sacrifice.[22] It can be traced back to the late seventeenth and early eighteenth centuries, which saw a shift within Western élite cultures toward anthropocentrism, toward the idea of impersonal order, and the idea that there was a true, natural religion. As polite society developed and as Hume put it "the ideas of men enlarged on all sides," men developed what Taylor calls a "buffered identity" arising directly from disenchantment.[23] Most importantly, their new take on the life of the spirit removed them in part from their communities; it involved "disintricating the issue of religious truth from participation in a certain community practice of religious life, into which facets of prayer, faith, hope are woven."[24] Admittedly, the movement called Neoplatonism that swept through Renaissance Europe revived notions of the earth being alive, of the universe being peopled by spirits, and of the world being governed by fundamental correspondences and relationships between all things. However by the end of the seventeenth century most scientists were moving toward belief in a much more mechanistic world. Science and what was called "magic" had originally advanced side by side, but as Keith Thomas has explained, even though elements of magic survived within orthodox religion after the Reformation, eventually a rejection of Neoplatonism marked the end of magic's whole intellectual basis. The idea that nature was subject to immutable laws took away the validity of miracles and the "Cartesian concept of matter relegated spirits, whether good or bad, to the purely mental world."[25] Yet another blow came from the commitment to experiment that characterized the new sciences, a commitment antithetical to belief in a world governed by enchantment.

The shift away from enchantment that was in progress within the West at the same time as the "discovery" and settlement of the "New World" did not happen overnight; rather it was a ragged and piecemeal process. A sense of enchantment stubbornly persisted in Europe, it was "one of the most serious obstructions to the rationalisation of economic life" as Max Weber put it, but some combination of Christian and other interests eventually brought about within the West a "disenchantment of the world" that drove certain values to take recourse within either the realms of fraternity or mysticism. As Weber explained in "Science as a Vocation" (1918–1919): "The fate of our times is characterized by rationalization and intellectualization, and, above all, by the 'disenchantment of the world.' Precisely the ultimate and most sublime values have retreated from public life either into the transcendental realm of mystic life or into the brotherliness of direct and personal human relations."[26] It is this lack of spirit, this loss of a sense of wonder interlinked with community, livelihood, and place that remains at the core of modern difficulties with land and the maintenance of the natural world however defined.

That said, a number of thinkers have argued that the historical roots of the devaluation of nature go even deeper still. The scientific revolution served to embed in new ways a hierarchical opposition between the human and the natural world but as we have seen from examination of the Bible, the roots of that opposition, the roots of a sense that human worth was connected to human separation from the rest of nature, went back much farther. Some think it goes back as far as mankind's adoption of settled agriculture. Writers such as Paul Shepard, Brian Morris, and James Serpell suggest that the move away from a hunter-gatherer lifestyle toward ways of living that required actively altering environments was a pivotal shift that marked the beginning of our ongoing problems ensuring our survival in relation to and alongside the non-human world.[27] Farming, after all, necessitates a wholly different attitude to the non-human world than the largely nomadic life of the hunt. Shepard argues that with this shift, man ceased to perceive wildlife as equals and ceased to relate to wild animals with humility and respect; instead, he adopted antagonism and hostility. Settled agriculture, after all, most often involves the subjugation or taming of wild creatures and the manipulation of the environment so as to foster and ensure sustained plant growth. As another scholar, Boyce Rensberger, writes, "the fact is that a farmer's success depends on his winning battles against pest and predators and even against nature's efforts to recolonize his fields with weeds."[28]

Arguably this implies that the farmer's relation to nature is unduly antagonistic, but it is the case that agriculture is highly dependent on rain and the absence of malevolent weather and that wild animals can bring irreversible havoc to subsistence agrarianism. While it is too pat to suggest, as one scholar has recently, that the hunter-forager lifeway is universally characterized by a harmonious, respectful, and reciprocal relationship to nature and in contrast the agricultural lifeway is characterized by a malevolent antipathy to the wild as opposed to the tame, there is considerable evidence that the hunting lifeway fosters an acute and unique awareness of mankind existing according to the vicissitudes of something greater than man—that is, existing at the whim of nature. Even the best early hunter, after all, cannot guarantee success. As a result there is repeated evidence from hunter-gatherer communities across time of their respect for balance, of an awareness of reciprocal relationship and kinship between all things, and of a sense of the precariousness of life. A predominance of hunter-gatherer traditions speaks of the need to respect what is hunted, of the hunted giving themselves up voluntarily to be eaten by man, and of the hunt being essentially outside of mankind's control. A useful book that has dealt with some of these issues is *Hunter-Gatherers: Property, Power and Ideology*, edited by Tim Ingold, David Riches, and James Woodburn. In it anthropologist Henry S. Sharp describes how certain traditional Chipewyan peoples of northern Canada believe that an animal "cannot be killed without its consent" and that animals choose to die for the hunters for whom they feel "pity" or empathy. Furthermore, failure to follow appropriate protocol and ritual during and after the hunt can result in animals rescinding their agreement to allow themselves to be killed in the future. Sharp explains, "Animal abuse, as regards the matter of killing, treatment of the carcass, wastage of the prey animal, and (in the past) allowing dogs to feed improperly upon an animal's parts can result in an entire species taking offence, all animals refusing to die for a particular hunter and even being so outraged as to abandon whole areas for a time, perhaps longer than a generation."[29]

A yet more nuanced, passionate, and fuller understanding of aspects of a hunting way of life came in 1981 from Hugh Brody's study of the hunting patterns of the peoples of the Canadian subarctic. *Maps and Dreams: Indians and the British Columbia Frontier* re-oriented how a great many Indian and non-Indian scholars viewed American land and the maps used to represent it. An elegantly written book, it disrupted centuries-old stereotypes about Indian land use but it was not without flaws. For example, it reinscribed several equally hoary stereotypes about essential Indian qualities and made its central character, the Beaver elder Joseph Patash, emblematic of his whole culture. Even so, Brody spent eighteen months in the subarctic, living with a small group of Beaver Indians who maintained a viable hunting economy in face of a projected oil pipeline and various other incursions on their way of life. He showed how their hunting lifeway, while it could appear from the outside to be haphazard, irrational, and its practitioners improvident, was actually deeply robust having survived centuries of disruption. It makes very subtle, intelligent, and sustainable use of land using rotational conservation, and it is based on freedom of access to and flexible use of large amounts of territory. A hunting way of life has little use for accumulated property but it has its own rationality, securing relative prosperity for its people with minimum effort, something that, as Brody points out, is "the very essence of sound economic practice."[30]

Brody admitted that the maps the Beaver drew, and which he publicized, can tell only part of the story, since they cannot do justice to the sophistication of a renewable resource economic system involving varying patterns of movement at different times of the year and shifts from one kind of resource harvesting to another. Yet they go part of the way toward explaining the "hidden" Indian economy that has survived generations of attack and incursion. They help explain why commentators puzzle over the fact that like the Inuit, the Beaver, Cree, and Slavey Indians of northeast British Columbia are "poor" but their tables are always laden with meat. Their maps unpack the seeming paradox fundamental to under-standing this kind of economy; as Brody puts it, "Living off the land in general, or by hunting, trapping, or fishing in particular, is associated with poverty, but a shift away from such harvesting creates the conditions for poverty." (p. 213) Indian maps showed that a hunting economy was a viable economy, as deserving of representation as the economic interests of non-Indians, and crucially it was a renewable, sustainable, and flexible way of life.

Brody's intention in the early 1980s was that the Indian maps he facilitated being made should "stand in the way of the white men's dreams" for expansion of the oil, trapping, and sport-hunting frontiers. He made the radical suggestion that exploitation of Canadian natural resources may not actually be in anyone's long-term interests, arguing that "Resources left in the ground are saved, not lost." However, the emotional heart of his book was spiritual. At its high point, when Indians meet with non-Indians at a public meeting to discuss plans for the giant subarctic oil pipeline, he describes how the Indians present unwrap a sacred map, a magnificent dream map. It spoke to the ancient ways of hunting when men "located their prey in dreams, found their trails, and made dream-kills. Then, the next day, or a few days later, whenever it seemed auspicious to do so, they could go out, find the trail, re-encounter the animal, and collect the kill." This, in a book full of references to what could be called a human hunting mind-set, where clock-time and planning are irrelevances and where the Indians when in hunting mode display many of the attributes of hunting animals, from highly receptive, watchful, relaxed stillness to sudden, decisive action prompted by "a sense of rightness." The moosehide dream map unwrapped was as large as a table top and had been kept for many years. Two Indians, Abe Fellow and Aggan Wolf, explained how the map revealed in intricate detail the path to heaven, all of which had been discovered in dreams: "Up here is heaven; this is the trail that must be followed; here is a wrong direction; this is where it would be worst of all to go; and over there are all the animals."[31] They went on to express the fear that the loss of their hunting way of life would mean that there would no longer be strong-enough dreamers capable of interpreting the map's directions.

Brody describes the hunting way of life as one that produces much plentitude even though it does not require or foster the accumulation of many material pos-sessions. This corresponds with the resentment early settler Europeans felt toward the hunter-gatherer peoples they encountered. They were sometimes described as "noble savages" in part because they behaved as the European nobil-ity did, living nomadically and moving seasonally, spending their time hunting and resting, and not straining themselves to meet with the recurrent demands of settled farming. Given that hunter-gathering is seemingly so pleasant a lifestyle, it is something of a puzzle as to why man adopted settled agriculture in the first place unless it was as a result of population pressure. But given that the bulk of mankind has done so, it may well be the case that the roots of the present-day Western relationship to nature lie with that shift from hunting to farming, from a life in reciprocal and respectful relationship to plants, animals, water, stone, to one where these things have to be controlled and spatially ordered so as to ensure survival. This penchant for order stemming from a survival need connected to farming may explain why the absence of order—wildness—has in Western traditions come to be associated with chaos and negativity. In turn, order has come to be associated with good.[32]

ON INDIAN REJECTION OF NON-INDIAN APPROACHES TO LAND AND SPIRIT AND THE NATURE OF ANIMISM

The earliest records suggest that outright rejection of the whole set of premises upon which Western Christian thinking was based was a persistent characteristic of Indian–non-Indian interaction at contact. Even through the filter of probable repeated translation over time, it is clear that this rejection was more often than not tinged with a firm helping of irony and/or sarcasm. For example, Benjamin Franklin described how when Indians had had explained to them "the historical facts on which our [own] religion is founded, such as the fall of our first parents by eating an apple," an Indian spokesperson stood and said: "What you have told us . . . is all very good. It is, indeed, bad to eat apples. It is much better to make them into cider. We are much obliged by your kindness in coming so far to tell us these things which you have heard from your mothers; in return I will tell you some of those which we have heard from ours." Franklin may well have been using the Indian voice on this occasion to make fun of his own people, but nonetheless, he was representing a kind of Indian puzzlement over the central spiritual narrative guiding Euro-American "discovery" that characterized his and previous eras. It is the same sort of puzzlement that Indian peoples repeatedly felt when Euro-Americans persisted in calling them not by their tribally specific names but by an alien invented pan-continental term—*Indian*. The word has now been reinscribed by indigenous Americans, but it is important to keep in mind that it was originally a term that invoked presuppositions Euro-Americans already had very much in place prior to Columbus's first journey. From the Euro-American perspective anyone they encountered at that time would perforce be an Indian, since Indian was then a synonym for all of Asia east of the river Indus. Indies was the broadest term Columbus could use for all of the areas he claimed under royal patent.[33] For generations of indigenous Americans the word remained a puzzle. As one unnamed Indian man asked the Massachusetts missionary John Eliot in 1646: "Why do you call us Indians?"[34] He might just as easily have asked for an explanation of another fiction—why non-Indians persisted in not perceiving the long-term Indian use of land.

Diversity is at the core of Native American approaches to the life of the spirit; but among what might be called traditional perspectives, animism has a key role. A sense that perception and communication are not the sole preserve of humans and that trees, stones, animals, and places have their own consciousness spans a number of native traditions It is a sense powerfully expressed by the Meskwaki poet and novelist Ray A. Young Bear, who describes a fundamental kinship between the human and non-human world within which the human is not superior but instead dependent upon a much larger spiritual and material equilibrium At the heart of this kinship relationship is place and what it is owed spiritually and materially. Young Bear writes:

> My maternal grandmother used to say it was crucial we have a place of our own. Listening intently, I learned that our lives were dependent upon a plethora of animistic factors immersed in ethereal realities. Basically, she instructed that the very ground on which we all stood, Grandmother Earth, was the embodiment of a former Supernatural being. She was all of nature, this Grandmother: She was the foundation for rivers, lakes, fields and forests; she provided homes and sustenance for insects, birds, reptiles, fish, animals, and human beings. She held everything together, including the clouds, stars, sun, and moon. Our sole obligation, my grandmother instructed, in having been created in the first place by the Holy Grandfather, is to maintain the Principal Religion of the Earthlodge clans.[35]

For Young Bear, "the tribal domain where animism and supernaturalism prevailed" is at the heart of Indian community.[36]

Connected to the heart of animistic approaches to the world is language in a different grammar and different conceptual register than we may be used to. It is a linguistic understanding that has been mapped conceptually in sinuous prose with specific reference to the Koyukon of Alaska by the British social anthropologist Tim Ingold drawing on the work of Richard Nelson. Ingold describes the "meshwork of storied knowledge" that characterizes these other ways of knowing, a knowledge discrete from the "colonial imaginary that sees the world spread out before it like a surface to be occupied, and whose contents are to be collected, inventoried and classified." This other way of knowing the world conceives of it as continual birth. Thus the fundamentals of grammar change such that names become verbs rather than nouns. The focus is on what is ongoing rather than on what momentarily is and knowing is more akin to storytelling.

Particularly interesting is Ingold's application of Gilles Deleuze and Félix Guattari's discussion[37] of how animals are perceived when it is not as anthropomorphized subjects or as a set of characteristics that may be classified. Ingold explains:

> The third way is to regard the animal as going on: not as a living thing of a certain kind but as the manifestation of a process of becoming, of continuous creation, or simply of *being alive*. From this perspective the wolf, for example, 'is not fundamentally a characteristic or a certain number of characteristics; it is wolfing' (Deleuze & Guattari, p.265). To say that the wolf is a pack animal, argue Deleuze and Guattari, is not to suppose that it lives in packs, or to enumerate the individuals of which each pack is comprised. Rather, it is to say that the wolf *is itself* a pack. It is, in other words, the 'going on' of wolfing, seen now here, now there, in its multiple instantiations.

Thus Ingold explains how hunting cultures like the Koyukon can go beyond nouns *without* going beyond language. This creates, reflects, and perpetuates an entirely different understanding of and relationship to animals and other beings. Thus to speak of an animal in this fashion as the Koyukon may is to enter into the process of its life: "speaking its name is part of the process whereby language itself is brought to life: the animal can be animaling in a language that is languaging." Ingold takes this active, engaged and dynamic language relationship further explaining how:

> In a languaging language—one not semantically locked into a categorical frame but creating itself endlessly in the inventive telling of its speakers—animals do not exist, either as subjects or objects; rather they *occur*. The name of an animal as it is uttered, the animal's story as it is told, and the creature itself in its life activity are all forms of this occurrence. Animals happen, they carry on, they *are* their stories, and their names—to repeat—are not nouns but verbs.[38]

The above discussion, while it makes clear some of the discrete characteristics of indigenous perspectives on land, spirit, and language, should not be read as suggesting all things indigenous or a pervasive indigenous emphasis on balance necessarily means that indigenous peoples always have acted or act today just as ecologists might prefer. Indigenous traditions are in this sense as flexible and interpretable as any other set of human mores and just as subject to issues of class and hierarchy. A good example of this is the whale hunt controversy surrounding the Makah Indian Nation of Washington State. There are about 1,100 enrolled Makah living on a remote 27,000-acre reservation across Cape Flattery on Olympic Peninsula in extreme northwest Washington. Despite considerable debate within the tribe and formidable opposition from environmentalists outside of it, in May 1999 the Makah resurrected a long-dormant tradition and hunted to death a gray whale, an endangered species until 1994. It was done in a fashion the Makah considered ceremonially and ritually appropriate. It reasserted treaty rights allowing the Makah to hunt whales dating back to 1855 but which they had not implemented since the 1920s. For about three decades from about 1860 the Makah had concentrated on commercial sealing until federal protection of seals was inaugurated because of seal depletion. Aside from a lack of gray whales due to commercial culling, a large part of why the Makah stopped whaling in the 1920s was because of an American assimilation drive that included various forms of cultural suppression. To a number of Makah, the resumption of whaling was a means of cultural revitalization, a way of teaching their young about a great Makah ritual heritage and of improving a diet too full of sugar and carbohydrate. In contrast, to a number of ecologically minded protesters, including the militant Sea Shepherd Conservation Society, the Makah were simply stupid for killing a whale while other sources of good food were readily available to them.

A juvenile gray whale was taken by the Makah while Makah women ceremonially lay down as per tradition. The next week the tribe held a large potlatch and invited other tribes. The environmentalist backlash was fierce, persistent, and aggressive, pitting animal rights against Indian "baby whale killing." Over 350 groups from 27 countries opposed the hunt. The President of the Makah Whaling Commission, Keith Johnson, dubbed the response "moral elitism."[39] Since 1999 Makah whaling has been piecemeal, family- rather than community-based, and stymied by various lawsuits. The 1999 hunt and subsequent hunts can be seen as a form of strategic essentialism carried out to articulate cultural autonomy in what is a post- or neo-colonial context for Indian peoples within the United States. In this new incarnation of Makah tradition, a gray whale gave its life to help assert and perpetuate Makah identity, an enterprise the majority of Makah felt outweighed other considerations. One might also argue that the Makah whale hunt was environmentally sound on a number of levels. It reinvigorated the Makah community and almost every part of the whale was used, not least the whale's symbolic and intercultural power to highlight a native people's rights to maintain their way of life in whatever sovereign form they chose. A similar determination has at points characterized other ways in which native peoples have given their values voice within Native American Indian literature and art and it is to these we now turn in the chapters that follow.

CHAPTER 4

~

Literature, Land, and Spirit

Man is not the lord of beings. Man is the shepherd of Being. Man loses nothing in this "less"; rather, he gains in that he attains the truth of Being. He gains the essential poverty of the shepherd, whose dignity consists in being called by Being itself into the preservation of Being's truth.

—Letter on Humanism, 1947, Martin Heidegger in D. F. Krell,
Martin Heidegger: Basic Writings, 1977

For the Amahuaca, the Koyukon, the Apache, and the diverse Aboriginal peoples of Australia—as for numerous other indigenous peoples—the coherence of human language is inseparable from the coherence of the surrounding ecology, from the expressive vitality of the more-than-human terrain. It is the animate earth that speaks; human speech is but a part of that vaster discourse.

—David Abram, The Spell of the Sensuous, p. 179

BEGINNINGS: NATURE, INDIAN IMAGINATION, AND EUROPEAN INNOCENCE

Early settlers to what would become the United States had much invested in the idea that native peoples were incapable of fiction, incapable of the conceptual and metaphorical dexterity it implies. Indians were thought of as being stunted in this regard, as literalists unable to see or think beyond what an image or a sign represents. As Hayden White explained:

> The lack of this fictive capability, the inability to "play" with images and ideas as instruments for investigating the world of appearances, characterizes the unsophisticated mind wherever it shows itself, whether in the superstitious peasant, the convention-bound bourgeois, or the nature-dominated primitive. It is certainly a distinguishing characteristic of mythical thinking, which, whatever else it may be, is always inclined to take signs and symbols for the things they represent, to take metaphors literally, and to let the fluid world indicated by the use of analogy and simile slip its grasp.[1]

Such thinking persisted despite very early recognition, for example from Amerigo Vespucci, that native peoples spoke a multitude of languages and that the old European insistence that there were only 77 different tongues in the world was flawed.[2] It was important because it justified settler behavior; if Indians lacked such a higher capability then it followed that they were fundamentally different from Europeans and they could be treated in fundamentally different ways according to separate standards. By the eighteenth century these ideas had been codified. The work of René Descartes and other aspects of the Enlightenment impetus privileged reason over other human characteristics. Writing was cherished as the means whereby reason was expressed and it was not thought that races lower down the chain of being from Europeans were capable of it, or at least not comparably so. Western culture used writing, as Henry Louis Gates, Jr. once put it so pithily, as "a commodity to confine and delimit a culture of color." Denying literary ability for those "beneath" Euro-Americans had its own significance for blacks in America, since it denied them the humanity that would have made slavery difficult to justify, but the principle applied to Indians too, if in different ways. Indian peoples, like black peoples, were condemned as lacking the dimensions to which writing gave both access and voice. Gates illustrates this with a little-known 1748 quotation from Hume that links this supposed absence of ability within non-European racial groups directly to nature itself, a self-verifying set of justifications that served to reassure those who were white that they were also right to enforce their "superiority" on others. Hume wrote:

> I am apt to suspect the negroes, and in general all the other species of men (for there are four or five different kinds) to be naturally inferior to the whites. There never was a civilized nation of any other complexion than white, nor even any individual eminent either in action or speculation. No ingenious manufactures amongst them, *no arts, no sciences* ... Such a uniform and constant difference could not happen, in so many countries and ages, if *nature* had not made an

original distinction betwixt these breeds of men. Not to mention our colonies, there are Negroe slaves dispersed all over Europe, of which none ever discovered any symptoms of ingenuity ... In Jamaica indeed they talk of one negroe as a man of parts and learning [Francis Williams, the Cambridge-educated poet who wrote verse in Latin]; but 'tis likely he is admired for very slender accomplishments, like a parrot, who speaks a few words plainly.[3]

Deemed childlike and comparable to animals, non-whites were thought of as having no sense of anything other than the present moment. Unable to register and thus retain the past, it was thought that they had no grasp of their own history and no means by which to analyze the past as it happened. Such thinking among elites in the West persisted overtly for a remarkably long time. As late as 1963 the Oxford University Regius Professor of History Hugh Trevor-Roper said: "Perhaps in the future there will be some African history to teach. But at present there is none; there is only the history of Europeans in Africa. The rest is darkness ... and darkness is not a subject of history."[4] Confronted with Africa's indigenous oral traditions, Roper, like Hegel before him, could find no version of history amenable to his method and so simply decided that African history did not exist. This sort of myopia had a centuries-long pedigree. Having defined how the past should or could be articulated and finding no immediate evidence of precisely such articulation, Western thinking has tended to ignore the vastness of other cultures' oral traditions and their diversity of means of honoring the past. It chose to characterize what it could not or would not comprehend as irrelevant or beyond comprehension and those associated with it as childish or animal.

Paradoxically, while Indians were thought of as having only a child's capability for understanding the complexity of representation, a significant number of early observers still remained convinced that Indians were more than capable of exhibiting the mental dexterity necessary to deceit. The idea that Indians were in general cunning, lying, and treacherous had deep-seated roots.[5] It can be seen as a direct inversion of a wider truth that Indian peoples were consistently tricked, hoodwinked, and misled especially through the misuse and misapplication of language, translation, and the bases of communication throughout settler history. We can trace that larger history of settler deceit most easily through study of land ceding and treaty history in the eighteenth, nineteenth, and twentieth centuries but also back as far as the sixteenth century to the curious use the Spanish made of a document, the *Requerimiento*, to "justify" attack and consequent usurpation of native lands. In a real sense the *Requerimiento* was a means whereby the Spanish lied *to themselves* that they were satisfying the requirements of international law as it was evolving at the time. It was a means whereby Spanish policymakers could claim they had extended the doctrine of just war to the Americas, a doctrine originally developed in Europe to provide a context for making war against infidels. Military commanders and ship captains would have the document "read" to the native peoples they were about to brutally dispossess from a safe distance in Spanish, a language those they were about to attack almost certainly did not understand. The document explained that native peoples had a choice to make peace or war and that if they failed to acquiesce to the Catholic Church and the Pope's right as the representative of God on earth to donate their territories to the Spanish monarch, then what would happen to them next would be their own fault. The Spanish promised that if natives resisted:

> We shall subject you to the yoke and obedience of the Church and of their highnesses; we shall take you and your wives and your children and shall make slaves of them, and as such shall sell and dispose of them as their highnesses may command, and we shall take away your goods and shall do to you all the harm and damage that we can, as to vassals who do not obey and refuse to receive their lord and resist and contradict him; and we protest that the deaths and losses which shall accrue from this *are your fault, and not that of their high-nesses, or ours, or of these soldiers who come with us.*[6]

This sort of collective lying to the self to maintain a positive national self-image while undertaking progressive and often acutely violent Indian dispossession was a trait shared by all three of the main colonizing nations (Spain, France, and England). For example in the English context in 1636 Peter Heylyn in his survey *Microcosmus* claimed that the "New" world was just like the "old" only somehow not coeval with it, its ways much more like a time three hundred years after the biblical flood. Since native peoples were enjoying a version of European prior history, the expropriation of their lands and resources somehow did them no injury according to Heylyn, given that the future of that land was in any case preordained to replicate the same patterns of power and ownership as in Europe. He explained:

> He that travelleth in any Part of America not inhabited by the Europeans shall find a world very like to that we lived in, in or near the time of Abraham the Patriarch about three hundred years after the flood. The lands lie in common to all Natives and all Comers, though some few parcels are sown, yet the Tiller claims no right in them once he has reaped his crop once. Their Petty Kings do indeed frequently sell their kingdoms, but that in effect is only taking Money for withdrawing further up the Country, for he is sure never to want land for his subjects because the Country is vastly bigger than the Inhabitants, who are very few in proportion to its greatness and fertility ... Sometimes whole Nations change their Seats, and go at once to very distant places, Hunting as they go for a Subsistance [sic], and they that have come after the first

discoverers have found these places desolate which the other found full of inhabitants. *This will show that we have done them no Injury by settling amongst them; we rather than they being the prime occupants, and they only Sojourners in the land;* we have bought however of them the most part of the lands we have, and have purchased little with our Swords, but when they have made war upon us.[7]

Of course, Indian peoples did lie to protect their interests and in particular to wage war. In fact, we have repeated evidence of colonists taking particular exception to Indians waging war against them when previously Indians had enjoyed their company or worked with them and learned their languages. For example, when Indian violent attacks started against Pennsylvania settlers late in 1755, the naturalist John Bartram noted, "most of y Indians which are so cruel are such as was almost dayly familiar at their houses eate drank & swore together was even intimate playmates."[8] As Paul A. W. Wallace explained back in 1945, "what gave the invasion a peculiar pall of horror was that local Indians—inoffensive, shiftless, companionable fellows as they had seemed a few weeks before—were among the scalping parties."[9] The settlers were appalled that Indians deliberately used their knowledge of the layout of settlements and their knowledge of English to make war. Some in Pennsylvania were multilingual, speaking German, English, and/or Dutch as well as indigenous tongues. Even so, such obvious evidence that Indian peoples were capable not only of linguistic dexterity but of strategic thinking and speedy adaptation did not upset long-held myths that they were somehow trapped in time and living exemplars of an earlier, perhaps Greco-Roman stage of European life. It was thinking encapsulated by Ferdinando Galiani in 1751, who wrote confidently of how spatial distance from Europe and time could somehow be interchangeable: "If one wants to discover the truth amongst what I said to have happened in far-off times, there is no simpler way than to look at the present-day customs of the illiterate peoples in far-off lands, the remoteness of place having the same effect as diversity of time."[10]

In sum, in the centuries following contact Indians were deemed incapable of the higher thought necessary to the creation and understanding of fiction, but they were nonetheless thought of as fully capable of deceit. Colonizing nations, for their part and on a larger scale, deceived not only Indian peoples in the attempt to dispossess them of their lands but also themselves, inventing logic and reasons why their displacement of Indian peoples and theft of their resources left them pure and devoid of guilt. The dominant non-Indian understanding of language, valorizing as it does language when divorced from the literal, has important links to the colonizing process in environmental terms. Literature as conventionally understood in the West is largely divorced from the real, it exists in spheres—the symbolic, the historical, the artistic, the imaginary—that are often thought of as separate from nature. Thus in a visceral and immediate sense, literature and writing are thought of as serving to sever humankind from its immediate environment. It is perhaps unsurprising, then, that settler societies, seeking to usurp indigenes and to dominate nature, might argue that those they disposed lacked the ability to manipulate language in an abstract sense. Linked as Indians were to the "wild," they were deemed too connected to the earth to transcend their immanent time and place through use of the written word. Key aspects of Western thought today still cling to this notion that writing per se has served to loosen our embeddedness to the earth. The philosopher David Abram, for example, traces our current lack of connection to the elements and earth back to the invention of writing, stating; "Only as written text began to speak would the voices of the forest and of the river begin to fade. And only then would language loosen its ancient associations with the invisible breath, the spirit sever itself from the wind, the psyche dissociate itself from the environing air."[11] Elsewhere he extends the point, highlighting how, relative to any individual's life, the letters of the alphabet can be said to have a timeless and placeless quality. "They could seem, to culture previously steeped in the fluidity of an oral universe, to be utterly unchanging forms, a most profound magic, as fixed and eternal in their significance as the stars."[12]

The history of Indian writing and perhaps of all writing shows this to be not quite true and not just because writing per se has a long history of drawing us back to nature, to the mythic, and to the spiritual. Writing after all is a medium, influential in its way, but it is primarily a form of communication not the thing communicated. Neither does writing as a medium necessarily dictate either what is communicated or how it is comprehended. The invention of an alphabet that represents the sounds made by the human mouth when speaking does not in itself make what is said more timeless or placeless, for what matters is how what is communicated is received and its cultural, political, and social context. There is also the argument that what is orally transmitted has an abiding quality that is more robust than what is communicated via the alphabet *because of* its potential fluidity and responsiveness to cultural context. Further, Abram's proposed solution to the idea that language has severed us from the earth—to write about place or nature, what he calls "writing language back into the land" does not *necessarily* connect us meaningfully, either in a cultural, political, or spiritual sense, to land, earth, or to nature. The reason is that such connections are not exclusively or even primarily to do with writing; rather, they are linked to wider issues surrounding how we receive meaning, our attitudes of mind, our communities, and our sense of what is sacred.[13] Indian writing in English from the earliest records shows that while how meaning was conveyed was significant, the politics of what was conveyed and what could not be conveyed was just as important. Indian writing, because of whose voice was aired, because of the histories invoked, because of the specific context of publication, whether Indian writers interlaced their language with naturalistic language or not, registered fundamental Indian loss—of spiritual context, linguistic diversity, and of land and of the stories those lands embodied.

That early Indian writing concerned itself so often with loss, specifically the loss of land, is too often underemphasized. Indeed, even when filtered through non-Indian sources and records and distilled onto the page via multiple Indian and non-Indian translations, our earliest records are still replete with Indian voices demanding explanation and redress for the loss of land and habitat. Even colonial representatives such as the powerful Northeastern British potentate Sir William Johnson would write of their terror following the brutalities of Pontiac's War in 1763 of yet more conflict caused not because of Indian actions, but because of colonists' "ungovernable passion" for land.[14] Very often, Indian violence against settlers was in direct response to severe hardship as a result of losing land. One sachem Checochinican's complaint to Lt. Gov. Patrick Gordon in 1729 can be taken as representative of a host of similar situations across the eighteenth-century frontier. He complained that his people were not permitted by their land's new owners even to cut down trees for shelter ever since, "the Land has been unjustly Sold, whereby we are redused to great wants and hardships." Yet another Delaware leader, Teedyuscung, is on record explaining violent conflict after 1755 by stating, "The Land is the Cause of our Differences; that is, our being unhappily turned out of the land is the cause." On occasion, European intermediaries such as Conrad Weiser showed a degree of self-reflection as to how central encroachment in terms of land and resources as well as a lack of good neighborliness made Indian–settler relationships deteriorate over time. He wrote: "Toward the white people as a whole [the Indians] have a deeply rooted prejudice and secret mistrust . . . they say that the white people should have remained on their own ground and lived there and not have bothered them. We came over here with no other purpose than to take their land away from them, to decrease their catch of game, fish and birds, to drive them farther into the wilderness, to make their life more difficult." But in the main, most colonial settlers gave little thought to Indian needs. A waiting game resulted in many areas where settler interests worked to worry away at what underpinned the Indians' presence until such times as their outright removal could be assured through war or massacre. Although much has been written about the English government acting as a buffer between Indian and English settler interests and about the English at least having some sense of a future accommodation being made between indigenous America and its settlers, in truth most settlers wished that Indians would vanish. Little serious thinking was done by them that might answer the question a Virginia trader was asked in 1750 by two Delaware, namely, "where the Indian's Land lay, for that the French claimed all the Land on one side the River Ohio & the English on the other side?"[15]

To many settler commentators, removing Indian title to their lands was a first and necessary step to reducing them to their rightful position relative to their new European neighbors. Thus 1654 English sources spoke of the need to displace Algonquian religion in order to "reduce ym to civility of life."[16] Early accounts teem with unease at how Indian peoples were living above their station, living a healthful, unstressed life, characterized by seasonal travel, hunting, and merriment—living in fact, the kinds of lives reserved in Europe only for the nobility. That they did so served to unsteady a whole constellation of non-Indian thinking about wealth, just reward, sin, and status. Indian good-living was an obvious and practically successful manifestation of separate standards, of a separate understanding of how man might live. Thus early eighteenth-century travelers in the St. Lawrence Valley such as Baron de Lahontan would write with disdain about the Iroquois he encountered that the "easiness of their Life, puts 'em on a level with the Nobility."[17] Disquiet about the obvious quality of Indian life was compounded by the fact so many early colonists chose to defect to Indian communities and to marry into Indian kinship networks. One French elite figure summed the situation up succinctly in terms of the coureurs de bois who routinely intermarried with Indians in the "New France" of the St. Lawrence Valley: "I cannot emphasize enough," wrote the Marquis de Denonville, "the attraction that this Indian way of life has for these youths."[18]

SPIRITUAL EXCHANGE: ON LOSING THE "PEARLES OF THE EARTH"

As part of this process of creating or re-creating a landscape of rightful hierarchies in European eyes, spiritual exchange played a key role. It helped to explain away both the moral inequity of settlers planting themselves on Indian land and the legal wrong of their taking the land of others who, by right of prior occupancy, clearly had primary claim to the territory by Europeans' own legal standards. Perhaps remarkably, even in the midst of initial colonization, such obvious truths were sometimes articulated. In 1609 the Virginia Company propagandist Robert Gray asked himself in print, "by what right or warrant can we enter into the land of these Savages, take away their rightful inheritance from them, and plant ourselves in their places, being unwronged and unprovoked by them." His answer to his own question was muddled. It suggested that Indian peoples invited their own colonization, that the process was inadvertent, and that in any case, with American land being so vast, English and Indian settlement could proceed apace without any detriment to Indian interests. He wrote: "the answer to the foresaid objection is that there is no intendment to take away from them by force that rightful inheritance which they have in that country, for they are willing to entertain us, and have offered to yield into our hands on reasonable conditions, more land than we shall be able this long time to plant and manure." Gray even tried to convince himself and his readers that exchange of resources played no role at all in the settler enterprise, writing; "We desire not, neither do we intend to take anything from them, *ex pacto jure foediris*; but to compound with them for that we shall have of them." The theft of Indian land and resource was thus rationalized as good business, a means whereby English know-how could develop what was woefully underutilized to the benefit of all. As so many underconfident writers have since, he sprinkled his dubious justifications with a garnish of Latin so as to suggest that they were both sagely authoritative and the distillation of ancient precedent.[19] Sometime in 1610 the governing council in Virginia would advertise to those back home that the English, "by way of merchandizing and trade, doe buy of them [the Indians] the pearles of the earth, and sell to them the pearles of heaven." In this way spiritual profit was added to the balance of exchange between settlers and Indians and the loss of the tangible justified through the offer of what was unsought and intangible. Elsewhere such an exchange was similarly characterized as inevitable; a providential circumstance God had created using Indian assets as a means of attracting European colonizers and so of spreading the gospel. As Samuel Purchas put it in the seventeenth century, "God in wisdom having enriched the Savage Countries, that those riches might be attractive for Christian suters, which there may sowe spirituals and reape temporals."[20] Here was a wondrous inversion: the very qualities that made Indian land attractive and worth possessing justified its possession in an exchange whose parameters were essentially one-sided. It was in essence, a version of the age-old rapist's lament. Indian intrinsic qualities were used as a justification for extrinsic actions done in the main against Indians' will and against Indian interests.

Preposterous spiritual exchange also lay at the heart of the judicial and theological ultimatum the *requerimiento* referred to previously. The lawyer behind it, Martin Fernández de Enciso, claimed in 1513 that although God had given Adam the whole earth, idolaters, such as foreign native peoples, in disavowing the only true God had committed such a sin of ingratitude that they had therefore "lost the earth." Native idolaters, like the biblical idolaters once conquered by Joshua in just war, had no spiritual claim to their own lands.[21] In fact, European discovery of the New World accentuated a number of philosophical and ethical problems that had troubled European thinkers before discovery itself. Saint Thomas Aquinas was sure, for example, that the rejection of the true Christ done by heathen Saracens was a sin, but he did not think that if a pagan had never heard of Christ he too was necessarily sinning. Dante summed up the problem toward the end of the *Divine Comedy*, touching on an awkward conundrum whose logic upset the whole matrix of thought supporting the Christian worldview. Dante wrote:

> For 'Here's a man,' thou sadst, 'born of some breed
> On Indus' bank, where there is none to tell
> Of Christ, and none to write, and none to read;
> He lives, so far as we can see, quite well,
> Rightly disposed, in conduct not amiss,
> Blameless in word and deed; yet infidel
> And unbaptized he dies; come, tell me this:
> Where is the justice that condemns the man
> For unbelief? What fault is it of his?[22]

In time this unease would be partially resolved with the offer of the Christian God as compensation for Indians' loss of land and resources, and it followed that if such was the compensation, then Indian peoples must be found to be in dire need of spiritual succor.

WRITING INDIAN LAND AND SPIRIT
IN THE TWENTY-FIRST CENTURY

How does this primal loss of land and of the cultural space within which communities' spiritual traditions flourish register within contemporary Native American Indian literatures? As we make the leap from the origins of colonization within the United States to today, how has the conceptual map changed for Native American voices, voices for so long denied recognition within what might be called the topography of the imagination? Because of the demographic inevitabilities that apply to any set of peoples on one continent engulfed by much larger sets of ethnic groups from another, Native American writing today is predominantly mixed-blood writing. Its remarkable success post-1968 has occurred variously either in opposition to or in concordance with various dominant stereotypes about mixed-bloodedness, about an essential Indian identity, and about the Indian spiritual and cultural connection to the land and to the environment. Here we have space only to testify to its inherent diversity and to make the central point that in contemporary Indian writing relationships to land and spirit are far from uniform or unchanging. As the twenty-first century progresses, it seems inevitable that aesthetic concerns will be in increasing tension with the political and social themes that have dominated Indian writing in the past and that the Native American literature will increasingly be obviously transnational, relating to land and spirit in new ways and in new contexts. Contemporary Native creative writing reflects the fact that the overwhelming majority of Native Americans as well as African Americans, Mexican Americans, Latinos, and Asians live in urbanized or industrialized areas. Indeed, if anything unites Native writers it may in fact be alienation from the environment, from nature, from a reciprocated sense of home. At the same time, it may be the beauty of the attempt, shared by other post-colonial writers such as James Joyce, to reconstitute spiritual and communicative relationships using a language alien to just such relationships. As Joy Harjo has explained, her work strives to reinvent the enemy's language because English denies "anything other than that based on the European soul."[23] The violent legacies of colonialism are not difficult to trace in much native writing and are especially evident in Leslie Marmon Silko's controversial and giant 1991 book, *Almanac of the Dead*. Here using violence against violence is portrayed positively and linked explicitly and implicitly to the oppression and rape of native women and the despoliation of the earth. Silko has described the book as long consideration of the "death orientation that . . . permeates the times we live in."[24] An internalized, domestic violence and lack of emotional attachment within some Indian communities is another legacy of colonialism, for example powerfully expressed by Chickasaw writer Linda Hogan in her 2001 book *The Woman Who Watches Over the World.*

Some of the best critics of Indian writing have bemoaned both the lack of analysis in print of Indian literary relationships with land and the environment and the insidious double bind contemporary Indian writers find themselves in. They may wish to write against romantic stereotyping of Indians as essential eco-warriors, but they may also have a profound desire to register and perpetuate moral, spiritual, and cultural attitudes to land unique to their ethnic group, to their communities, and to their familial contexts. As Lee Schweninger recently put it, contemporary native authors "carefully balance a resistance to reductive stereotyping and a firm belief as expressed through their literature that there is such a thing as a meaningful and useful contemporary land ethic."[25] Like their critics, different Native American authors relate to the ecological Indian stereotype in different ways. Some, such as the Spokane Coeur d'Alene writer Sherman Alexie, have expressed chagrin at European despoliation of American land but find it risible that contemporary Indians coping with some of the highest poverty rates in the country should be automatically connected with environmentalism. He is quoted as having said, "White people only like Indians if we're warriors or guardians of the earth. Guardians of the earth! Have any of you ever been to a reservation? A guest house is a rusted car up on blocks out behind a H.U.D. trailer."[26] For others, such as Winona LaDuke, the historical loss of indigenous peoples is directly linked to wider global species extinction. She writes:

> The last 150 years have seen a great holocaust. There have been more species lost in the last 150 years than since the last Ice Age. During the same time, Indigenous peoples have been disappearing from the face of the earth. Over 2,000 nations of Indigenous peoples have gone extinct in the western hemisphere, and one nation disappears from the Amazon rainforest every year.[27]

For Paula Gunn Allen, discussing Indian writing of the Southwest, Indian peoples and American land are one. She has written explicitly:

> We are the land. To the best of my understanding, that is the fundamental idea embedded in Native American life and culture in the Southwest. More than remembered, the earth is the mind of the people as we are the mind of the earth. [] It is not a matter of being "close to nature." The relationship is more one of identity, in the mathematical sense, than of affinity. The Earth is, in a very real

sense, the same as ourself (or selves), and it is this primary point that is made in the fiction and poetry of the Native American writers of the Southwest.[28]

A number of critics have also argued that land should be central to how Indian writing is interpreted; in fact, that it should be seen as central to identity in Native American fiction. Robert Nelson, for example, has argued that in Indian novels such as N. Scott Momaday's *House Made of Dawn* (1968), Leslie Marmon Silko's *Ceremony* (1977), and James Welch's *The Death of Jim Loney* (1979) land is what provides the basis for a re-centering of self-consciousness. "Acquisition of a 'realistic' vision of the landscape is, in these works," he explains, "a prerequisite to the acquisition of a verifiable cultural identity." Nelson even suggests that land is the answer to the oft-repeated conundrum of how critics might transcend the limitations that stem from their evaluation of native fiction by primarily ethnocentric criteria, that is, the problems that arise from reading Indian fiction as culture. Nelson's analysis of three of the key works of the Native American canon suggests that it is physical landscape, rather than social fabric, that is the common referent defining and validating Indian identity.[29] To be more exact, he suggests it is the relationship between the individual and physical context that creates identity in Indian fiction. As Nelson makes clear elsewhere, this has implications. It means that relationships between humans and landscape may actively drive the plot of Indian stories and that landscapes can function within them as characters rather than as backdrops or settings. Land can be seen to be at the heart of the process of triumphing over alienation, a journey that has been and remains central to key works of Native American contemporary fiction and poetry. There is much to suggest that this relationship, where distance from sacred space is distance from the self, is reflected in native languages, such as Tlingit and the language of the Chukchi in northeastern Siberia, which have a richness and variety of terms to express the position of an object in the relation to the speaker. By comparison, English demonstratives lack such locational range.[30]

For Louise Erdrich, one of the foremost native writers of her generation, land is similarly central. In her essay, "Where I ought to be: a writer's sense of place," she quotes Alfred Kazin's comment that the most striking feature of American writing in general is "our writers" absorption in every last detail of this American world, together with their deep and subtle alienation from it." Erdrich looks at a number of writers, including William Faulkner and Willa Cather, noting their preoccupation with the change and disruption brought to America in the wake of white modernization, and how they wrote with a melancholy awareness that they lived in a culture destroying the character of the vast spaces that made up the continent. In contrast for Native Americans, Erdrich says, their life on the land is part of what that white culture has disrupted and torn apart. She concludes, "Contemporary Native American writers have therefore a task quite different from that of the other writers I have mentioned. In the light of enormous loss, they must tell the stories of contemporary survivors while protecting and celebrating the cores of cultures left in the wake of enormous destruction. And in all this, there always remains the land."[31]

The way such "cores of cultures" are depicted is necessarily related to the area or groups from which they come. It is perhaps not coincidental that some of the seminal early novels in the wave of Native American fiction that began in the late 1960s were set in the Southwest, an area where Pueblo and Navajo cultures had been able to keep more links with their terrain and their past than many other native groups. Novels like N. Scott Momaday's *House Made of Dawn* and Leslie Marmon Silko's *Ceremony* drew on a rich heritage of myth and ritual associated with specific places to tell stories of difficult and hard-fought survival. Yet if part of the political significance of such novels was to reassert and celebrate the value of a denigrated culture, or, as Arnold Krupat puts it using Kwame Anthony Appiah's phrase, "to authorize a 'return to traditions'," later works are more concerned with registering the complexity and hybridity of modern Native American life. They show an acute awareness that there is no return to a putative authenticity, but through their writing generate a sense of the place that fissured native identities now inhabit often by making the unhomely a home.[32] The often impoverished and painful lives that Louise Erdrich's characters lead on or off the reservation fuse both white and Indian inheritances. She transforms the bleak spaces of North Dakota, to which the Chippewa were forcibly removed, into a Chippewa landscape by investing its lakes and water with the imagery of renewal and power that had been associated earlier with the Chippewa Great Lakes home.

Leech Lake Reservation author David Treuer, whose characters' "homes" include a housing strip called Poverty, a parking lot, a derelict train, and the high rise construction sites of the Twin Cities, has argued that critics and reviewers often misread what is happening in these texts. They look to Native American writers to offer representations of true Indianness, to be guarantors of access to cultural authenticity, instead of reading their work as literature, that is as nuanced, many-stranded imaginative writing. To agree with this is not to make land and spirit irrelevant. Louise Erdrich argues that every writer must have a place where they feel they ought to be, because a sense of relating to a place is a constant human need, made even more acute in the modern world. "In our beginnings," she says, "we are formed out of the body's interior landscape. For a short while, our mothers' bodies are the boundaries and personal geography which is all we know of the world. Once we emerge, we have no natural limit, no assurance, no grandmotherly guidance like the Tewa, for technology allows us to reach even beyond the layers of air that blanket earth. We escape gravity itself . . . by moving into sheer space, and yet we cannot abandon our need for reference, identity, or our pull to landscape to mirror our most intense feelings."[33] It is this human connection to land and place, however fractured, violated, stretched, and/ or powerful it is, that so often links contemporary Indian writing and gives it animating force. While we now have a much firmer sense of the great diversity of

Indian responses to modernity and of the impossibility of making unassailable generic, pan-tribal statements about Native peoples, there is nonetheless still truth in University of Montana emeritus professor William Bevis's 1987 insight about the animate and inanimate inclusiveness at the heart of much native writing. He wrote:

> Nature is "home," then to Native Americans in a way exactly opposite to its function for Boone. Nature is not a secure seclusion one has escaped to, but is the tipi walls extended, with more and more people chatting around the fire. Nature is filled with events, gods, spirits, chickadees, and deer acting as men. Nature is "house."[34]

Even where the distance from nature in a welcoming restorative sense and from "home land" has become so great as to become dark in some Native writing, as perhaps it does in Louis Owens's 1991 book, *The Sharpest Sight*, it persists still.

CHAPTER 5

❧

Art, Land, and Spirit

You use a glass mirror to see your face, you use works of art to see your soul.

—George Bernard Shaw[1]

As with so much about approaching Native America, a central hurdle is language and the conceptual matrix it embodies. Or to put it another way, a foundational problem with Anglo-American words and the categorizing they embody is that they are limiting: They put aspects of human activity and understanding in separate silos that in truth do not really exist or, if they can be said to exist, reflect interests outside of the Native American world. This is the case with many words and ideas, including *art* and *literature*. In a great number of Native American languages there is no direct linguistic equivalent for the word *art*. However, this does not mean that native artists are or ever have been unreflective about the art work they produce or that native communities lack a set of aesthetic or value-laden criteria for evaluating what is produced. Throughout history native peoples have valued "worked" or elaborated objects as peoples have the world over, because they give visual and tactile pleasure and have an almost indefinable enhanced power because of that quality. Yet what we might think of as native art encompasses much more than the visual; it has tended to include and perhaps even prioritize oral expression and dance. Furthermore, there tends not be a distinction made within Native American traditions between what is beautiful and what is functional, or between what connects to the life of the spirit and what does not. Thus Indian "women's arts," such as coiled baskets, woven blankets, and beaded moccasins, can have just as much artistic and spiritual value as Indian artwork produced in other forms. The notion of the secular in contrast to the spiritual often simply does not apply. Immanuel Kant's aesthetic theory put forward in 1790, challenged by European artists in the first decade of the twentieth century, that functionality limits the extent to which a work of art can achieve formal beauty and express ideas is generally redundant in the Indian context.[2]

In fact, ideas about design relating directly or primarily to function or ideas about beauty relating primarily to how something externally have limited purchase within much native art. Instead, across native traditions we find much reverence for beauty, but it is most often conceptualized in relation to broader ideas such as harmony and balance. In this sense, Native American art is boundless. It is part of intimately linked sets of kinships, between animate and inanimate forms of being, between humanity and the rest of creation, between place, self, and community that provide spiritual and material strength. Thus much Native American Indian art, like oral tradition more generally, is essentially inclusive; it is a part, as the Ocoma poet Simon Ortiz describes it, of "the actions, behavior, relationships, practices throughout the whole social, economic, and spiritual life process of people."[3]

Historically a lot of what has been designated Indian art has been concerned with spiritual work and with the processes that accompany recognizing and accessing powers connected with specific plants, places, animals, and celestial alignments. For example, Inuit peoples tell stories of powerful earth-dwelling or sea-dwelling spirits that have miniature animals that live on their bodies. These tiny animals travel to the human world and allow themselves to be captured in the hunt, thus enabling human life to be sustained. For thousands of years Inuit peoples have worn small amulets carved in the images of these entities so as to seek their cooperation and to honor them. This speaks to a wider belief shared by many indigenous communities in a basic reciprocity between the spirit world and the world of humans and the plants and animals that sustain them.[4] A small but illustrative example of that binding reciprocity comes from a late nineteenth-century missionary who wrote that among the Dené, "a hunter returning home empty-handed would not say, 'I had no luck with bear or beaver'," but rather "Bear or beaver did not *want* me."[5] The historical record is littered with evidence of this fundamental connection between in particular hunting communities, their spiritual beliefs, and their art. Thus the French traveler Captain Marchand wrote in 1801, "What must astonish most is to see paintings every where [sic], every where sculpture, among a nation of hunters." It was art he noted, that was "not deficient in a sort of elegance and perfection."[6] This was no small compliment, given that according to Thomas Kuhn "in early modern Europe, painting was regarded as *the* cumulative discipline."[7]

This is not to suggest that Native American art is incomprehensibly different or extraneous to American art per se. Indeed one of the many ironies connected with the obsession within the art world for what is uniquely Indian and "authentic" in the sense of being unadulterated by contact with the non-Indian world is that there is much evidence of Native art itself always having valued the exotic and the unusual and therefore of having happily and consistently incorporated imagery and materials from elsewhere. Like artists in many other places across the globe, Indian art has a long history of dialogue within and across Indian communities, and for at least the last 500 years it has responded to the encroachment of other, non-Indian individuals and communities.[8]

Too often Indian art and things Indian in general are put in a special category and defined as being outside of the modern world and its history, but in fact Indian art was a key part of the mix of things Americans used to explore and comprehend modern life and aesthetics, in particular at the beginning of the twentieth century. Americans studied Indian art alongside non-Indian modernist works and found Indian art promoted in the most modern places from department stores to world's fairs. Part of how Americans came to understand twentieth-century artistic creativity came from the attention American art paid to indigenous works of beauty and handicraft. One might even suggest that the Native example legitimized the pervasive interest at the time in formal abstraction. Indian art was welcomed as a tangible representation of what Anglo-American culture recognized it had now perhaps irretrievably lost, a sense of integrated community, a sense of the authentic and of a reciprocal, sustaining link with the natural world. The popularity of Indian art in the early twentieth century, in particular among the avant-garde, was part of what T. J. Jackson Lears identified as "antimodern longings for liberation."[9] These were bound up with a desire for intensity and for a better-realized self in a world that had come to seem perilously sterile, overcivilized, and unreal. Perhaps these feelings have only intensified since as we grapple today with ever-newer levels of artifice in the twenty-first century. Yet we must be grateful to Lears for painting the candystripe picture of the complex process of modernity developing that he did, for it helps us to recognize how its seemingly contradictory impulses (the modern and the anti-modern) in fact act in unison so as ultimately to fulfill the needs of an increasingly powerful corporate state.

The love of things Indian, especially Indian art—what Elizabeth Hutchinson has dubbed the "Indian craze" from 1890–1915—allowed non-Indians to rediscover a lost sense of place, a sense of home in a world that seemed increasingly to lack that sense both materially and spiritually.[10] If we look closely at the spiritual side of early twentieth-century American homelessness, we find that Americans turned to Indian art, as they had in the past, at a time of spiritual unrest. Faith seemed under profound threat and the intensity of belief and the solidity in particular of American Christianity was at risk. Moral and emotional connections had frayed. Without the sort of moral and spiritual framework that had characterized life for previous generations, educated Americans felt unanchored and expressed a gnawing sense of loss. Protestantism had by this time lost its hard edges in a gradually secularizing world, and its lack of influence among the expanding urban, immigrant populations seemed especially marked. On every level, including those encompassing gender, class, race, and age the old hierarchies had shifted and were losing their grip. It was a transition as Lears points out that the nineteenth-century German philosopher Friedrich Wilhelm Nietzsche had foreseen. He predicted that with Christianity's decline, "it will seem for a time as though all things had become weightless."[11] The shift from production to consumption brought with it a new set of values. Whereas before elites had circulated a clear message about hard graft, thrift, civic responsibility, and deferred gratification now the ethos was all about individual fulfillment, leisure, spending, and a detachment from active political civic engagement.[12] The material sense of place that modernizing Americans sought was in part delivered by a perceived link between Indian art and the land. In a decentered, migratory world Indian art seemed to offer a firm and timeless link to American soil and a sense that even amid constant change there were values as old and unchanging as the earth itself.

Being part of their times and responsive to it, Indian artists promoted their work as being authentic, as authentic as the soil itself and just as enduring. For example the Winnebago painter, illustrator, and educator Angel DeCora told the nascent Indian reform group the Society of American Indians in 1911: "The Indian's art like himself is indigenous to the soil of his country, where, with the survival of his latent abilities, he bravely offers the best productions of his mind and hand which shall be a permanent record of the race." DeCora was perhaps the best-known Indian artist of the day; and for her, Indian art was a means whereby the essence of Indian ability could be retained for future generations even as Indian cultures transformed as they adapted to the modern world. As she told her educated middle-class Indian listeners, "The Indian in his native dress is a thing of the past, but his art that is inborn shall endure. He may shed his outer skin, but his markings lie below that and should show up only the brighter."[13]

Modernist art may in the main have been highly self-referential and concerned itself primarily with sculpture and painting, but as Hutchinson has shown, it was also fascinated—crazed, one might say—with Indian aesthetics displayed on decorated objects. In sum, Indian crafts were an important if neglected part of mainstream American art and an important part of how Americans assuaged what John Ruskin called "the anxieties of the outer life."[14] In their homes middle-class Americans created oases of primitivism—"Indian corners" replete perhaps with Navajo weaves, woven baskets, and Iroquois false face masks. The urban consumer found it easy to buy "authentic" Indian art if need be by mail-order, such that he or she could create their own reservation of Indian materials in their own home. They could bring something of the great outdoors and of the quintessence of America into the city, articulating in material form the abstract feelings and freedoms they felt were being eroded through urban living. Such corners said something about the intellectual caliber of their owners and they testified to their taste for the natural, the fine, the well-made, the manly, and the imaginative in a world that seemed increasingly ephemeral, trashy, unnatural, feminized, and mundane. In a word they evidenced what constituted good taste at the turn of the century.[15] Interestingly, while the Indian artefacts so assembled by middle-class Americans were gathered by them so as to assuage what were in large part spiritual losses, little or no attention was paid to their spiritual provenance or possible spiritual power. Dedicated collectors such as the political cartoonist Udo Joseph Keppler (son of Joseph Keppler Sr., founder of *Puck* magazine) bought a Seneca false face mask and was warned by the Cattaraugus elder Edward Cornplanter (Sosondowa) about the dangers of handling "dangerous materials."[16] This did not prevent him triumphantly displaying it as part of his collection in his study even though his own and his father's close association with Indian peoples would have made the spiritual context of false face masks something he understood.[17]

In the Indian schools of the era Indian art was used as a way to encourage Indian entry into the industrialized world and, just as importantly, Indian adoption of the lifeways best suited to an industrializing America's needs. Perhaps half of all Indian young people at the beginning of the twentieth century were exposed to the industrial schools' particular brand of education with some 307 Indian schools claiming they had 21,568 enrolled in 1900.[18] Art was part of a wider onslaught that sought to kill Indian ways within Indian peoples and to induce a respect for the non-Indian conceptualization of life as existing within separate silos. Indian children were required to divide their lives into periods of "work" and non-work, and to conceive of art not as an integral part of a balanced, communal lifeway but as a separate species of activity that required difficult and sustained effort according to a predetermined timescale. Such artistic "work" was encouraged as a means of fitting Indian peoples into larger processes of exchange where the bulk of human effort was linked to its trade value in a wage economy. Thus Frances Sparhawk, secretary of the Indian Industries League, wrote in 1893 of Mrs. Mary Eldredge's Navajo weaving project in Jewett, New Mexico, "The room is not merely for the weaving of their old-time Navajo rugs, so justly famous, but its purpose is expressly to be a place of initiation for these women into work of many kinds, and into our ways of doing work; and to lead them up to modern methods of weaving; also, as far as possible, to teach them to exchange their present desultory methods of work for that regularity necessary to wage-earners."[19] It seems it was not so much Indian art that mattered as much as the inculcation of the work ethic and, perhaps, the removal of the web of spiritual, family, and community rhythms that supported its production. Rather than learn traditional methods from elders on their own lands and in their own homes, Indian children were taught in generational isolation in designated non-Indian institutional spaces often by white women or by Indian figures like DeCora who had established a privileged position as an arbiter of Indian art as an assimilationist tool.

THE AUTHENTIC IN INDIAN ART

Elizabeth Hutchinson along with others such as Erika Bsumek, Phoebe Kropp, Molly Mullan, and Chris Wilson have shown that Indian art at the beginning of the twentieth century was the vanguard of a larger process of mainstream aestheticization of Indian art that consolidated in the 1930s. It spoke to the same desires as the wider arts and crafts movement that shared an emphasis on the decorative. As Stella Tillyard explained, this was a protomodernism of sorts, in that it repositioned the artist within society so that he or she became the spokesperson for core values that seemed about to perish for good within industrial life.[20] It was connected to what Warren Susman has described as the intellectual "discovery" of the concept of culture in the 1930s and a growing sense that as a valuable entity in the world, culture could be maintained, devalued, or even destroyed.[21] Perhaps for as long as there has been the demarcation "Indian art" there have been concerns about preserving and maintaining its authenticity. This is because so much of the wider circulating value of the phenomena "Indian art" has been dependent on essentialist ideas about Indian peoples, ideas about them existing in some sense outside of time and consequently being more "real" than the rest of us. Thus the Chilocco Indian Agricultural School advertised its shop with an advert that read:

> A great injustice has been done true Indian Art by dealers in fake Indian curios. Believing that palming off factory-made imitations is calculated to degrade Indian Art in the eyes of the innocent public, an Indian Curio Store has been established at the Chilocco Indian Agricultural School, Chilocco, Okla. Blankets, Rugs, Moccasins, Baskets, Beaded Work and all manner of Indian hand-work are kept on hand. Indians on the reservation send these goods here to be sold, so you know that you are getting the "real article" when you buy Chilocco goods.[22]

Thus Indian artistic history and colonial history is difficult if not impossible to separate. The need to establish and maintain authenticity in Indian art is part and parcel of a wider need on the part of the dominant society to fit Indians and their art into capitalism. It is partly a symptom of the success of that process that the need to establish and maintain Indian artistic authenticity is now as likely to be expressed by Indian artists and dealers as it is by non-Indian artists, dealers, and buyers.

Paradoxically, one of the ways promoters of Indian art have elevated its exchange value and status has been by denying its link to the need to make money. To make Indian artists appear more authentically different from non-Indian artists, James Houston, for example, the promoter of the West Baffin Island Co-operative in the 1950s, argued that Inuit sculpture was in no way connected to making money.[23] Instead he linked Inuit sculpture with spiritual practice, capitalizing on the widely held belief that indigenous art is more valuable and more authentic if it is made so as to serve a spiritual purpose. Houston said of Kopeekolik, one of the cooperative artists: "As far as he is concerned, there was no connection between carving and commercial gain—he had proved himself a carver of walrus, and that was enough." Houston also invoked Herbert Spencer's thinking that "primitive" peoples were so closely tied to an awareness of their environment that they were unable to function at a higher or abstract level. Thus he suggested in "Contemporary Art of the Eskimo" in 1954: "In his art we see life through the eyes of a hunter as he perfectly portrays the moving things around him with the keen, trained senses of one whose very life depends upon observation."

Elsewhere Houston linked the ancient and the modern and reiterated the same limited notions of Inuit mental abilities, "It is impossible to know the objectives of the ancient Eskimo carvers since no written record accompanies their work. It is not easy either to analyse the motives of living Eskimo artists, because they seldom give utterance to abstract thought."[24] The illusion Houston perpetuated that the Inuit artists he promoted were somehow culturally ossified, pure and unsullied by the modern world, served a useful purpose in terms of gaining recognition for their work and providing financial help where it was much needed, but it was also part of long tradition of conceptualizing native art as primitive, tied irrevocably to nature and fundamentally outside of the artistic contexts that apply to non-Indian artists. According to Houston, Indian art was neither political, reflexive, nor self-aware; instead it was intuitive, "natural," and without intellectual context. Houston felt that just like Artic wildflowers, "Where nature allows, their art flourishes." In the same way, Inuit art for Houston had no internal or external critical matrix, it existed seemingly as an expression of instinct: "Because he has not been exposed to any formal training, or been overwhelmed by the great works of any especially talented people, the Eskimo has no troublesome yardstick of good art or bad art or formalized carving techniques to inhibit him."[25]

But we must remember that not everything about stereotyping and the projection of characteristics onto ethnically different others is a priori bad. While Houston infantilized Inuit art, made Inuit artists into primitive others, and connected them to an instinctive animal nature alien to the rest of human culture, he also pulled off a neat trick. He made Inuit art seem extrinsic to commercialism and patronage and therefore very much worth investing in since its generation and appeal seemed to stem from timeless and invaluable impulses. Houston also suggested that Inuit art was guided by aesthetic standards that were wholly discrete from those of the art world in general and that this should continue. Most importantly, he helped Inuit art gain profile and prominence and in so doing gave Inuit people an ongoing income. Houston and his relationship to twentieth-century Inuit art in turn invokes a larger history of commodity art sales and of performance for tourists as a means whereby Indian peoples have ensured their own cultural and political survival.

The history of Indian use of ethnography and museum data in the commercial production of "authentic" Indian art is equally complex and revealing. That such a history exists flies in the face of the approach to professional anthropology put forward by Vine Deloria Jr. in his 1969 book, *Custer Died for Your Sins*. Here Deloria suggested that native peoples had never had and never would have much use for anthropologists or their research. Yet in truth, there is a significant record of Indian peoples taking what they had a use for from anthropologists. Consider for example the use young Indian artists selectively made of anthropology from 1927–1955 at Bacone College, Tahlequah, Oklahoma. Given the history of Indian removal to Oklahoma and the high levels of assimilation in Indian territory, they "relearned" tribal histories, ceremonies, and practices from the library so as to better demonstrate their "authentic" identity as Indian artists. Research became integral to the Bacone curriculum since as Lisa K. Neuman has pointed out, "the expectations of patrons and the standards of art competitions required that Indian artists not only produce works in what had come to be defined as the traditional flat style of Indian painting, but that they also produce representations of traditional or even pre-contact tribal cultures."[26] Even so, columnists of the 1950s would write of artists such as Acee Blue Eagle that he was "not a scholar, but rather an instinctive artist" even while also admitting elsewhere that he "spends scheduled time every week sketching small items in museums and studying how his ancestors treated the head, arms, legs, and feet in their art."[27] It seems that the imperative to view Indian artists as "authentically" linked to a pre-contact reality brought about a blindness to the realities of removal, and a blindness to the very real history of Indian cultural attack and displacement, a history that made salvaging aspects of lost culture important to Indian peoples even if it had to be done through the potentially skewed lens of professional anthropology.

Another example of the same phenomenon is the Seneca Arts & Crafts Project sponsored by the Rochester Museum in New York State and funded in the depths of the Depression by the Temporary Emergency Relief Administration and after 1935 by the Rochester City Council and the Works Progress Administration. The scheme was controlled entirely by the part-Seneca director of the Rochester Museum, Arthur Parker. He hit upon the idea of getting contemporary Seneca to copy the "authentic" Seneca materials described and collected by his intellectual hero Lewis Henry Morgan in the previous century but lost in a 1911 fire. The project lasted for six-and-a-half years and everything produced became the property of the museum so that it might trade it within the museum and collector's world. This was good business for the museum and a means whereby Parker felt he could better equip his own people for the commercial world. He was convinced that the creation of "manufactures for trade" that were "typical of the days when Indian art was original and pristine" would allow the Seneca to achieve their own salvation.[28] Yet what Parker demanded from the project was ethnographic reproduction rather than contemporary Seneca art. As he put it in a letter to the president of the Tonawanda Council of Chiefs: "the workers are required to make duplicates of ancient patterns which the Rochester Museum supplies, suggests, or authorizes various persons to make" in order to "produce such material of any kind or sort as may be of use to the museum."[29] To add irony to irony, the collection Parker used as the model for the work his artists produced had itself, in part, also been created by Seneca under instruction. In 1848, Lewis Henry Morgan had advised the New York State Museum to set up an Indian Cabinet where Iroquois arts and crafts could be preserved as the "unwritten history of their social existence." He set about collecting Seneca objects that were in use at the time and simultaneously commissioned Tonawanda Seneca to make traditional items to be accompanied by records of how they were produced. It is entirely possible, therefore, that Parker in the 1930s was actually commissioning simulacra, or copies of copies, of Seneca material culture. That is, that he was continuing a scientific project of salvaging what was, at least in part, a constructed past.[30]

But perhaps we should not be surprised by the constructed nature of elements of Indian art in the past given the constructed nature of "art" as a cultural category. Some, such as Shelly Errington writing for *Cultural Anthropology*, argue that art as a cultural category was invented simultaneously with collecting and that, in fact, the two are inconceivable without each other. Errington's focus is what she calls "high primitive art," the "authentic" work by "untouched cultures" that has commanded the highest of prices at auctions and galleries. She cites its death knell as coming in 1984, when even the mainstream art audience was stunned by the controversy that surrounded the Museum of Modern Art's attempt to show " 'Primitivism' in 20th Century Art." In linking art to collecting, Errington highlights the implications of the mechanics of display and how "art" is constituted by a hierarchy of permanence in terms of what can and cannot be somehow framed and displayed. Thus the market for monumental pieces is extremely limited no matter how much such pieces are praised as art—as Errington puts it, "Whose living room could accommodate an Olmec head—even if it could be bought?" "Art" made of ephemeral or fluid materials—flowers, bamboo, barkcloth, sand for example, has therefore tended not to get displayed, and artistic material that combines soft and hard parts has tended to lose the soft parts over time with profound epistemological and aesthetic consequences. Thus as Errington explains, what has come to constitute the collected canon of "authentic" art from those peoples previously deemed "primitive" is "usually the size and durability that money can transport, dealers can store, and collectors can conveniently display." Errington in fact would prefer that we confine the word "art" to objects "conforming to the cluster of associations and practices articulated at the end of the 18th century in Europe."[31] It was the eighteenth century, after all, that called for the separation of "art" from life, culminating in Kant's ideas about purely aesthetic objects being useless, that is, being purely for contemplation. Uselessness in this sense, along with what we might call "displayability," has, up until relatively recent decades, played a key role in the reception of Native American art alongside the wider imperative for Native American Indian art to appear "authentic" in order to succeed within the global art market.

Another part of how "authentic" Indian art gets constructed and received concerns its relationship to individualism, not least because an individual's stamp on a given artwork is the usual way of establishing ownership and the extent of reproduction an artwork has been subject to. This is true even though the notion of art as an original creation produced by a talented individual is, in the Western context, actually relatively recent.[32] As explored previously in this volume, for many traditional communities, overt individual identification of this sort is complex, unusual, and not necessarily socially sanctioned. Yet many Indian artists are happy today for their work to be identified as their individual expression and to differentiate their work from the larger continuum of life within their respective communities. Thus, for example, Indian potters have, since the 1970s in particular, signed the bottom of the pots they have made and taken part in competitions (such as those organized by the Southwestern Association for Indian Arts) and competition for gallery space that encourages further differentiation and thus better sales. However, for other Indian artists the individual's relationship to community precludes the sort of individual artistic ownership more usual within the U.S. art economy. If the artist and art itself is part of a community and indecipherable from it, then its identity is not the individual's alone. As the modern Santa Clara Pueblo scholar Rina Swentzell put it, "How does one talk about the community when it's all moving so fast? The older way of seeing community is seeing people as integrally connected. That's why the word Art never came up. Because in a basic way everybody was connected to what the group needed in order to survive."[33] One implication of Swentzell's remark is that art as a conceptual category is in itself a symptom of unintegrated communities, an indication of a lack of connection that requires "art" as a cultural production to act as a salve or balm. Yet, it is difficult to deny how profoundly Indian art over time has been deeply dependent on specialization by individuals, and it is clear that within a number of traditions, the individual's spiritual dreams and visions are fundamental to artistic production.[34]

The fundamental inclusiveness of much Indian art has also served to exclude it from the category of "high art" outside of primitivism, at least until the advent of postmodernism and its encouragement of new ways of perceiving.[35] Perspective has been perhaps the key representational language throughout centuries of Western colonialism and it is a way of depicting space and form that tends to fundamentally separate the see-er from the seen. As critics such as Norman Bryson have explained in his 1983 book, *Vision and Painting: the Logic of the Gaze*, it is a way of seeing that excludes context and as such it represents a particular set of relationships to power where what is seen is subject to he who sees.[36] In contrast, the recent shift toward postmodern aesthetics removes this wall and subverts these power relationships, allowing for the possibility via installation and performance of the inclusion of ceremony, of a sense of place and of community. Postmodernist changes to visual art can be said to have provided a conceptual matrix of use to the provincial or marginalized and/or indigenous artist. This is because as Brian O'Doherty explained in 1986 in *White Cube: The Ideology of the Gallery Space*, "The mark of provincial art is that it has to include too much— the context can't replace what is left out, there is no system of mutually understood assumptions."[37] Whether "authentic" Indian art requires such almost infinite context is another matter, but it is the case that Indian art has over time suffered in terms of its critical reach and reception because context, community, and place have most often been integral to its worth and full appreciation.

An added complexity that connects directly to the broader discussion of the contested and thorny issue of Indian identity and blood quantum in the next chapter is how Indian art today confronts the marketplace. The 1990 Indians Arts & Crafts Act made it a federal offense for anyone who is not a member of a federally recognized tribe or recognized by a state or federally recognized tribe as an "Indian artisan" to claim to be a tribal member when selling Indian art. The Act therefore enshrined a relationship between Indian art and the blood classification schemes from 1887 that underpin much tribal enrollment. Many Indian peoples were excluded by the 1887 Dawes Act and their descendants are therefore in turn excluded from selling Indian art today. Irrespective of 1887, tribal membership requirements vary significantly with some tribes requiring one-fourth Indian blood and a small number one-half, while some allow any descendant of a tribal member to be enrolled regardless of blood quantum. Scholar Frederick Hoxie has connected the passage of the 1990 Act to tribal lobbying, which he argues "has produced an American law that can penalize people whose lives violate an official ethnohistory. In this new world there are no adopted Indians, no multitribal Indians, and no official difference between enrolled Hopis, who have a relatively 'high' blood-quantum requirement, and enrolled Cherokees, who do not. There are also no Indians who exist outside the federal system: no Monacans, no Indiana Miamis, no Brothertons, and no Ohio Shawnees."[38] We have no definitive statistics on how many people of Indian descent are not enrolled or who are not eligible to be enrolled in an Indian tribe, but there are a good number of historical and contemporary reasons why someone would not wish to be. The law is particularly invidious when we consider the significant number of Indian children who were removed and adopted by white families and who thus find it near impossible to demonstrate the requirements for tribal enrollment. The status of recognized "tribe" is equally fraught. There are 556 tribes recognized by the U.S. government but a number of others, such as the Abnaki of Vermont, never consented to a treaty with the United States and thus have never been "recognized." Yet others have abandoned tribal status voluntarily or as a result of Congressional legislation such as during the policy shift begun in the mid-1940s when over 100 tribes were "terminated" in terms of their relationship to the United States government.

Added to all of the above, the Indian Arts & Crafts Act has proved formally unenforceable due to lack of funds and has caused a great deal of division among Indian peoples. Formulated in a year when Indian peoples were heavily represented in popular media (Kevin Costner's highly romantic *Dances With Wolves* won the 1990 Academy Award for Best Picture and *Northern Exposure* was airing on TV), the law was flawed and as William J. Hapiuk, Jr. has explained in the *Stanford Law Review*, its objectives would have been better served by a certification trademark system.[39] The litigation and prosecution the law has engendered have been a poor means by which to attempt to preserve cultures. The market for Indian art, from wood carvings to "ethno-kitsch," was big business in the 1980s with a 1985 congressionally mandated study by the U.S. Department of Commerce estimating annual sales of Native American jewelry and handicrafts at $400 to $800 million. There is and was a need to protect Indian art, but the Act simply caused rancour within the Indian art world. Or example, the prominent Cherokee artist of Cherokee heritage Jimmie Durham, who was not an enrolled tribal member, refused to seek membership or certification and had his exhibit cancelled in 1992 at the American Indian Contemporary Arts Gallery in San Francisco. He said, "I've lived all my adult life in voluntary exile from my own people, yet that can also be considered a Cherokee tradition. It is not a refusal of us, but a refusal of a situation and of imposed-from-without limits."[40] Bert Seabourn, whose work is hung permanently at the Vatican, was refused certification by the Cherokee. Others, such as Jeanne Walker Rorex, niece of the well-known Cherokee sculptor Willard Stone, also refused to seek certification on principle. Hapiuk quotes one artist, Eugene Pie, who compared the Act to Nazism, stating "No one else has to prove anything. Black artists don't have to prove they're black; white artists don't have to prove they're white. I think the government still feels we're possessions, that we're part of the National Park System, standing at the cabin door."[41] Pie's comments are incendiary, but resonant.

Thus authenticity, as externally and to a lesser extent internally defined, dictates the wider context for Indian art. Furthermore, it seems that in a number of dominant contexts Indian peoples are stuck with a wider cultural fundamental identification between themselves and the artistic. As Henry Louis Gates put it in one of his discussions of authenticity, "like it or not, all writers are 'cultural impersonators' "; similarly, it seems, Indian artists cannot escape a wider identification of their work with "authentic" and totalizing notions about their cultures.[42] A number of thinkers within Indian Studies have railed against this. Richard White pointed out the logical flaw in identifying everything Indian as artistic and in perceiving everything Indian as sacred. White argued "it is the sheerest romanticism to believe that all native groups had well-developed pottery, weaving or pictorial traditions, that all these societies were essentially spiritual and

artistic."[43] Similarly, unless tradition is deemed to be an infinitely malleable concept, it is difficult to argue that all Indian art is necessarily "traditional" or that it
has in the colonial or neocolonial era existed outside of a wider non-Indian market. Indeed, some have argued that the very collection of Native American arts
and crafts is in itself negative, a form of colonization. Art critic Richard Shiff
writes of it as:

> a form of colonization, an appropriation of the world of the other to make up a
> lack in one's own. This is colonization by metonymic exchange, the redemption
> of product (artwork) for process (conduct of life, system of values). As aggres-
> sive consumers, the colonizer-collectors control what is to be desired in the life
> process of the "native", for the collectors create the market for certain goods,
> inducing their production. The resultant industry both determines and symbol-
> izes the conduct and perhaps even the values of the Indian producer (this com-
> mercial circuit might be seen as a case of ideological colonization). Commercial
> gain rewards the Indian producer for creating signs of a life deemed more valu-
> able to the Euro-American consumer. The collectors return to the values of
> living in harmony with the land by purchasing products of those they think
> never left nature's estate.[44]

If Shiff's point is true, the question then arises—can Indian art escape this
nexus? Can Indian art exist outside of the market's desire to buy what it perceives
to have been irrevocably lost—a connection to land and to nature that Indian culture is imagined to have uniquely retained? For that matter, can Indian art pros-
per outside of what Russell Lynes described in his 1949 study, *The Tastemakers*,
as the ongoing American thirst for culture, culture that is definably American in
opposition to elite European art forms? Indian peoples have been awarded the
consolation of culture, status as culturally intense in opposition to the American
mainstream that has in the modern era defined itself as culturally eroded, vapid,
and hollow. Yet, as Lynes wrote, "Through the story of the history of our taste has
run a constant theme—if America is to be great, America must have culture."[45]
Thus Indian art circulates in terms of the market in an invented reality, reflective
not of Indian history or Indian diversity of experience but of nonIndian desires
and regrets. It is seen as inherently regional, as the product of nonalienated labor,
of a symbiotic relationship between the artist and his community, a wondrous
balance of the useful and the creative. Just as importantly, it is perceived as outside
of shifting fashions, as taking its lead from the soil and from timeless values
embedded in place. This, despite the long history of forced Indian migration,
of Indians as front-line experiencers of modernity, urbanity, and of industrial
labor and despite equally long histories of intra- and intertribal discord.
Yet the future of the mantle of romance that has settled over Indian art

seems secure. If we are to heed David Harvey's diagnosis in *The Condition of Postmodernity*, the more mobile capital becomes, the more the dominant cultures of the world will nostalgically yearn for a lost identity steeped in signifiers of place.[46] Capital grows ever-more liquid, suggesting that the desire for identity signified through relationship to place will only increase.

Of course, the Native American art worlds of today are multifaceted and those outside of American Indian communities know little of Indian art's use within and among Indian communities. Some Indian artists deliberately "other" audiences, or infantilize them by making central use of Indian language terms as well as very specific Indian symbolism; thereby excluding those without a deep linguistic and conceptual involvement in their specific Indian community. Thus the sculptor and writer Jimmie Durham has at times deliberately withheld translation in works that incorporate a text in Cherokee. In conversation with Jeanette Ingberman he said of his audience, "What I want them to know is that they can't know that. That's what I want them to know. Here's a guy having his heart cut out with an obsidian knife and he's saying something in Cherokee and I don't want people that come into the gallery to know what he's saying . . . The first text is the real things, turquoise, words, gold, emeralds, obsidian and flint, the second text is the Cherokee counterpoint, and the third text is that you don't know what the Cherokee means."[47]

American Indian artists and critics continue to ironize and fight stereotyping, resistance that includes attacks on the very bases of the language of art criticism.[48] Recent thinkers have argued that what is most needed today is a greater awareness that indigenous American art cannot rightfully be separated from indigenous spirituality. For example, for the non-Native University of South Dakota scholar Leroy N. Meyer, "indigenous "art" cannot be parsed from indigenous "religion." Nor can indigenous social organization be parsed from "religion." Our aesthetic interpretation of culture requires a widening of the hermeneutic circle of understanding, as Gadamer called it.[49] Much, not least the advice of practicing Indian artists, supports Meyer's recommendations. As Meyer notes, as far back as 1926 the University of Nebraska scholar Hartley Burr Alexander spoke of the deep integration within a number of Native American traditions, a conceptual holism whereby everything is in one reality: "real life and dream life, fact and symbol, are all of one piece . . . One is always struck by the *littéralité* of the Indian understanding, even where he is thinking of the supernatural." Alexander knew that a Native American worldview "reveals itself while self-transforming in ritual forms, constructing a religious image for life as a whole."[50] Meyer argues that what Westerners might think of as transubstantiation is key to Native American artistic and religious endeavor, quoting as an example Frank Fools Crow who once introduced Crazy Horse's pipe just before prayer by explaining how Crazy Horse received the pipe: "he felt something crawling up his leg, and when he touched it, it was a snake, which became his pipe." Thus Meyer advises that Western Euro-American concepts of aesthetics are abandoned as far as native art is concerned, even though some basic distinctions within some communities do seem at least superficially to be comparable. He quotes William Powers point that although there is no distinction in Lakota between craft and art, for example, there is a linguistic distinction made between *wokayke* (costume) and *hayapi* (clothing). Since performance is often key to native art, Euro-American distinctions between "fine" and "performing arts" cannot be easily applied. He cites as examples Navajo dry-painting and peyote ceremonial fire-sculpting by the "fire-man" of the peyote ritual. In both cases the act of painting and fire-sculpting is in itself aesthetic, something Western artists only began to investigate in the twentieth century. Similarly the Platonic idea of enduring and fixed perfection, of a finished artwork, often has little place in Native aesthetics where key phenomena such as song, fire sculpture, or totem poles are transient. Song and music in particular are not traditionally thought of as external to people at all, rather they are part of a cosmic whole of which members of a community are part. Thus Oglala Lakota are described by William Powers as having a regard for song as living part of nature:

> Music . . . is *there*, occupying a niche in the natural universe with a humanlike capacity to be born and to die, to undergo changes, to be renewed or "cured" if you will (as the language suggests). Music is not so much composed from the whole cloth as it is, metaphorically, reincarnated, as is true, so the Oglala believe, with humans. The term *yatun* "to give birth to a song" is perhaps the closest gloss to "to compose," but the connotation of *tun* is "to give rise to something *that has already existed in another form*."[51]

CONCLUSION

How does all of this help us to understand native art and artwork today? One way of seeing Indian art in the twentieth century and beyond is to perceive a gradual move away from American Indian arts as ethnography toward American Indian arts as art. We can trace this shift through institutionally significant events. In 1931 there was an explicitly nonethnographic "Exposition of Indian Tribal Arts" and in 1941 an analogous specific exhibition at the Museum of Modern Art curated by René d'Harnoncourt. In the 1960s and 1970s Native American art history became an academic discipline in its own right, much advanced by the 1971 publication of J. J. Brady's *Indian Painters and White Patrons*; the establishment in 1962 of the Institute of American Indian Arts; booms in Indian pottery making and in Indian jewelry; and in 1975 the creation of the *American Indian Art* magazine.1985 then saw a high profile bringing together of African Oceanic and American Indian material from museums who juxtaposed works by Henri Matisse, Henry Moore, André Derain, and Pablo Picasso so as to suggest affinities between tribal aesthetics and those of modernist artists. Finally in 1992 major exhibitions were mounted at the National Galleries of Canada and the United States, "Land/Spirit/Power" and "Arts of the American Indian Frontier," signaling a new level of recognition that Indian art was mainstream as art.

While American Indian art has stopped being ethnography and increasingly been classified as "art," being Indian and being tribal has become, if anything, more complex. Intellectually, key cultural studies scholars such as James Clifford have perhaps permanently destabilized concepts such as culture and brought to our attention the inherent messiness involved when we refer to culture in any reified, essentialist formulation. It may or may not be a good thing for Indian art if culture is accepted as being as Clifford puts it, "deeply compromised" as an idea. He makes an excellent point that the old anthropological shibboleths about cultures existing in bounded, coherent, collective wholes are now impossible to sustain. As he explains, "In a world with too many voices speaking all at once, a world where syncretism and parodic invention are becoming the rule ... it becomes increasingly difficult to attach human identity and meaning to a coherent 'culture' or 'language'."[52] Yet where this leaves Indian art and indeed much about the assertion of Indian sovereignty, which remains bonded, often by necessity, to such essentialist ideas, is unclear. For reasons that are both extrinsic and intrinsic, it is difficult for "Indianness" to transcend "culture" at its most basic, often blood-based, definition.

Today, the question of who controls Indian art, its contextual scope, and the extent to which it represents the tremendously diverse communities from which it stems is more important than ever. It seems that the constellation of conceptual thinking surrounding the word "art" in terms of what is produced by native artists is here to stay, but the challenge will be how native artists will retain or achieve sovereignty over how their work is sold, displayed, and circulated. As the executive director of the Southwestern Association for Indian Arts put it:

> For the non-Indian or outside looking in, the term "art" is a convenient classification to make sense of a dynamic and integral component of the Native American worldview, to make the Indian world intelligible to in terms of Euro-American experience. Indian art is the sense of motion and creation expressed symbolically in objects and is to be understood as a way of living. Indian arts have always been dynamic, challenging conventions and adapting, reinterpreting, and improvising. Indian art reflects a particular community's aesthetic that is firmly rooted within the daily lives of the people and their religion, along with cars, fast food, and mass media. A new generation of Indian artists continues the intimate and vital dialogue between life experience and artistic expression. Tradition is constantly changing and it needs creativity in order to remain alive because creativity breaks apart old thoughts in order to reassemble the parts into new thoughts. But we must ask ourselves what

happens when art is controlled by a hermetic world of scholarship and art markets and the artists themselves begin to fall victim to the chimera of a Romanticized past."[53]

The challenge is how and whether Indian art can transcend Western and transcultural criteria of quality, whether it can retain or generate a preferred relationship to Indian spirituality and Indian land and whether the often inherently challenging nature of good art can be preserved when highly contested representational issues are at stake. Consider, for example, the negative native and nonnative reaction to the work *Offensive/Defensive* (1998) by Edward Poitras (a member of Canada's Gordon First Nation and a treaty Indian of Metis and Indian ancestry). Poitras received a strong reaction for seeming to criticize reserve Indian communities as stifling and limiting in contrast to city life. He showed two pieces of turf outside Mendel Art Gallery, in Saskatoon, Saskatchewan—one prairie sod from Gordon Indian Reserve and the other from the Gallery lawn—each had been interchanged. The urban gallery sod on the Reserve died but revived soon after while the Reserve sod did really well immediately on the city gallery lawn. People objected that the installation's message was that cultural survival is only possible in the city, but in truth Poitras intended to suggest only that personal identity is more likely not to be challenged in urban areas; on the smaller community of the Reserve a person would have to fit in with community mores.

Perhaps the bulk of Indian art today speaks to issues to do with sacred places, community, and the symbolism of spirituality. In one sense this is such a truism it hardly bears repeating. It has not changed for centuries and neither should it. Examples are legion but a nonrepresentative sample is instructive nonetheless. Consider, for example, the hauntingly beautiful work of the Iroquois artist John Fadden provided at the close of this chapter whose work often dwells on key figures of Iroquois cosmology such as Sky Woman or the personification of Corn. Sky Woman, *neh nih Che yonh en ja seh*—when the world was new—was pushed from the land of the sky people through a hole opened up by the uprooting of the great tree of light. Birds helped her land on the back of a great turtle and a muskrat brought her up to earth from beneath the waters that she walked on so as to make the earth we know. The story of the good- and bad-minded twins to which she gave birth speaks to the importance of respecting nature—and of maintaining peace and harmony.

Similarly the Anishinabe artist Leland Bell from the Wikwemikong Unceded First Nation on Manitoulin Island, Ontario, Canada sees his artistic purpose as being primarily spiritual and not unlike the spiritual work carried out over the centuries by the Midewiwin medicine society. Leland, whose work often centers on circularity, peace, and serenity, is on record as saying, "My quest is not so much to become famous and to become rich but to find those colours that nobody else could see. Whether I find them is not important. It's the task of searching for those colours which is important."[54] For First Nations Anishinabe artist Rebecca Belmore a defining principle is both cultural and environmental— "we are of this land"; for the Crow-Blackfeet artist Susan Stewart her work is "an emotional and spiritual response to nature. My work is not literal; it's a feeling, it's an essence. I'm trying to pull from a place that's deep within me. I'm having a dialogue with nature."[55] For a number of artists, the survival of Indian peoples is tied fundamentally to the expression of a spiritually informed relationship to land. For example, the Six Nations, Ontario painter, sculptor, and filmmaker George Longfish believes for Indian peoples to survive, "one of things we need to be able to do is to find where our power is. Basically we are a spiritual people. We are able to heal ourselves that way and to have a reverence and a respect for the land, or to use it up. Predominantly the Indian people are the caretakers of the earth." Indian art is also frequently talked of by Indian artists as an expression of community, a means of expressing Indian peoples' relationship to place. As the Flathead-Cree-Shoshone artist Jane Quick-to-See Smith points out, "Native peoples have something like three thousand languages from Patagonia to Point Barrow, with no word for art in the Western sense, yet art is deeply integrated in daily life. There is an integration of art with life. It's such a natural process, all part of that sense of art in daily life. On the reservation you'll be working in the kitchen, cooking, you've got a child on your hip, and you're doing beadwork at the same time. It's part of your life."[56]

While the above is true, one could equally argue that what links the bulk of Indian art is a sense of powerfully culturally specific dissent, a dissent unique to the indigenous experience but representative of a consciousness often shared in different forms by artists worldwide. Installation and performance artists like the Luiseno Nation figure James Luna of La Jolla Reservation in California may or may not allude to the spiritual, but they nearly always deliberately challenge their audiences by poking at the often ugly realities of reservation life, exposing the aggression felt by Indian peoples when confronted by repeated instances of their own cultural misrepresentation and the hypocrisies inherent in the idea of the "authentic," "spiritual," and "real" Indian. One might argue that by focusing so thoroughly on the issue of Indian authenticity Luna's work simply reinscribes its potency. Such thinking suggests that a contemporary Indian artist should surely be able to think of something more important to do than ridicule non-Indian stereotyping even if such work often has a ready (post-modern, liberal, and disproportionately non-Indian) audience?[57] On the other hand, Luna's performances, while often punishingly drawn-out, clearly serve an educative purpose and have great capacity to heal both wounds rent by cultural conflict and traumas stemming from war service and addiction. They are also often funny. Quite who is laughing at whom and how wholesome and generous the laughter always is, is another matter.[58] For Luna, performance and installation are uniquely adapted to Indian artistic endeavor, they "offer an opportunity like no other for Native people to express themselves in traditional art forms of ceremony, dance, oral traditions and contemporary thought without compromise."[59]

Other contemporary artists have spoken out explicitly against the corralling of Indian artists into a box marked "spiritual" and "nature-loving" and—perhaps most radically—marked "tribal." The Tuscarora photographer and painter Rick Hill has described his work as being concerned with transcending such limitations. He is on record as saying, "We're constantly confronted with things non-Indian, and therefore to me it's only logical—and this is what bothers me about Indian art-that we should address the things that impact on our lives, instead of pretending that all Indians are in this spiritual nirvana somewhere. We have to deal with the reality that the waters are no longer clean, the skies are no longer clear, that not all Indians like being Indians, and that there is still a battle on for hearts and minds." For the Seneca artist G. Peter Jemison, Indian art cannot escape wider political realities. He has said, "The very act of showing Indian art is political."[60] For the Ojibwe artist Carl Beam, as an Indian artist, he transcends tribalism and his work is essentially hybrid and culturally composite. He has said, "I don't need the tribal bonds. I'm not saying the tribal rituals aren't useful. They are. They help people to belong to an alienated world. There are so many forces that want a piece of your soul. But a tribal culture is only a temporary resting place."[61]

Post-contact Indian art can only be fully understood once we take on board the often unlovely realities of contact and once we comprehend the linguistic and conceptual baggage that accompanies the idea of "art" in Indian and non-Indian contexts. Searching for "authenticity" in Indian art is perhaps only a symptom of the art market and of late capitalist malaise. As suggested at the beginning of this book, we would be better advised to follow Arnold Krupat's recommendation given in the context of Indian literature and film that we should look for and recognize what he calls *both/and* modalities of thought that incorporate what is Indian and what is not, what is Indian by adoption and what is not, as opposed to what we may be more used to—Aristotleian, analytic, *either/or* modes of thought.[62] Such an approach moves us away from a sterile discussion of degrees of "Indianness" and toward a a more mature recognition that assimilation to non-Indian artistic modes does not wholly preclude resistance to non-Indian ways.

Montage Skull. (Courtesy of John Kahionhes Fadden)

Berry Picking. (Courtesy of John Kahionhes Fadden)

Peacemaker's Birth. (Courtesy of John Kahionhes Fadden)

Peacemaker Affinity Animals. (Courtesy of John Kahionhes Fadden)

CHAPTER 6

~

Environmental Justice, Place, and Indian "Sacrifice"

We started in chapter one with discussion of the idea that much that has been problematic about dominant societies in the West and their relationship to nature has stemmed from the anthropocentrism at the core of the biblical story. We began with the suggestion that the West's spiritual ideas about an omniscient God who made man in his own image were, at least in part, where things had begun to go wrong. When the Judeo-Christian God gave man dominion over the earth and its inhabitants, it provided those who sought to exploit nature with a moral, social, and spiritual framework for doing so. Perhaps ironically, the ecological movement that today might be said to hold out most hope for redress and ecological fairness for indigenous peoples is in turn anthropocentric. The environmental justice movement again puts humans at the center of environmental discourse, redefining the environment as "the place you work, the place you live, the place you play." Some mainstream environmentalists argue that this replicates the same thinking that caused environmental despoliation in the first place; man after all, through thinking of himself as at the center of the world especially since the seventeenth century has used world resources shamefully for his own limited ends. Environmental justice activists counter this critique by linking it to equally hoary binary thinking separating man from nature. They argue that man must be at the center of the solution to environmental problems because he has been at the heart of what caused those problems in the first place. They highlight that the real issue is *which* segment of mankind is considered.

In this sense, the environmental justice movement represents a important fundamental democratization of environmental thinking, a democratization that opens up greater opportunity for indigenous voices to be heard and for the indigenous human presence on urban, suburban, and "wild" land to be meaningfully considered. In terms of social justice and intellectually, the movement has much to recommend it. Certainly, to broaden established ideas about the need to protect "endangered species" so that they include endangered humans and endangered human cultural systems indigenous or not makes real sense. The idea of an "endangered species," while it may help to garner support for the preservation of specific areas, also decontextualizes that species, dangerously isolating it from its deep-rooted historical and cultural interconnections with humans and others. The idea was very effectively critiqued in 1991 by the anthropologist Stephen Feld, known for his work with the rain forest communities in Papua New Guinea. He wrote:

> When I read that we lose 15–20,000 species of plants and animals a year through the logging, ranching and mining that escalates rainforest destruction, my mind immediately begins to ponder how to possibly calculate the number of songs, myths, words, ideas, artefacts, techniques—all the cultural knowledge and practices lost per year in these mega-diversity zones. Massive wisdom, variations on human being in the form of knowledge in and of place: these are co-casualties in the eco-catastrophe. Eco-thinout may proceed at a rate much slower than cultural rubout, but accomplishment of the latter is a particularly effective way to accelerate the former. The politics of ecological and aesthetic co-evolution and co-devolution are one.

Putting people at the heart of environmental problems almost inevitably sheds a spotlight on what most people do in the largest sense, that is, that they take part in a capitalist system committed to ongoing growth. Globalization and its associated new levels of competition have made sustaining American growth increasingly difficult especially since the 1970s; and the environment, since its protection is generally perceived as a cost rather than as contributory to profit, has suffered acutely as a result. Environmental woes cannot be separated analytically from capitalism and in particular from the fact that an increasingly small number of people now control American wealth. Since the nation's founding American wealth has always been concentrated in the hands of a comparatively small number but this has noticeably accentuated in recent decades. According to Michael Parenti writing in 1995, the 800,000 people who make up America's top capitalists and their managers have more money and wealth than the 184 million Americans aged over 16 who at that time worked for a living and drew salaries. This means just one percent of America owned sixty percent of all corporate stock and business assets.[2] More recent figures from the economist Edward N. Wolff suggest that the current picture is even more skewed toward the rich. As of 2007, 1 percent owned 34 percent of all privately held wealth and the next 19 percent—a group made up of managers, professionals, and small business owners—owned 50.5 percent, meaning that overall, 20 percent owned 85 percent of American wealth, leaving just 15 percent of wealth for the bottom 80 percent—those who draw wages and salaries. The years 1983 to 2004 saw particular concentration of American wealth such that by the late 1980s the situation was comparable to how it had been in 1929. Of all the financial wealth created in those years just 6 percent of it went to the bottom 80 percent of Americans.[3] The number of billionaires worldwide rose between 2007 and 2010 by nearly a third and just over a thousand individuals now own a combined wealth of $4,500 billion, equal to a third of the output of the U.S. economy.[4]

Interestingly, according to other recent studies, most Americans seem to significantly underestimate these disparities and at the same time to significantly overestimate the country's capacity for social mobility.[5] This may or may not substantively alter if the current Western financial crisis continues to deepen. Whatever transpires, it suggests a general popular lack of awareness of who and what needs to change if environmental imperatives are taken seriously and the human species is to survive in the long term. As James Speth pointed out in his recent study on the issue, *The Bridge at the Edge of the World: Capitalism, the Environment, and Crossing from Crisis to Sustainability*, what is needed is for capitalism to become humanized. Echoing John Maynard Keynes, Speth suggests that mankind has reached the stage when growth is no longer needed. Power, held disproportionately in corporate hands, needs to change how it works; that is, corporations need to change from separating ownership from management, change the emphasis away from maximizing stockholder wealth, limited liability needs to be rethought, as does the externalization of social and environmental costs and the invidious relationships between corporations and governmental politics. Pie in the sky? Perhaps, but if the dramatic environmental challenges now facing us are real then the magnitude of change necessary to address them is commensurately huge. What is becoming increasingly clear in this globalized world, is that infinite economic growth is incompatible with a world of finite resources. Governments can offer only empty hope while they remain as they are, wedded indissolubly to corporate power operating within only a partially effective regulatory framework.[6]

ENVIRONMENTAL RACISM AND TOXIC WASTE

Given the unequal nature of American society, it is perhaps unsurprising that environmental degradation and suffering has impacted disproportionately on the poor and the places where they work and live. There is now extensive literature linking poverty and environmental degradation and linking race to environmental degradation, what has been dubbed "environmental racism," a term coined in 1987.[7] A pivotal text in the latter area was Robert Bullard's path-breaking 1990 book, *Dumping in Dixie; Race, Class and Environmental Quality*. Bullard went on to write much more on this theme and to help advance key early avenues where people of color got together and worked to get over their differences in leadership and style so as to advance the multiethnic environmental justice case in contexts such as the First National People of Color Environmental Leadership Summit. One particular instance of environmental disparity linked to race, which Bullard and others have stressed, is the risks people of color face who live close to American hazardous waste landfill sites. In 1983 the U.S. General Accounting Office reported that three-quarters of such sites were close to poor, mainly African-American and Latino communities.[8] Bullard, who currently leads the Environmental Justice Resource Center at Clark Atlanta University, conducted a 2007 study that found that more than half of the 9.2 million people who live within three miles of a commercial hazardous waste facility are black, Latino, or Native American and that neighborhoods with more than one hazardous waste site tend to have higher proportions of minorities and poor people. The limited number of relatively recent studies on the environmental inequality faced specifically by Native Americans include a book by Gedicks that traces mining company and governor's office efforts to break up an Indian and sportsman alliance against mining in Wisconsin as well as work by Sachs and Small.[9]

An instructive recent example of environmental racism is the huge mound of coal ash that has been shipped from Kingston, Tennessee to Arrowhead, outside Uniontown, in Alabama's Black Belt. The ash came from the rupture of a holding pond on December 22, 2008 at a Tennessee Valley Authority coal-fired power plant that sent 978 million gallons of ash into a nearby river. Roane County, where the accident happened, is richer and whiter than Perry County, where Arrowhead is. It is 67.5 percent black and almost a third of its residents live below the poverty line. Locals say the coal ash stinks and are suing Phill-Con, the landfill's operator, in state and federal courts, claiming that dust and odors from the ash have made them ill. Coal ash is known to be full of toxic metals such as arsenic, lead, mercury, and selenium, and it tends to leach out into ground-water. It can also release dangerous concentrations of radioactive uranium and thorium. Meanwhile the Alabama Department of Environmental Management and the EPA (Environmental Protection Agency) say that Arrowhead was chosen for good reasons such as the fact that it is on a railway line, which takes away the need to transport the ash by road. Phill-Con, for their part, insist that their actions were in full compliance with state, local, and federal laws. The two business enti-ties that originally hired Phill-Con filed for bankruptcy in January 2010, thereby effectively halting the lawsuit that seeks to stop the dumping.

Key political figures, mostly Democratic, have tried to tackle this sort of envi-ronmental racism with limited success. In 1994 President Clinton signed Executive Order 12898 on Environmental Justice for Low Income and Minority Populations, but this did not enshrine any rights enforceable by law. Hilary

Clinton, then-Senator, put forward the Environmental Justice Renewal Act thirteen years later, but this died in committee. The Obama presidency gave environmentalists considerable hope for change but recently key figures have expressed their disappointment over the administration's enthusiasm for nuclear power, including the proposal to triple federal loan guarantees for new reactors, as well as its embracing of offshore drilling and the notion of "clean coal"—the as-yet-unproven idea that carbon dioxide from coal-fired power plants can be captured and stored.[10] Further disappointment has stemmed from the administration's failure to push a climate change bill through Congress and its failure to designate the polar bear as endangered by global warming. The Obama administration's support for nuclear has also caused it to come under fire specifically over environmental racism against blacks. New nuclear sites are planned near existing ones in the majority black Burke County, Georgia, across the river from the Savannah River nuclear weapons facility. The Savannah River flows between a nuclear weapons site on the South Carolina side and currently functioning and proposed electric utility reactors on the Georgia side. It is already the country's fourth most toxic river according to the Environmental Protection Agency (EPA) while the 310 square miles adjacent to the Savannah River, principally in Aiken and Barnwell counties of western South Carolina, is a secured U.S. Government facility with no permanent residents. It is also a designated Superfund site.

Superfund sites are instructive from an environmental justice perspective. They are hazardous waste areas that have been placed on the EPA's National Priority List based on a scoring process that rates its current or potential health impact. The original "Superfund" was created by the Comprehensive Environmental Response, Compensation, and Liabilities Act of 1980 in the wake of a national tragedy that unfolded at Love Canal, New York. Lois Gibbs, a housewife-activist, managed to publicize a link between toxic waste that had been buried underneath her hometown decades earlier by Occidental Petroleum and human illnesses in the area. She succeeded in prompting a "Superfund" to be set up that taxed known polluters and used the money to clean up sites where the polluters were unknown or could not do the work. However, that tax law expired in 1995 and the $3.8 billion the fund held at its peak was finally used up in 2003. Superfund now gets its funds from the taxpayer and from money the EPA recovers from polluters for work it has done at their sites. Overall its budget has very significantly not kept up with inflation.

To its credit, in recent years the EPA has made efforts likely to help waste sites linked to Native American populations gain Superfund status. In 2003 the EPA reported that there were 602 hazardous waste sites on or impacting on Indian country and 55 NPL (National Priority List) or NPL-equivalent sites affecting 50 tribes. NPL sites are given priority for further action under CERCLA, the Comprehensive Environmental Response, Compensation and Liability Act. Recently EPA headquarters directed regional Superfund site assessment personnel to consider health and environmental concerns unique to tribal populations and tribal resource uses—both on and off reservations—when scoring sites under the Hazard Ranking System that dictates which sites get on the NPL. As the EPA's Inspector General put it in 2004, "due to subsistence lifestyles, spiritual practices, and other cultural behaviours, tribes have multiple exposures from resource use that could disproportionately impact" on them.[11] This is a positive step forward; but since in 2010 around 67 percent of Native American Indians live off-reservation and the 2000 Census reported that 45 percent of those identifying as American Indian and Alaska Native alone resided in urbanized areas, it is by no means a global solution to the cumulative environmental injustices Native peoples face. Living as many do in poor and racially mixed environments often without the resources to mount powerful defenses against the encroachment of environmental hazards, Indian peoples are likely to remain at a specific disadvantage as environmental degradation and pollution reach new heights in the early twenty-first century.

Native American reservations have proved particularly attractive to toxic disposers who as a consequence have become embroiled in a number of controversial disputes.[12] For native communities, often struggling under the weight of endemic poverty and deprivation, the huge amounts of money available make hosting nuclear waste on their land a tricky and potentially hideous dilemma. To some scholars, the contemporary relationship between Native Americans and toxic waste disposal is a further wave of Indian genocide, this time concentrated via attacks on the Indian environment. However, the issue is complex and the Indian response to nuclear waste has been as diverse as Indian peoples and their interests have always been and remain. Yet it is worth recognizing that overall, while a number of tribes have actively pursued options to cite waste on Indian land, most have decided not to.[13] That said, at points public pressure has played a decisive role, as in 2007 when the Skull Valley band of Utah's Goshute tribe were urged to forego plans to offer their land for toxic waste storage. Goshute tribal leadership had struck a deal with a corporation, Private Fuel Storage, to store up to 44,000 tons of high-level nuclear waste on a 100-acre site on their 18,000-acre reservation. The Nuclear Regulatory Commission had approved a license for the deal in 2005, but a year later rulings by the U.S. Interior Department blocked the inauguration of a transfer facility essential to the project and the land-lease agreement the Goshutes had signed with Private Fuel Storage, a limited liability corporation representing eight strongly resourced nuclear utilities.

It is not difficult to see why the option of welcoming nuclear fuel onto Goshute land seemed reasonable to an element of Goshute leadership. Their community ranks among the nation's most economically and politically vulnerable and it is already surrounded by toxic industry. The U.S. Army stores the nation's largest stockpile of chemical weapons close by, there is a bombing range as well as a proving ground that has tested the acutely deadly VX nerve gas,[14] toxic incinerators and an industry accused of being the nation's biggest air polluter, Magnesium

Corporation. Only about 25 members live on the Skull Valley Band of Goshute Indians Reservation, an hour's drive from Salt Lake City in Tooele County, Utah with the remaining 100 members living in surrounding Tooele County towns, Salt Lake, or elsewhere. The decision to accept the waste caused fundamental rancor and dissent within the tribe, including accusations that the decision was made by an "executive committee" who agreed an undisclosed amount in return for accepting nuclear waste onto Goshute Land that it did not intend to share with the rest of the tribe. However, Leon Bear, the pro-dump Goshute tribal chairman, has stressed the tribe's sovereign right to make the deal and the absence of any viable economic long-term alternative for his people. "We can't do anything here that's green or environmental" he states, "Would you buy a tomato from us if you knew what's out here? Of course not. In order to attract any kind of development, we have to be consistent with what surrounds us."[15] Other tribal members have spoken out vehemently against such logic, arguing that what is left surviving on Goshute land (e.g., cedar and sage with profound sacred significance) is even more precious and more deserving of protection *because of* the surrounding threats to life and because of its age-old links to traditional lifeways. In August 2010 the Interior Secretary Ken Salazar said that the Obama administration had not as yet decided whether to appeal the standing decision not to site a nuclear waste facility on the Skull Valley Goshute Reservation, but pressure to change the status quo continues to mount in light of the Obama administration's commitment to what it seems will be a future national nuclear renaissance. Goshute land was to have been used to store used nuclear fuel above ground and as such it would have been a key link in the chain of getting nuclear waste to Yucca Mountain, Nevada, currently the U.S. government's sole proposed permanent storage facility for radioactive nuclear waste.

Yucca Mountain, in turn, is home to historical rivals the Western Shoshone and Southern Paiute. The former, who refused a $23 million compensatory award from the Indian Land Commission in the 1970s, have persistently asserted title to the land at Yucca Mountain and have wholly rejected nuclear waste.[16] The latter have been more open, at least to exploratory discussion and studies. Then in February 2009, the U.S. Department of Energy announced it would lessen its efforts to make Yucca Mountain home for the United States' used-up nuclear fuel and said it would look into alternative long-term strategies, an approach that seems to be in concert with voices from within the Obama administration. However, in June 2010, the Nuclear Regulatory Commission ruled that the Energy Department could not in fact withdraw its application to make Yucca Mountain a nuclear waste repository. This leaves the ultimate decision on Yucca Mountain pending and open to new thinking should there be a change in the prevailing political weather.

Aside from some of the more obvious reasons why a number of Indian peoples around Yucca Mountain might not want a permanent nuclear waste storage facility sited near them on land known to be seismically active, there are supremely significant spiritual and cultural matters to consider. The area is on the northern boundary of the Mojave Desert and southern boundary of the Great Basin Desert and it is the place to which a number of Indian peoples trace their creation. It is said that Southern Paiutes know themselves to have been created at Nuvagantu (Charleston Peak), 25 miles away from the proposed waste site in the Spring Mountains area. It is at the core of Tuwiinyaruvipu, the Storied Land. Yucca Mountain, within aspects of Western Shoshone and Southern Paiute thinking, has *Puha* or power. It is said that Southern Paiutes cross over the mountain on their way to the afterlife. As Valerie Kuletz has explained in her moving book about Southwest nuclearism, *The Tainted Desert*, certain Timbisha or Tumpisattsi Shoshone, the closest tribe to the Yucca Mountain Project, have an intersubjective and interconstitutive relationship to what is animate and inanimate in the region. Rather than perceiving the area as a deathly, hell-like desert, the Timbisha, like a number of other Indian peoples, perceive it as full of places and place names signaling water and life. Kuletz quotes Catherine Fowler, a Timbisha spokesperson:

> The Tumpisattsi live in their valley where their ancestors have lived since the time of Creation. Some archaeologists have written that our ancestors came here less than one thousand years ago from the Great Basin, but we learned differently. It was told by the old ones that Coyote brought the people to this place in his basket. When he fell asleep, the people crawled out of the basket and went away in all four directions. This happened at *Wosa* (Coyote's "burden basket"), now called Ubehebe Crater on the maps of the [Death Valley] Monument.
>
> Our history is not what has been written in books. Our history is in the Creator's belongings: the rocks and the mountains, the springs and in all living things. The old ones taught us that Coyote did not leave the people until he finished his job and traveled through *Tupippuh Nummu* ("our homeland"), naming all the places for the people to use for places to stay and to obtain all they needed.
>
> At the places that Coyote named for them, the *Nummu* found a good living in their homeland.[17]

Elsewhere Kuletz quotes the Shoshone spiritual leader Corbin Harvey articulating how alive the Yucca Mountain region is spiritually and how essential a reciprocal human and non-human spiritual relationship is in maintaining a positive environment there:

> Whereever you go, in places like these, there are spirits out there trying to hold themselves together. We are the ones with the voices, and we have to talk to those spirits, and so that's what we're doing by having our spiritual gatherings.

When we get together and pray and talk to the spirits of everything that's out here for a few days, then the spirit is happy. The water is happy. The air is happy, and so on. This practice is very important to the people. [We have to] keep this spirit alive here, so it will have a voice and keep talking to us and helping us. That part is very important to us all . . . People were brought here because this is medicine water. It's a medicine canyon, a medicine rock, and medicine water.[18]

[handwritten margin note: so powerful stroces connection to land]

Yucca remains a bellwether in terms of Native American environmental justice. The situation is highly problematic but at least Indian peoples have recently gained the right to reject proposals to site waste on their lands. In the past such matters were decided by state and federal regulations that did not take into account the wishes of specific bands, tribes, and communities. It took until the late 1980s before Congress gave Native Americans the authority to enforce their own standards and regulations and to make their own contracts with the EPA. As Marjane Ambler has explained, pivotally, this gave tribes such as the Umatilla in Oregon, the Sioux in South Dakota, the Kaibab-Paiute in Arizona, the Kaw in Oklahoma, and the Choctaw in Mississippi the ability to reject proposals to site hazardous waste landfills on reservations and to regulate the use of reservation lands.[19] Much more work needs to be done not just on waste siting decisions but also on the scope of toxicity in general and its specific impact on Native America and others. One survey involving just 25 Indian reservations found 1,200 hazardous waste generators or other hazardous waste activity sites were located on or near them.[20] Further, although toxic-waste siting is an acutely important and headline-grabbing Indian and environmental issue, something more prosaic may in fact be of more day-to-day significance to more Indian peoples, the amount of illegal dumping of all sorts of materials that is regularly done both by corporations and others on reservation lands without tribal permission. Dumping is also done by natives themselves, either for their own financial profit or as a service they sell to others.

NATIONAL SACRIFICE AREAS AND IDEAS ABOUT INDIAN IDENTITY

They're unusable, period. That's where you've got to start it. The only ultimate outcome of hostility is simply unfaceable.

You're never going to win a war with nuclear weapons.

I foresee no way we're ever going to be able to use them. We're thinking 90% of the time about something we can't do.

Years ago I reached the conclusion that our nuclear weapons arsenal was not adding to our security. If anything it was adding to insecurity and instability. We have become the victims of the momentum of the vested interests of the nuclear weapons people.

The changes in my thinking occurred starting about 1980, mostly because I came to the realization that the political people in the United States were actually talking about nuclear war being fightable and winnable.

—Statements from retired U.S. admirals and naval officers, 1986.[21]

I will show you fear in a handful of dust.

—T.S. Eliot, *The Wasteland*, 1922

Pro-nuclear voices claim nuclear power should in fact be seen as part of the world's arsenal with which to combat climate change in a context of dwindling accessible oil supply. On most continents now there are proposals to site new reactors even though such developments will inevitably require heavy governmental subsidy. Political belief in a nuclear future is maintained even though the United Nations Climate Change talks refused to give nuclear power greenhouse gas credits in 2000 and in 2001 the United Nations Sustainable Development Conference refused to label nuclear a sustainable technology. However we choose to view nuclear power one thing is clear—waste is an associated problem and a powerfully enduring one at that. If nuclear power continues to be promoted as key to our future, then it seems we must make peace with the idea that whole areas of the earth will be sacrificed to its containment, if indeed waste *can* be contained long term. Much about nuclear waste is contested, perhaps especially the amount of radiation exposure that is acceptable to humans. Compared to other countries, the U.S. strategy for dealing with nuclear waste is underdeveloped and, in comparison with a number of European countries in particular, the amount of radiation deemed acceptable for a member of the public to be exposed to is considerably higher.[22] Furthermore, a number of factors currently make the need to find a U.S. nuclear waste repository, whether at Yucca Mountain or elsewhere, increasingly critical. One is the billions that up until 2009 have already been spent on evaluating Yucca Mountain's suitability as a site seemingly to avail. Another underdiscussed factor is that of global security. Some 65,000 tons of nuclear waste is now in temporary storage throughout the United States—a national vulnerability as the recent earthquake and disaster at Fukushima Daiichi, Japan, demonstrated. Time is pressing. Under current law, the inventory of spent nuclear fuel will soon exceed the amount that can legally be stored at Yucca Mountain even were it to be sanctioned as a storage site. A second site therefore needs to be agreed to as soon as possible. Furthermore, commercial reprocessing of nuclear waste does not offer an appropriate solution, particularly abroad, where the plutonium it generates holds the possibility of fostering a nuclear arms race or in the wrong hands, a terrorist-led threat to world peace. Instead, to preserve world peace and national security the United States probably actually needs to be in a position to take spent nuclear fuel from smaller states.

Given this, one can only sympathize with politicians faced with making an impossible decision, what to do with waste no one wants that will have negative effects for generations to come? Despite successive administrations' efforts no obvious answer presents itself. As the Blue Ribbon Commission on America's Nuclear Future tasked to examine the question by President Obama in 2010 recently concluded in its draft report, the program to manage nuclear waste in the United States "has been troubled for decades and has now all but completely broken down."[23] In the United States, the land that has been most studied with a view to siting nuclear waste at great cost to the taxpayer is disproportionately Indian, and the people first in the queue to make that national and international sacrifice are Indian peoples. Indian sacred and on occasion subsistence geographies and American nuclear geography are inextricably entwined. As Valerie Kuletz has made clear, "the sociological populations most severely affected by the pollution created by these installations, most disturbed by the blasting engines of fighter aircraft over their homes, most displaced by military land withdrawal and acquisition, and most endangered by the above- and below-ground testing of nuclear weapons over the past five decades are American Indians."[24]

The idea of a "National Sacrifice Area" was put forward in a 1973 National Academy of Sciences report on the Southwest that concluded that some areas could be used for national priorities such as energy irrespective of the permanent environmental damage that such exploitation would cause.[25] The fact that Indian lands have disproportionately been designated for "national sacrifice" without Indian agreement and while Indian peoples remain on or near them and remain using the land points to one of the largest ironies in Native American historical politics. That is, the fact that a significant amount of the land on which Indians were allowed to survive in the nineteenth century, land deemed worthless desert or "badlands" and relegated as unsuitable for farming, has since the latter half of the twentieth century turned out to be exceptionally rich in energy resources. In this sense, Indian peoples have been earmarked to make sacrifices *because they have already made profound sacrifices* in previous centuries. America's desert regions have been isolated for sacrifice because they have yielded the perceived ingredients for America's Southwestern nuclear landscape. It is land that includes much of New Mexico, Nevada, southeastern California, and parts of Arizona, Utah, Colorado, and Texas; a region that has all five of North America's major deserts: the lower Great Basin desert in Nevada and the southeastern edges of California, the Navajo desert in the Four Corners area, the upper Chihuahuan desert in New Mexico, the upper Sonoran desert in California and Arizona, and the Mojave desert in California, Nevada, and Arizona. Over the last 70 years lands within this area have become the world's most extensive peacetime overtly militarized zone.[26]

Using "deserts as dumps" as a concept has been subject to scrutiny within the scientific community, but too often such discussions reproduce a sometimes sophisticated variant of the truism that "the solution to pollution is dilution." That dilution's specific impact on desert communities, including Indians, is generally given insufficient attention. Simultaneously, the degree of risk from nuclear contamination in particular is contextualized within an elite language that can be contested only on its own terms within set parameters, the language of high-level mathematics. An example is repeated reference to risk assessment in this context, as when waste management specialist at the University of New Mexico Bruce M. Thomson in a discussion of the engineering choices for deep geologic disposal of waste in the 1992 volume *Deserts as Dumps?* wrote dismissively of a general "morbid fear of radioactivity that often bears little relation to the actual hazards as determined by risk assessment."

Risk assessment merits deep consideration especially with reference to nuclear contamination. It is usually a quantitative scientific method where the potential for loss and the probability of occurrence is expressed mathematically. Both factors are notoriously difficult to measure and that measurement process can be subject to error. Prescient voices such as the Lebanese American financial expert and Professor of Risk Engineering at New York University Nassim Nicholas Taleb, who criticized the risk management methods used by the finance industry and linked them in recent years to the current ongoing global financial crises, have described risk managers as little more than "blind users" of statistical tools and methods.[27] The associated new science of pathways and consequence analysis that was born as a result of the atomic age is subject to analogous critique for being disproportionately quantitative and reductive. Scientific evaluation of risk in terms of the risks that matter most for most of us, for example the chances of developing cancers from toxic dumping, atomic bombs, radon, and pesticides, is notoriously difficult. Cancer often has multiple possible causes and can take years to develop. Direct links between cancer clusters in an area and specific risk factors are often hard for scientists to establish within a statistically significant margin of error.[28] Brian Wynne of Lancaster University, U.K., has done interesting critical work on risk, exploring how expert dismissal of typical public refusals to accept scientific knowledge claims work. He explores how risk as science gets prioritized by experts and policymakers while the public's wider concerns about, for example, their dependency on scientists for information about risk, about how trustworthy or otherwise scientific data and its interpretation is, about how the political economy can drive innovation through science are downplayed as public ignorance or misunderstanding of the science. As Wynne explains, when policy gets reduced to science—in this case risk, the public's relationship to science and technology deteriorates.[29]

Much more confident in science and its ability to wholly transcend cultural, social, and political influence is *Deserts as Dumps*'s other editor, energy consultant

Charles C. Reith, who concludes simply and with admirable honesty that: "if the scientific community demonstrates that deserts are the best among the Earth's ecosystems for waste disposal, then those who live around deserts have an obligation to accept this particular land use."[30] Reith's belief in his own ability to allocate national and perhaps global obligation is remarkable, but calm reflection suggests that this is surely not a decision that should be made by one person however eminent a scientist. Reith and other scientists' openness to deserts as suitable sites for waste disposal and storage might well strike the layperson as odd since there is much that is relatively obvious about deserts that makes them problematic in terms of the long timescale and profound engineering imagination needed to make nuclear waste disposal feasible. After all, near-surface disposal of low-level radioactive waste requires isolation for tens of thousands of years and non-degradable chemical wastes need to be isolated forever. Quite a number of deserts are in tectonically active areas; for example, the proposed Yucca Mountain site that is only 12 miles from Nevada's Lathrop Wells volcano. Most deserts have developed because one or more basins have filled, making moving water that could carry contaminants a distinct possibility near a desert disposal site. Deserts are also formed by weathering, erosion, and deposition, all of which points again toward their having the potential to transport toxic materials by wind or other means. Water in desert regions is even more valuable than elsewhere, and many deserts are on top of precious large freshwater aquifers as is the case with Yucca Mountain, a proposed high-level waste site located over the only usable aquifer in the region and the third largest aquifer in the whole of the United States.

Despite these issues, American desert lands have been coveted by scientific, military, and industrial forces keen to develop the United States' nuclear capacity because they, and some would say their inhabitants, were perceived as peripheral. As Hal Rothman has explained with reference to the siting of the Los Alamos nuclear facility on the Pajarito Plateau:

> Ironically, the very attributes that protected the Pajarito Plateau from the systematic colonization that engulfed much of New Mexico before the 1940s made it made it attractive for this secret project. Seeking a remote locale to hide those researching the possibility of creating the single most dangerous human weapon invented up to that time, federal and military officials wanted a place with minimal distraction and little chance of discovery or subversion. The Pajarito Plateau fit such requirements. It had never become thoroughly integrated into the economy of modern America, and in the 1940s it remained as it had always been: remote, peripheral, and marginal to the mainstream ... The region did not offer industrial society enough to justify development.[31]

Or, to give voice to how one tribal judge and health commissioner put it in 1995, shedding new light on the mainstream political support given to Native American sovereignty rhetoric of recent years:

> The U.S. government targeted Native Americans [as hosts for nuclear waste dis-posal] for several reasons: their lands are some of the most isolated in North America, they are some of the most impoverished and, consequently, most politically vulnerable and, perhaps most important, tribal sovereignty can be used to bypass state environmental laws.
>
> How ironic that after centuries attempting to destroy it, the U.S. government is suddenly interested in promoting Native American sovereignty—just to dump its lethal garbage . . . [and] serve as hosts for the nation's nuclear garbage dump.[32]

Oddly, while such land has been deemed suitable for sacrifice, it has also in its time been revered as quintessentially American. In fact, Indian districts now dealing with the ongoing legacy of uranium extraction include some of the most iconic landscapes in America, land such as the Monument Valley district on the Navajo Indian Reservation, which straddles the Utah/Arizona state line. This is the land-scape made famous by John Ford in movies such as *The Searchers* (1956) and *Stagecoach* (1939); by Stanley Kubrick in *2001: A Space Odyssey* (1968); and by Robert Zemeckis in his films *Forrest Gump* (1994) and *Back to the Future III* (1990). It was from Monument Valley uranium that scientists made the first three atomic bombs tested in July 1945 at what is now the White Sands Missile Range, New Mexico, land near the Ndé or Mescalero Apache Reservation. Mining stopped in the Monument Valley area in 1969 after 3,900 metric tons of uranium oxide had been extracted. The experience for Navajo of working as miners was in itself finan-cially discriminatory but the ongoing associated health issues have been much worse, causing the Navajo nation to declare a ban in 2005 on further uranium min-ing in the area. As of September 2011, a cleanup at just one of several hundred radioactive sites on the Navajo reservation, Skyline Mine, is coming to a close at a cost to the EPA of $7.5 million. The clean-up was prompted at least in part by a film made about the Navajo elder Elsie May Begay and her family, whose home was found to have radiation levels up to one hundred times what the United States deems an acceptable level. Two of Elsie May Begay's sons have died—one from lung cancer and one from a tumor. She herself has thyroid cancer.

The kind of nuclear sacrifice Southwestern Indian peoples have been required to make has been neither consistently elective nor a sacrifice consciously made. For example, the Western Shoshone and Southern Paiute had their lands com-mandeered in 1951 in clear violation of the Treaty of Peace and Friendship at Ruby Valley 1863 so that the Nevada Test Site/Nevada National Security Site might be created.[33] About a third of the testing from 1951 to when testing (other than the subcritical) ended in 1992 was done directly in aquifers. With approximately 300 million curies of radiation remaining in 1992 by Energy Department estimates, the site remains one of the most radioactive places in the United States with the water particularly radioactive. It is only about 65 miles from Las Vegas and is often formally referred to in a final irony for those aware of its history as a "United States Department of Energy reservation." It also adjoins the highly secure Area 51 military base so beloved of conspiracy theorists. One could argue that Indian peoples have been bombed by American forces testing and practicing their weapons in the hope that these experiments would help keep larger American populations in the Cold War era safe. As Chief Raymond D. Yowell of the Western Shoshone is quoted as putting it, "We are now the most bombed nation in the world ... The radiation has caused Shoshone, Ute, Navajo, Hopi, Paiute, Havasupai, Hualapai and other downwind communities to suffer from cancer, thyroid diseases and birth defects."[34] There is also evidence that in the early days of Los Alamos Indian peoples unwittingly became part of experiments to test the effects of radiation at Pajarito Plateau and in the Rio Grande valley.[35]

Further Indian sacrifice is linked to Hanford, southeastern Washington. As the General Accounting Office disclosed in 1991, 444 billion gallons of liquid radionuclide and hazardous waste were pumped into soils around it from 1944 until 1972 and millions of gallons of water from the Columbia River were pumped into the cores of eight of Hanford's nine nuclear reactors. Currently an estimated 150 square mile plume of contaminated groundwater exists underneath the Hanford site. The people most immediately at risk from what happened at Hanford are the eight Indian tribes in the region for whom the Columbia River is a central and intimate resource. They include the Confederated Tribes of the Umatilla Indian Reservation in Oregon, the Nez Perce peoples in Idaho and the Yakama Nation. Building Hanford originally meant the forced relocation of the communities at Hanford and White Bluffs and more than 1,500 people including the Wanapum Indian community. Prior to 1800 the 10,000-mile Columbia River Plateau was home to perhaps 8,000 Cayuse, Umatilla, and Walla Walla peoples. Deadlines for the Hanford clean-up continually recede, but the latest completion date is 2047. The current cost is more than $1 billion per year.[36]

This chapter does not attempt to describe all the Indian land sacrificed to national interests through nuclear activity, but no discussion of the theme can ignore the largest known nuclear tests ever conducted in the United States—the blasts at Amchitka Island off the southwest coast of Alaska in 1965, 1969, and 1971.[37] The 1970 "Cannikin" blast was 5.1 megaton, 385 times as powerful as what was dropped on Hiroshima. It is hard for most of us to imagine force of this magnitude, but one senior military witness to both atomic and nuclear atmospheric testing has provided a moving description of what much less force than this feels like. He said in an interview:

There is nothing that you can read, nothing that you can see in pictures, even motion pictures, which prepares you for what it is. 110-kilotons, which we now consider a moderately small bomb, nineteen miles away is just like the end of the earth. An enormous pulse of heat and incredible light. Even with your back to it, the light almost seems to infuse your skull from the inside. And then the blast like no other blast because it persists—it pulses a couple of seconds log. And then finally this enormous fireball, and then the glowing cloud going up in the stratosphere in this wicked purple light.[38]

Amchitka is part of the Alaska Maritime National Wildlife Refuge designated by President Taft in 1913 and was a highly significant Arctic bird sanctuary and a critical haven for sea otters, walruses, and sea lions. A key industry off the coast of Amchitka was the fishery, catching salmon, halibut, pollock, and haddock. Amchitka itself had not been permanently occupied by Unangen or Aleut peoples since around 1832, but the surrounding islands and the local waters were an Unangen mainstay. For indigenous Unangen, nuclear testing was yet another horrific blow to their lifeways after centuries of Russian, European, and American oppression that had included slavery and led to profound population loss. Yet it seems that both wildlife and Aleut peoples were deemed appropriate for yet further sacrifice from 1965 to 1970 and no Aleut peoples were consulted about the blasts. Their effect on wildlife was devastating, killing thousands of animals and birds. It is also thought that the Cannikin blast ruptured the earth's crust and caused a new radioactive aquifer to be formed. Both local Aleut peoples and workers involved with the tests are known to have suffered from exposure to radioactive carcinogens.[39]

Aside from whatever national strategic benefit was gained from the Amchitka tests, one other major good came from them—they prompted the name and foundation of the international organization Greenpeace. In 1998 Pam Miller and others working on behalf of Greenpeace were to find that radioactive materials were leaking into the environment as a result of Cannikin and as a result of the 1969 blast Long Shot, but more recent studies by University of Alaska scientist Mark Johnson funded by the Department of Energy suggest leakage is now minimal.[40] There is much to suggest that although leakage is not happening now in this geologically dynamic area, it may well occur in the future and that regular testing of the ocean environment around Amchitka and of food in the area likely to be used for human subsistence is essential. For those keen to know more, the best recent book on Amchitka is Dean Kohlhoff's 2003 *Amchitka and the Bomb: Nuclear Testing in Alaska*. Other indigenous populations profoundly affected by nuclear testing include the populations of Bikini Atoll and Enewetak Atoll of the Marshall Islands where tests were conducted from 1946 to 1958 that caused severe environmental contamination and human malady. Castle Bravo in 1954 was the first U.S. test of a dry fuel thermonuclear bomb and through a miscalculation back at Los Alamos, it yielded a then-unprecedented 15 megatons, a figure in turn eventually displaced in 1961 by the Soviet Union's Tsar Bomba, which yielded the equivalent of 50 megatons of TNT. The Kiribati (Christmas) Island peoples have also suffered as a result of testing carried out by the United Kingdom from 1957 to 1958 and in 1962 by the United States. Research in 1998 by Durham University, U.K., found that one in three servicemen exposed to the tests died from cancers linked to them. A court case continues as 1,011 former servicemen fight for compensation, but it makes no reference to civilian Gilbertese residents who may also have been exposed to radiation.[41]

How then, can we begin to conceptualize key aspects of the Indian relationship to things nuclear and to "national sacrifice"?

First, it is undoubtedly appropriate to deconstruct the latter term. To "sacrifice" what cannot be replenished and what is central to life, is not sacrifice but simple, massive, and intergenerational destruction. Furthermore, Indian nuclear sacrifice is not sacrifice as it is generally thought of—a conscious, voluntary act done on some level by the entity who will experience the loss. It is more like scapegoating, which is not true sacrifice, merely the projection of loss onto another with the hope of still gaining the benefits associated with true sacrifice. Here I am reminded of Thomas Pricen of the University of Michigan and his thoughtful discussion of what it means to sacrifice what he calls an "ultimate source," for example, a natural source such as an aquifer for which there is no substitute. He writes: "Spiritually speaking, ultimate sources are sacred. To sacrifice an ultimate resource is sacrilege. In contrast, to sacrifice the benefits otherwise derived from using up an ultimate source—to refrain from stripping topsoil, from draining an aquifer, from driving an organism to extinction, from opening the ozone layer, all for commercial gain—to sacrifice these benefits is to elevate human action."[42] Following Pricen, we might do better to think of National Sacrifice Areas as National Sacrilege Areas. Certainly, there is little about the permanent and near-permanent damage to the environment and to native peoples and others that nuclear sacrifice entails that fits conventional understandings of sacrifice as it is routinely understood, that is, as something that is, at least in part, a spiritual activity.

Were we to look to Christian theology for some defense of sacrifice in this context, it would be difficult to find. Instead, much of the Bible emphasizes the importance of doing what is right, applying mercy, and showing good judgement rather than making sacrifices. Thus in Isaiah, Proverbs, Psalms, and elsewhere in the Old Testament we find injunctions such as "To do justice and judgement is more acceptable to the Lord than sacrifice."[43] In Hosea God is quoted as saying, "For it is love that I desire, not sacrifice, and knowledge of God rather than holocausts."[44] For Jesus, in Christian thinking the ultimate and incessant sacrifice, true sacrifice and love of one's neighbor were inseparable. He is quoted in Matthew, "If you bring your gift to the altar and there recall that your brother has anything against you, leave your gift at the altar, go first to be reconciled with your brother."[45] Thus the Christian conception of sacrifice is in fact the opposite of how it is used in terms of National Sacrifice Areas with their associated effects on Indian peoples, their lands, and beyond. Christian sacrifice is an ethical phenomenon; one sacrifices to morally and spiritually grow one's self.

Anthropologists, for their part, have now more or less dispensed with any universal theory of what sacrifice means, but it does seem that the nuclear exchange—the loss of what sustains life in return for some new, seemingly transcendent knowledge—fits a recognizable Western tradition of sacrifice.[46] This was described pithily by Dennis King Keenan in a book oozing with theory that appeared in 2005 called *The Question of Sacrifice*. Here Keenan made the simple but profound overarching point that in the Western tradition sacrifice brings rewards to those organizing the sacrificing on multiple levels:

> In the genealogy of Western sacrifice, one can trace an increasing interiorization, spiritualization, and dialecticization of sacrifice. Throughout this genealogy, sacrifice has predominantly been understood as a necessary passage through suffering and/or death (either of oneself or someone else) on the way to a supreme moment of transcendent truth. Sacrifice effects the revelation of truth that overcomes the negative aspect of sacrifice. In a word, sacrifice pays.[47]

Indeed, it seems that in modern America, specifically, sacrifice as an idea has always paid handsome dividends. Sacrificial thinking, as the Boston University scholar Susan L. Mizruchi has explained in her 1998 book, *The Science of Sacrifice*, has tended in particular to coalesce around those Americans categorized as "strangers"—in the nineteenth century blacks, women, immigrants, the working class, and, Mizruchi might have added, Native Americans. Mizruchi's book is especially valuable because it demonstrates that much of modern social scientific thinking has sacrificial thinking inextricably embedded within it. As Mizruchi puts it, sacrifice "is a foundational script of our multicultural becoming."[48] Incorporating Mizruchi's insights about America and sacrifice, it becomes clear that the notion of a National Sacrifice Area where most of the sacrifice is borne by Indian peoples and their resources is in its own way, a falsely comforting one. It suggests a cleansing process that does not and will not occur since, as key anthropological thinkers have explained, sacrifice is usually conceived of as bringing about a sudden and violent cleansing of sin alongside the release of new sorts of power.[49] Yet in terms of Indian nuclear National Sacrifice no cleansing process will occur, since the pollution cannot in fact be contained within Indian lands. To the contrary, nuclear sacrifice of things Indian through Sacrifice Areas will inevitably and over thousands of years necessarily involve further sacrifice for non-Indians. Radiation, unlike the spiritual notion of sin, cannot easily be renounced, fenced in or put aside.

None of this necessarily ignores the number of Indian peoples who may feel prepared to shoulder a burden of nuclear sacrifice as a patriotic duty. Data on the matter is sparse but the idea is not as unlikely as it might seem. It is worth noting that across time Indian peoples have displayed a preparedness to protect their country expressed through war service and economic contribution to American wars that is significantly disproportionate to their numbers. Americans were surprised, for example, by American Indian support for the First World War effort. Approximately 10,000 joined the U.S. army for conflict overseas, 2,000 more joined the Navy, millions of Indian dollars were spent on war bonds and reports reached home of the bravery of Joseph Oklahombi (Choctaw) in the trenches. Such support of the defense of the nation has continued into the twenty-first century in countless ways although it is insufficiently recognized. The recent book, *Serving their Country: American Indian Politics and Patriotism in the Twentieth Century*, by Paul Rosier does however contain some useful information on World War II Indian patriotism. At least 25,000 Indian people, 800 of them women, served in the armed forces, and the efforts of Indians on the home front were exemplary with, for example, the Quapaw tribe donating $1 million to the government. Recent mainstream films have made the Indian contribution to wartime intelligence better known but what is less well known, is how pivotal the Indian desire to protect Indian peoples and their sacred land was in prompting war involvement. As one Navajo code talker, Albert Smith, put it, "This conflict involved Mother Earth being dominated by foreign countries," and he felt it was an Indian "responsibility to save her."[50] Native patriotism and exemplary military service continues today, an example being the first female U.S. soldier to die during the U.S.-British assault on Iraq, the Hopi Indian warrior Lori Ann Piestewa. The points above should not however, be taken as implying that Indian and environmental concerns are necessarily always the same in and around areas of nuclear sacrifice. Sometimes the opposite is the case. For example, Nevada and eastern Californian Indians have adopted cattle ranching, often by necessity in the wake of the destruction of pinyon forests, and their business interests, along with those of other cattle ranchers, are often in direct conflict with environmental imperatives.

In sum, little about nuclear power is simple and appropriately, neither is the indigenous response to it. Nuclear power is unlikely to go away, and blanket anti-nuclearism is not an adequate response to nuclear's position within current global politics. Since native peoples have a unique understanding of what it means to live with it in the modern world, we are well advised to take heed of their experience. Interestingly, one of the foremost native voices who has considered nuclear technology, the Cherokee-Appalachian writer Marilou Awiakta, grew up on a nuclear reservation at Oak Ridge, Tennessee and like this book's author, she has little time for simplistic anti-nuclearism. Instead, in her latest work, *Selu: Seeking the Corn-Mother's Wisdom*, she urges us to see nuclear energy as in itself sacred and to focus on survival. She diagnoses our current global malaise as a result of suicidal human greed and of the compartmentalizing philosophies that underpin it. She writes:

> All around us we see life "dying back"—in nature, in our families, in society. Homo Sapiens [sic] are literally killing their own seed and the seeds of other life forms as well. One cause of this is suicidal violence is greed. And that greed feeds on the philosophy that Earth is not our Mother, but an "it" that can be used and consumed. This philosophy even extends to the "conquest" of outer space. History shows that when the people in power call Earth "it", they consider all connected with her to be its, too—objects to be dominated, controlled, consumed, forgotten. They are—we are—expendable.[51]

Awiakta and others see the world's embrace of nuclearism as a symptom of the psychological and spiritual. They suggest that our deathly attraction to nuclear weapons is a result of an inherent human desire for annihilation and rebirth, a desire that in previous eras was satisfied through ritual and via myth. Tracing the same theme, American psychologist of war Robert Jay Lifton and his colleague E. Olson have made the following rather chilling argument:

> Expressed boldly, there may be a need to destroy one's world for purposes of imagined rebirth, a need which lends itself either to suicidal obliteration or to transformation and regeneration. This need takes advantage not only of every variety of individual and social aggression but fits well with the psychological principle of touching death, either imaginatively or literally, as a precondition of new life. Thus, nuclear weapons can achieve vivid symbolic representation in our minds precisely because of their promise of devastation.[52]

If such a reading is correct, then perhaps the "cure" for the nuclear disease does indeed lie close to its primary material source in the United States—in Indian country. Awiakta, along with a number of writers of color such as Alice Walker, Paula Gunn Allen, Leslie Marmon Silko, and Carol Lee Sanchez, argue that to cope with our current nuclear realities we must turn back to premodern methods of spiritual, material, and psychological survival. Such a change would involve a fundamental reordering of much about how global excess and global defense is managed. The last 30 years have seen an unprecedented acceleration of existing patterns, with the rich north and south having seen considerable growth in household and corporate wealth. After all, environmental injustice in Native America mirrors a wider set of environmental injustices globally. The repercussions of luxury emissions by the mostly urban rich living within the Northern Hemisphere are being dealt with spatially by those who live in poor countries that emit only subsistence levels of greenhouse gases.[53] This book does not advise categorically on how we might rectify such fundamental inequities, it argues that one of the ways we can begin to do so is by thinking broadly about them through the lens of land, spirit, and indigenous history.

INDIAN LAND RENEWAL AND THE POLITICS OF WILDERNESS

Perhaps the largest problem if we are to understand and support contemporary environmental justice in Native America is seeing the wood for the trees, that is, comprehending the wider context to the conflation of Indian identity with environmentalism and, just as importantly, recognizing the ways in which non-Indian activities limit, control, and direct Indian relationships to land. A good example of the need to see beyond simple representations becomes clear if we deconstruct a recent upbeat *National Geographic* article about how Native peoples are currently setting an example of how to restore the environment. The article looked at a series of native projects as we will below. The main one involved the Santa Clara Pueblo who live on a reservation eight miles downstream from the Rio Grande. They are working to restore the watershed along Santa Clara Creek so as to make thousands of acres alive again with native plants, beaver, and cutthroat trout. Their idea, it seems, is not to recreate "pristine wilderness" but simply to manage land as a number of Indian traditions recommend, that is, in a sustainable way that encourages diversity and advantages in native communities. Tamarisk, Siberian elm, and Russian olive have been removed from 650 acres along the Rio Grande and 75 acres of wetland restored. In an area left devastated by fire, 1.7 million seedlings have been planted and the hope is that with new streamside-growth beaver will return and with them dams, ponds, and eventually meadows. According to the pueblo's recreation director, Stanley Tafoya: "What we are trying to do is restore our resources. The older people want their grandkids to enjoy the canyon we once knew."[54] This is indeed a good news story but although the article infers that the environmental work being carried out is simply a result of Santa Clara Pueblo ownership of the Black Mesa Golf Club hotel-casino and the Dreamcatcher Cinema in Espanola, there is in fact a great deal more to the story.

If we take in more context it is, actually hard to separate what is happening at Santa Clara Creek from a larger ongoing narrative of poor and/or toxifying land use in and around Santa Clara homelands—homelands suffering as I write from the impact of the fourth fire begun outside of the reservation. In truth, a major trigger for the Santa Clara demanding to take over management of their lands from the BIA was a botched May 2000 "controlled burn" carried out by the National Forest Service in the nearby Bandelier National Monument area. According to an opaque document produced on February 26, 2001 by the Forest Service, the "Cerro Grande Prescribed Fire Board of Inquiry Final Report," the original reason for starting the fire was ironically, "to reduce hazard fuels in the burn area," that is, to avoid fires spreading in the future. The Cerro Grande fire destroyed over 235 buildings in Los Alamos and White Rock and damaged 47,000 acres including the upper part of Santa Clara Canyon. Chillingly, the fire spread to Los Alamos National Laboratory, but official sources maintained no radiation was released as a result.

As I write yet another fire, Las Conchas, is burning in New Mexico, again on Santa Clara lands. It may well turn out to be the largest fire in New Mexico's history. The fear is that it could spread to Area G at the Los Alamos National Laboratory where it is believed 20,000 drums of contaminated plutonium waste is stored under fabric tents. It is worth noting that the Los Alamos National Laboratory currently has plans to greatly expand its plutonium production with a new "Chemistry and Metallurgy Research Replacement" project, a project that will require a great deal of water. This, in spite of the fact that as well as being forested and prone to wildfire the region is actively seismic and in the immediate future likely to be acutely prone to drought. It is thought that the Las Conchas fire was caused by a falling aspen tree hitting a power line, but the real question is, of course, what underlying causes make fires in the area spread so fearsomely? According to geologist Grant Meyer at the University of New Mexico in Albuquerque, the answer lies with a build-up of fuels from the forestry industry as they try to suppress fires, climatic warming caused by industry and land-use changes that have caused a decline in annual amounts of snow as well as rising temperatures.[55] Las Conchas is likely to leave perhaps 15,000 acres of Santa Clara Pueblo burned and to fundamentally burn the watershed, leaving the pueblo chronically exposed to flooding as happened after the Cerro Grande fire.

Thus it becomes clear that while indigenous Santa Clara environmental work on the Santa Clara Creek is positive, the larger context to their efforts is much more complex, involving non-native mismanagement of surrounding lands and the throbbing terror of life lived in proximity to nuclear toxicity. As this chapter has made clear, the spiritual well-being of native populations and native land cannot be separated. Los Alamos rests on land sacred to the Santa Clara Pueblo, a number of whom have made clear that their sense of the sacred has been fundamentally disrupted both by fire and by nuclear radioactivity. Native elder Marion Naranjo has stated:

> The Pajarito Plateau on which Los Alamos National Lab was built is a sacred place to the native pueblo people since time immemorial. Look at the Bandelier National Monument, our ancestors lived there, but right now it is threatened by this fire. There are nineteen fingers in the Pajarito Plateau that you call canyons. Those are sacred to us. That is where the springs are. Fire is scared to us, as it replenishes life. Cloud is sacred to us, as we wait for rain. Rain is sacred to us, as it keeps everything alive in the desert. But after Los Alamos was built, our spiritual belief system has been shattered. Now when

we look up at the sky and see cloud, we wonder, is there radioactive elements in the cloud? When we get rain, we wonder, could it bring poison to our communities. We're afraid of our own rain. You talk about Area G as if it is an inanimate place, but all those plutonium-contaminated drums are sitting on one of our largest sacred Kivas. The lab is destroying our spiritual belief system.[56]

Rather than perceive Indian peoples as ecological do-gooders as the *National Geographic* suggests, it is more appropriate to recognize indigenous responses to the attacks on their own lands for what they are: urgent attempts to re-establish balance within a wider environmental context of imbalance and prolonged and often mismanaged external systematic exploitation of resources.

Of course, any efforts to restore or maintain Indian lands through Indian auspices and/or aided by federal funding is welcome and deeply worthwhile, even if there is often so much more to the story than generally gets presented. Thus the world is grateful for the 3,900 acres of Sinkyone land in the "Lost Coast" of California, which has now been made into the country's first intertribal "wilderness" area, a place where the Sinkyone people work to "fix the world" ceremonially each year. The InterTribal Sinkyone Wilderness with its elder redwoods is a "sacred ecosystem" as its executive director Hawk Rosales explains, and the hope is that under native management salmon will return on water such as Wolf Creek. An imponderable is whether a broader renewal of Indian lands in the future will come about within capitalism rather than in any sense outside of it. The Indian renewal projects mentioned here are small in comparative terms, and the task of working on them has not always been carried out by native peoples themselves. The 2,100 acres reclaimed by the Seminole in Florida is a case in point. Like a lot of land not managed for resource extraction or industry, it will be attractive to tourists and could be seen simply as part of the portfolio of assets owned by the tribe, a portfolio that includes the Billie Swamp Safari and the Big Cypress Entertainment Complex. In 2006 the Seminole also spent $965 million to gain control of 68 Hard Rock tourist destinations in the United States, Canada, Europe, Australia, and Puerto Rico. Their internal system of tribal self-governance is both developing and vibrant, and their greatest problems in recent years have centered around managing the sudden wealth flows that followed the 1988 sanctioning of Indian gaming.

It is important to recognize that irrespective of gaming wealth, Indian peoples across the United States have shown a commitment to managing their lands in an environmentally sustainable way. One example is the stunningly scenic Mission Mountains Tribal Wilderness in Montana, which the Confederated Salish and Kootenai Tribes designated as wilderness in 1979 after intervention from Kootenai "yayas" or grandmother elders. Today the 89,500-acre site maintains grizzly bear protection at levels more stringent than almost anywhere else in the lower 48 states. The Tribes' attempts to protect the Mission Range from development can be traced back to 1936, and of course to the period before the Hellgate Treaty of 1855 when an area of perhaps 20 million acres occupied by Salish (Flathead), Pen O'Oreille, and Kootenai Indians was ceded in return for around 1.3 million acres now known as the Flathead Indian Reservation.

Another example, also referenced by the *National Geographic article*, are the Confederated Salish and Kootenai tribes. They have found the wilderness concept useful as they continue to resist the centuries-long drive to secure and maintain their displacement. Tribal Ordinance 79A states:

> Wilderness . . . is the essence of traditional Indian religion and has served the Indian people of these Tribes as a place to hunt, as a place to gather medicinal herbs and roots, as a vision seeking ground, as a sanctuary, and in countless other ways for thousands of years.[57]

The Tribes' version of wilderness is replete with the language authors such as William Cronon and others have so powerfully deconstructed. It involves man "treading lightly" as a sometime visitor, and it seems, Mission Range being a tribal sanctuary, a place not unlike a tribal museum, where tribal peoples can retreat so as to find again what has been lost. Echoing the federal Wilderness Act, in part because no other definition of wilderness existed at the time, the 1982 ordinance defined wilderness as "an area where the earth and its community of life are untrammelled by man, where man himself is a visitor who does not remain. An area of wilderness is further defined as an area of undeveloped tribal land, retaining its primeval character and influence, without permanent improvements or human habitation, which is protected and managed so as to preserve its natural conditions."[58] Some sort of formal definition is a necessary vehicle for achieving an aim within most political contexts, but what and is unique about the tribal aims here is the desire to protect both a way of life and of a sense of the sacred embodied in stories and cultural experiences tied to the land. At a very basic level, the Confederated Tribes looked to find a way to preserve their own version of the good life unpolluted by ever-increasing numbers of incoming migrants since contact. In 1978 Pend O'Oreille Mitch Smallsalmon recalled, "A long time ago . . . all over this land, the people's medicine was here . . . It was good! Their home life was good, they were growing up in a good way, the children of the long-ago people. The land was clean, the air was clean, everything was good." At another level the Tribes' idea of wilderness is spiritual, a way of showing respect both for ancestors and to future generations. Its recent Comprehensive Resources Plan describes fundamental values that require them to respect and live in harmony with each other and with the land. Land is thought of as borrowed from future children. Thus they require of themselves that they act on a spiritual basis when dealing with the environment; preserve the abundance of animals, plants, and fish and maintain hunting and fishing based on need and traditional use.[59]

Elsewhere the Nez Perce, or Nimi'ipuu, who were forced in 1877 from the mountains of Oregon's Wallowa Valley, have been able to regain 16,286 acres of what is now known as its Precious Lands Wildlife Area or Hetes'wits Wetes. This happened with help from the Trust for Public Land, a nonprofit organization founded in 1972 by a number of professionals with the intention of applying a "modern business approach to conservation." The Trust, particularly since 1999 and the inauguration of its Tribal & Native Lands Program, has done much to protect sections of Indian Country. It claims to have worked with over 70 tribes to protect over 200,000 acres under the program. Again, a very specific definition of wilderness applies to the Nimi'ipuu Precious Lands. They are managed by the Nimi'ipuu rather than the federal government but no Nimi'ipuu live there. Instead the tribe has set up an office in an adjacent town named Joseph. Contemporary Indian conservation in this instance has succeeded in part because it practices conservation in ways the dominant society understands, that is, in ways that exclude any permanent human presence within wildlife zones. There is also a compensatory dimension to a number of these schemes: Indian conservation projects often get generated in part because of less environmentally favorable wider land-use choices made in the region. The Nez Perce management plan for Precious Lands, for example, was developed under the auspices of the Pacific Northwest Electric Power Planning and Conservation Act of 1980 with funding from the Bonneville Power Administration with the express purpose of mitigating wildlife habitat losses that resulted from the installation of four dams on the lower Snake River in the 1960s and early 1970s. Bonneville is a non-profit federal agency that markets about 40 percent of the electricity consumed in the southwest.[60] For some time a coalition of sport and commercial fishing groups, conservation groups and taxpayer advocacy groups have been demanding the removal of the four lower Snake River dams as part of the Columbia River salmon recovery plan. The Columbia River Basin once supported the world's largest runs of Pacific salmon and steelhead salmon but now some populations are extinct and others severely depleted.

Finally, the *National Geographic* article which has been the springboard for this section turns to the Red Lake Reservation in Minnesota where there is the only hook-and-line commercial fishery in the United States, a result of a management plan created by Chippewa, state, and federal agencies along with the University of Minnesota. From 2006 to 2009 fishing with gill nets was sanctioned and instead tribal fisherman caught by hook and line only up to 50 freshwater walleye pike commercially per day. This was the result of prior commercial over-fishing, which in the late 1980s legally took one million pounds of walleye from the lake a year and because of Red Lake band "subsistence" netting, which some Indians used as a license to sell thousands of pounds of walleye on the black market. It is worth noting, contrary to the implication in how the circumstance is described in the *National Geographic*, that in this instance the danger of over-fishing was a lesson Red Lake Indians selling on the black market relearned in the early

1990s along with everyone else in Minnesota.[61] However few other employment options were available to local Indian peoples and over-fishing had been fostered in the first instance by the federal government who encouraged commercial fishing from 1917 as part of First World War efforts and expanded it again during World War Two. Further problems for fish came in 1951 with the building at the main outlet of Lower Red Lake by U.S. Army Corps of Engineers of a concrete flood-control structure designed to stop the flooding of communities and farmland downstream from Red Lake. This impeded spawning walleye. In 1997 the Red Lake Band closed its commercial fishery and the next year implemented a complete walleye moratorium. In 2009 the Red Lake Band of Chippewa resumed limited commercial walleye netting. In 2010 state and federal officials and the Red Lake Band of Chippewa signed a new five-year agreement to continue working together to maintain the Upper and Lower Red Lake fisheries, extending a prior agreement in place from 1999–2009 that brought the walleye population back to health. Such cooperation is a success story, bringing walleye populations back from the brink in 1997 when a spawning assessment collected just four fish. The danger for fish and humans alike in the Red Lake regional area is now peat mining, which has the potential to increase, bringing with it rising mercury levels in fish populations and a host of issues related to acid mine drainage.[62]

This chapter's discussion of environmental justice in Indian country highlights acute problems and underdiscussed sets of histories. It reminds us that we must be just as vigilant about representation and scope of analysis in this context as any other. In Indian country environmental issues cannot properly be separated from the operations of capital, the ongoing legacies of colonialism, and the varieties of thinking that underpin both.

CHAPTER 7

~

Vanishing, Reappearing, and Disappearing Indians on American Soil

Context is all, as the conclusion of the previous chapter implied. Too often the wider context to developments in Native America have been ignored so as to create attention-grabbing headlines. Instead events are presented either as isolated instances or as a unique conflagration of circumstances. Toxic waste and the environmental injustices experienced by native peoples discussed previously are part of centuries-old processes that have operated on American soil against indigenous peoples as individuals, bands, tribes, and on a pan-Indian basis. Processes of attrition have made use of disease, encroachment, displacement, military, cultural and spiritual attack, forced assimilation, law, trickery, deceit, and varieties of intellectualism so as to edge native peoples out of American discourse and minimize their impact on American affairs. These processes reflect an abiding non-Indian desire to make Indians disappear that has a sustained, revealing, and, in terms of national self-reflection, blinkered history. Yet these in turn have been interrupted by a more recent history of Indian reappearance within certain scholarly work and within the American census coupled with a new appreciation of aspects of Indian sovereignty that is almost as remarkable. It is to this fundamental issue of the Indian presence on American soil and how it is thought about that we now turn.

Let us begin with Indian vanishing. The American nation-state convinced itself that Indians were about to "vanish" in a material sense until at least 1800 when the focus shifted to an equally steadfast belief that Indians would certainly vanish culturally if not also materially. Both versions of the same idea worked to satisfy non-Indian desires to gain control of Indian land. Throughout the long and unsavory history of the creation of reservations and then of the allotment of Indian land into individual sections via the Dawes Severalty Act of 1887 accompanied as it was by an ongoing and forceful program of Indian cultural assimilation to non-Indian ways, American beliefs stayed the same—one way or another Indians would disappear. The notion justified first Indian removal from their homelands and then consistently informed American policy. Yet as Brian Dippie's 1982 book, *The Vanishing American: White Attitudes and U.S. Indian Policy*, showed, in the final decades of the nineteenth century Americans started to fear that their steadfast efforts to smooth seemingly inevitable Indian decline might have been a mistake. The loss of a unique American cultural heritage seemed imminent at this time and efforts to ensure Indian cultural conservation began in parallel with similar efforts to preserve wild animals and natural resources. Within the academy, the foremost proponent of what became known as "salvage anthropology" was Franz Boas. He and his school of anthropologists sought to "save" and ossify Indian culture for storage in American museums before, it was thought, it disappeared forever. The 1920s thus saw one of the strongest of the periodic peaks in Indian nostalgia that have always featured in American history. Yet it was a Boasian understanding that cultures primarily made sense internally and could be judged only from the inside that would inform the great shift in Indian policy represented by the Indian Reorganization Act of 1934. Known as the Indian New Deal, changes in the 1930s saw a new comprehension from the dominant American society that Indian cultures had value, deserved investment, and, just as significantly, required the restoration of their land so as to culturally and materially develop. For all its flaws, embedded as they were in the stereotypes of the time, the New Deal provided an essential platform from which the twentieth-century regeneration of Indian numbers and communities could proceed. Reformers such as John Collier idealized Indian culture, especially the agricultural communities in New Mexico and Arizona, for the very qualities non-Indians had once decided marked Indians out as inferior. The centrality of spirituality and religion, the power of community, and a perceived lack of an historical dynamic were now admired as positive rather than as heretofore denigrated as "primitive" attributes.

The "vanishing Indian" myth may have been fatally wounded following the sea change represented by the New Deal but the idea takes many forms and requires much effort to displace. Success in this regard across the twentieth century has meant that Indians have "appeared" rather than vanished in a number of different ways. They have "reappeared" from the past in terms of estimates for numbers at contact and "appeared" in the present in terms of demographic counts within the United States since the 1960s.

INDIANS APPEARING: INDIAN POPULATION NUMBERS AT CONTACT

The debate over contact population numbers is a deeply poignant and significant one since it casts a defining light on how we view the human cost of conquest and consequently how Euro-Americans may think of themselves as an historical force. As remarkable as it may seem today, up until the 1920s the 1560 estimate by the Spanish priest Bartolemé de Las Casas that only 40 million Indians died in Latin America between 1492 and 1560 was generally thought of as being a gross exaggeration.[1] During the late 1920s, at a time when government reports and intellectuals more generally were beginning to recognize the horrifying conditions on Indian reservations, a scholarly debate broke out over Columbian contact numbers that stimulated a wave of new anthropological research.[2] Despite this swing toward a new approach from the late 1920s until the watershed of the 1960s, scholarly orthodoxy tended toward conservative estimates. James Mooney in 1910 and 1928 estimated that at the time of "first extensive contact" for individual tribal populations in regions north of the Rio Grande there were only 1.15 million Native Americans (that is, American Indians, Eskimos, and Aleuts).[3] Anthropologist Alfred Kroeber calculated the figure as 8.4 million in 1934 and 1939, philologist Ángel Rosenblat came up with 13.4 million in 1935, and Julian Steward calculated 15.6 million in 1949.[4] In retrospect, given how much the consensus on the appropriate range for these numbers has altered over time and the fact that the limited ethno-historical evidence on which they have been based has remained the same, the comparatively fine detail in these numbers is ludicrous. Even so, the numbers arrived at were the result of much intellectual effort and detailed calculus. In this regard they are reminiscent of Bishop James Ussher's equally deliberate 1650 calculation that the world was created precisely on the night preceding Sunday, October 23, 4004 BC. Like Bishop Usher's, these calculations owe most to their operating premises and to the beliefs that inform them.

The 1960s changed everything, including indigenous contact population estimates. Like the 1920s, it was a decade marked by investigation into Indian conditions and by reform pressure that stimulated policy change. The plea was for Indian "self-determination" instead of the termination of relationship with federal bodies that had been policy in the 1950s. It was a call echoed in the 1961 "Declaration of Indian Purpose" produced by the American Indian Chicago Conference, repeated by the National Indian Youth Council, founded in 1961, by the Alaskan Federation of Natives, formed in 1966, and by the controversial American Indian Movement formed in 1968. Strong Indian involvement in the war in Southeast Asia spurred further Indian activism. What came to be known as the "Red Power" insurgency was to last from 1969 to 1973 and to range from nonviolent political demonstrations to occasional armed resistance. Amid all this, a new outlook on Indian loss stemming from contact gained sway. Anthropologist

Henry Dobyns picked up (some suggest became obsessed with) the work of an earlier geographer from Berkeley, Carl Sauer, and his emphasis on disease as a key determinant. Sauer and his school had emphasized the importance of respecting early counts, estimates and documentary data, and stressed the importance of epidemics in prompting catastrophic decline in Indian numbers. Dobyns in turn argued that European pathogens could have cut a swath through Indian population numbers long before actual face-to-face encounters between European settlers and Indians had actually occurred. He therefore suggested that a huge jump in estimates was appropriate and that there were up to 18 million Indians north of Mesoamerica when Europeans began to make contact.[5] Subsequent scholars, such as David Stannard, have gone even further, arguing that there were in fact 100 million Indian deaths, a loss that constitutes "the most massive act of genocide in the history of the world."[6]

Without doubt, the intellectual implications of fully assimilating the thinking put forward by Dobyns and other "high counters" were and remain enormous. It means accepting that Indian losses occurred of a magnitude unmatched at any other time in history, caused not only by the ugly realities of the colonial process but by a conjunction of factors including the introduction of a suite of European diseases to which American populations were uniquely susceptible. It means accepting this as the starting point for the story of European life on the American continent and dealing with its moral and cultural implications. These involve dispensing with long-held heroic American narratives where Indian absence and dispossession are put forward as a minor footnote in a story of generally glorious American progress. The exemplar for such narratives within the historical discipline was written by the historian Frederick Jackson Turner in 1893; but still today few textbooks mention Indians in significant detail after 1812, and it is possible to write acclaimed popular books praising America as an empire without discussing the obvious in-depth—that the first sets of peoples the United States displaced were its original, indigenous owners.[7] At the same time, superb scholars are able to win awards for books about presidents such as Lincoln in spite of, or perhaps in part because of, such books turning a blind eye to Lincoln and his generals' ugly legacy in Indian country.[8] Comprehensive recognition of the extent of Indian death brought about by contact along Dobyns's lines would deal a fundamental blow to such historical innocence, a malevolent and immature condition that Graham Greene once said was a particularly American failing. He described it as "innocence ... like a dumb leper who has lost his bell, wandering the world, meaning no harm."[9]

Yet we must bear in mind that since 1966 few scholars have approached Dobyns's heights in their estimates, and his work in terms of its scholarship and premises has been much critiqued.[10] Meanwhile the debate over contact population numbers has continued apace. The respected Cherokee demographer Russell Thornton estimated in 1987 that there were over 5 million on the U.S. mainland in 1492 with another 2 million in present-day Alaska, Canada, and Greenland combined. He suggested that a 75 million aboriginal figure was a reasonable esti-mate for the hemisphere.[11] Douglas Ubelaker estimated an aboriginal population north of Mexico of 1.85 million in 1988, while Kirkpatrick Sale in 1990 argued the correct figure was actually 15 million for all of the United States and Canada. William Denevan estimated 3.79 million in 1992, the same year that A. J. Jaffe estimated one million.[12] Perhaps the most forthright of all the critics of Dobyns and other "high counters" has been David Henige. He accused Dobyns of conjuring *numbers from nowhere* in his attempt to answer what Henige concluded was "a thoroughly unanswerable question." In a sarcastic, funny, and strongly felt 1998 book, "Numbers from Nowhere," Henige explained that he simply could not concur with the assumptions that underpin the "high counters'" work, namely that early European observers could count accurately, did in fact do so and communicated this accurately within written sources. He also felt that the impact of disease had been highly overestimated.[13]

While demographers continue to attempt to nail jelly to the wall with reference to indigenous American Indian numbers at contact, nondemographers can be sure only that the consensus has radically shifted over time. It now seems certain that Indian populations were much larger than was thought in either Mooney or Kroeber's days and that, as a corollary, those societies are likely to have been much more complex than previous commentators had imagined. Despite Henige's reservations it also seems probable that Old World diseases played a key role, that is, that the nonstrategic transfer of disease pathogens was not insig-nificant in the "conquest" of the New World.[14] Furthermore, Indian population decline was unlikely to have been uniform and the effect of epidemics was prob-ably central but not necessarily a determinant long-term. Rather, repeated pum-melling from cyclical bouts of disease would have had a devastating effect when compounded with, as key commentators Thornton, Miller, and Warren put it, "the indirect effects of wars (and genocide), enslavements, removals and reloca-tions, and the destruction of the 'ways of life' and subsistence patterns of American Indian societies accompanying contact with Europeans."[15] Disease was important but it should not be overemphasized at the expense of other fac-tors that may have exacerbated its impact such as relocation, forced labor, and changes in diet. As Thornton explains, "Native American societies were removed and relocated, warred on and massacred, and undermined ecologically and eco-nomically. All of these effects of colonialism caused population decline through reduced fertility as well as increased mortality."[16]

MORE INDIANS APPEARING: CONTEMPORARY CENSUS

Few things about how and whether Indian peoples are enumerated are simple but they are always revealing. Given the early American conviction that Indian peo-ples were vanishing it is perhaps not surprising that the country did not then bother to count Indian peoples in a coherent fashion for over a century.

Although the first decennial census in the United States in 1790 collected data on race, American Indians were not to be counted as a separate group until 1860. Even then, those on American Indian reservations and those in American Indian territories were not included. It took until 1890 for Indian peoples to be fully enumerated throughout the country, a point at which Indian numbers are deemed to have reached their all-time nadir at just 228,000 individuals. Thankfully since then Indian population numbers have made a spectacular recovery depending on how one interprets the figures. The 2000 census listed 4.1 million Indian peoples made up of 2.5 million American Indian and Alaskan Native, 1.6 million American Indian and Alaskan Native as well as one or more other races. In 2010 the estimated population of American Indians and Alaskan natives, including those of more than one race stood at 5.2 million, some 1.7 percent of the total U.S. population.[17] Without doubt these figures suggest that there has been repeated underenumeration within federal population censuses even when we factor in variables such as rapid Indian population growth in the last several decades and the impact of improvements made in healthcare provision on reservations.

Why then, have so many Indians "appeared" relatively suddenly within census enumeration? Certainly the biggest change has stemmed from the shift to self-identification starting in 1960 and, to a lesser degree, from shifts in how Indians have been defined by the Bureau of the Census.[18] This is not to suggest that identifying oneself as Indian has necessarily become easier or any less fraught with controversy. Neither is it the case that recent figures are in any sense necessarily an accurate representation of the extent of Indian identity within the nation. Indeed, just in terms of federal definitions, "Indianness" is an identity defined in 33 different ways in assorted pieces of legislation.[19] Although contemporary America has seen burgeoning numbers choosing to claim Indian identity, there has been a steadily increasing reluctance both among scholars and within Indian communities to grant legitimacy to such claims. These are conflicts linked to the inconsistent and often illogical legacy of the Indian relationship to the federal government. Generally, the government body with responsibility for Indian concerns, the Bureau of Indian Affairs, demands one-quarter Indian blood quantum and/or tribal membership before an individual can be counted as Indian. Various tribes have differing requirements, but around two-thirds of all federally recognized tribes specify a minimum blood quantum, and most often it is one-quarter. This means that significant numbers of individuals who live as Indians, think of themselves as Indians and who are accepted by other Indians as Indians, can nonetheless find themselves excluded from legal status as Indian. For example, since 2000 Americans have been able to choose more than one race with which to identify themselves. However, those who register Indian ancestry from more than one tribe risk exclusion if their tribe specifies that the one-quarter Indian blood quantum registered comes from their tribe only.

Some have explained the rise in the number of Americans self-identifying as Indian as the result of "ethnic-switching" because of a variety of factors. One is a perception that being Indian carries a certain cultural cachet; another is the fact that a legal Indian identity carries with it various rights, protections, and privileges. These can include certain economic rights guaranteed by treaty, such as subsistence rights in designated lands, exemption from state property tax, and the right as an Indian parent for your children, should it be deemed necessary that they be removed from their home, to be placed with another family member in keeping with the dictates of the 1978 Indian Child Welfare Act. This Act was intended as a means of redressing what had been an up to 35 percent loss in some states of Indian children to foster and adoption care within non-Indian families, a phenomenon perceived by many as a symptom of cultural incomprehension on the part of predominantly white, middle-class social workers. Those legally defined as Indian are also protected from prosecution for using certain prohibited items, such as eagle feathers and the pseudo-hallucinogen peyote. They also enjoy further rights under the 1990 Native American Graves Protection and Repatriation Act; are allowed to market their work as "Indian produced" under the 1990 Indian Arts and Crafts Act; and can benefit from "Indian preference" in federal employment, particularly within the Bureau of Indian Affairs and the Indian Health Service.

Tribal reliance on rolls written in the past as a means of identifying Indian people is in itself a legacy of colonialism. It is highly problematic at best and has been wholly rejected by a significant number of Indian individuals since traditional methods for retaining and passing on knowledge within many tribes were and remain oral and the legal characteristics of tribal enrollment today are inconsistent with what are usually thought of as "traditional" concepts of tribal membership.[20] As the Ojibwa-Sioux activist and long-term federal prisoner Leonard Peltier put it, "This is not our way. We never determined who our people were through numbers and lists. These are the rules of our colonizers ... I will not comply with them."[21] Tribal rolls were often compiled in the nineteenth century by non-Indians in a most biased, overcomplicated and unsystematic fashion at a time when a fundamental and deep-seated program of Indian discrimination and attempted cultural obliteration was taking place. The Dawes Rolls, for example, were compiled between 1898 [the time of the Curtis Act] and 1906 by the Dawes Commission as an attempt to persuade tribes who had resisted the Dawes Act of 1887 to go along with its dictates. This was one of the most invidious pieces of legislation ever passed by Congress, since its purpose was to pulverize Indian cultures and force assimilation to the lifeways of the dominant culture within a single generation. It required Indians accept allotment of tribal land according to status. In return they would be extended citizenship and the proceeds from the sale of unallotted tribal lands were to be used for Indian education. However, what actually got assimilated into the mainstream were not Indians themselves, but Indian land. Close to two-thirds of Indian lands nationally went into white ownership, an estimated 86 million acres by 1934 when policy changed.

Even though the Dawes Commissioners enrolled only a small percentage of those who applied and acknowledged that they had denied many people of indubitable tribal ancestry, the Dawes Rolls remain the basis for the award of Certificates of Degree of Indian Blood (CDIBs, in Canada known as Indian status cards) for people of Cherokee, Choctaw, Creek, Chickasaw, and Seminole blood. Unsurprisingly, Indian people actively resisted the enrolment process which has meant that their descendants have been disenfranchised from their rightful status. However, numbers were also bolstered in other ways. Non-Indian people made it onto the rolls, including non-Indian spouses of Indians and, on occasion, on remarriage, their non-Indian children and their subsequent non-Indian partners. As well as the notorious "five dollar Indians" (non-Indians who paid this amount to bribe unscrupulous census enumerators), there were also African-American slaves with no Indian ancestry formerly owned by Oklahoma tribes who were made into tribal members. It is impossible to know how many there are today of these so-called "non-Indian Indians." From the perspective of some Indian communities, however, the issue may be of interest only to outsiders since, as noted above, for a number blood quantum is not the primary determinant in reckoning belonging. It is also worth noting that the history of non-Indian cataloguing of Indian numbers is not without its own sarcastic brand of humor. There is evidence, for example, of Sicangu Lakota peoples who, when queuing for a census that would determine rations, ensured that they were counted more than once. Census enumerators duly recorded names that translate as "Dirty Prick" and "Shit Head." Whether these fictional individuals are still in receipt of government largesse or indeed, still paying federal or state taxes, is not known.

INDIAN DISAPPEARANCE IN THE FUTURE: BLOOD QUANTUM

Although Indian numbers have been growing, reckoning descent and identity via blood quantum carries with it inbuilt, serious problems. It also perpetuates anomalies. Acquiring and maintaining Indian identity today requires effort and in many cases certification. By comparison, to be socially attributed as black or African American is much easier. From the Civil War African American descent status operated according to the "one-drop rule," or rule of hypodescent, a form of establishing identity that had power within American state courts up until 1970. In truth, there is much to suggest that Indian peoples would be well advised to reconceptualize how tribes, bands, and communities recognize each other since the existing system is likely to ultimately serve interests other than their own. Indian enumeration using blood quantum was thought up by the U.S. government rather than by Indian peoples themselves at a time when the stated aim of that government was to annihilate Indian peoples as discrete, viable cultures. As the notorious assimilationist, founder, and superintendent of Carlisle

Indian School, Pennsylvania put it in 1892, "all the Indian there is in the race should be dead."[22] It therefore seems odd that so many tribes should themselves adhere to the blood quantum system of defining Indian identity. It is particularly unsuited to tribes that are small and therefore need to marry outside of their own group in order to persist. More importantly, if tribes and the government continue to adhere to blood quantum as a means of reckoning identity in the long term, there will potentially cease to be any Indians left to count. Perhaps unsurprisingly given their history of progressive engulfment since 1492, Indians today have the highest rate of intermarriage of any group. Therefore, continuing to adhere to or to tighten existing blood quantum requirements in the long term could bring about Indian self-destruction, at least in terms of how Indians are enumerated and formally defined. Given that the numbers of "mixed-blood" Indians are continually increasing, some within Indian communities argue that by choosing blood quantum instead of traditional modes of community membership, native nations are "committing the ultimate act of self-colonization in that not only are they excluding a growing number of their 'mixed-blood' brethren, American Indian people are, in a self-colonizing act, breeding themselves out of an "authentic" Indian identity."[23]

Native peoples in the United States today can find themselves in a double bind that stems directly from the limiting of identity that accompanied the subdivision of native lands in 1887. The 1887 General Allotment or Dawes Act set blood quantum as the primary means of identifying Indian status, deeming those of one half or more Indian blood as the only ones eligible to own Indian land via a federal land grant. Those who were not deemed sufficiently "Indian" in terms of blood quantum were summarily disenfranchised and their treatied entitlements to land and to federal benefits removed. Subsequently it has been in Indian peoples' best interest in terms of maximizing federal benefits allotted for Indians, to maintain blood quantum divisions. The long-term impact of blood quantum since 1887 has been the creation of a situation that structurally, at least, encourages the perpetuation of a colonial agenda by Indians themselves. As M. Annette Jaimes put it in her essay "Federal Indian Identification Policy: A Usurpation of Indigenous Sovereignty in North America,"—"the limitation of federal resources allocated to meeting U.S. obligations to American Indians has become so severe that Indians themselves have increasingly begun to enforce the race codes excluding the genetically marginalized from both identification as Indian citizens and consequent entitlements."[24] This has persisted despite blood quantum being replaced in favor of self-identification as part of the 1972 Indian Education Act because certain federal and state authorities still cling to blood quantum to define "Indianness." The Census Bureau accepts self-identification but other agencies define "Indianness" variously, either via residence on a reservation or according to a range of fractions of Indian blood. For a number of Indian peoples, the 1972 change is yet another equally insidious shift in terms of maintaining Indian sovereignty; as Ted Means put it in 1975, it is "the federal attempt to

convert us from being the citizens of our own sovereign nations into benign members of some sort of all-purpose U.S. 'minority group,' without sovereign
rights."[25] According to the Lakota social worker and writer Hilary Weaver, some
of the harshest arbiters of native identity are, in fact, native peoples themselves.
This is in part also a legacy of federal policies of the past that served to set
mixed-bloods against full-bloods and "progressive" pro-acculturative Indians
against those who were determined to retain traditional lifeways. Other aspects
of the wider federal system have prompted intertribal conflict over Indian status.
In 1979, the Samish and Snohomish of Puget Sound, for example, were declared
"legally extinct" by the federal government partly because other Native groups
such as the Tulalips did not consider them to be genuine. Similarly, one of the
largest tribes in the 1990 census, the Lumbees of North Carolina, had difficulty
gaining federal and social acceptance as legitimate indigenous communities
because of intertribal disputes over timber resources. After a long fight they
received only limited federal acknowledgment in 1956 with the proviso that they
receive no federal services.[26]

Blood and direct descent have therefore an important role within intra- and
intertribal politics and within Indian thinking more generally. Reference to
"memory in the blood" in one form or other is a characteristic for example, of
each of the Kiowa Pulitzer Prize winner N. Scott Momaday's major works. The
idea is so central to so much of native writing that a critical text, *Blood
Narrative*, has been devoted exclusively to the nexus of blood-land-memory.[27]
This is not to suggest that Indian and non-Indian ideas about blood and geneal-
ogy are the same or, for that matter, that an Indian emphasis on blood can routinely be dismissed as racist. Indian thinking does not necessarily imply that
Indian identity is diluted as the degree of Indian blood decreases. Instead, as
scholars such as Eva Garroutte point out, Indian ideas about kinship differ greatly
from those of non-Indians and it is important that we recognize that "there are
indigenous essentialisms quite different from the biologistic, social and scientific
varieties" dependent on the idea of race.[28]

Predictably, there is considerable debate about how Indian identity will come
to be reckoned in years to come and over how Native American political purchase
might operate. Growing intermarriage rates with non-Indians are linked to perhaps the biggest structural shift of late within Indian life, the shift from rural to
urban living. At the turn of the twentieth century only 0.4 percent of Indians lived
in urban areas, whereas in 1990 it was 56.2 percent, a transformation aided by
government relocation programs begun in the 1950s. The 2000 census showed
that at most only 36 percent (0.9–1 million) of American Indians and Alaska
Natives lived on reservations or in other Census-defined tribal areas. Even though
growth rates are higher for Indians living away from Indian-owned land, the shift
toward urban living combined with increases in Indian intermarriage seem likely
to reduce the strength of tribal identity and further decrease the extent to which
Indian languages are spoken. Lakota demographer Russell Thornton has argued

that these are changes that may make it appropriate in the future to speak primarily of Native American ancestry or ethnicity, rather than of specific tribal members or of "full-blood Indians." In his view, "a Native American population comprised primarily of 'old' Native Americans strongly attached to their tribes will change to a population with a predominance of 'new' Native Americans who may or may not have tribal attachments or even tribal identities."[29] Not everyone agrees. Nancy Shoemaker argues plausibly that in fact the tribe will remain the primary Indian entity of the future. Candid about the fact that Indian population numbers are such a small percentage of America's overall population figures, she feels that therefore Indians are never likely to have a strong voice as a cohort within American politics as a whole.[30] Her conclusions are strengthened by estimates about future Indian numbers. Although Indians are the ethnic group whose numbers are currently growing fastest through natural increase, even if projected growth is maintained, the proportion of Indians within the United States will still only be around 1.96 percent in 2050.[31]

If the tribe is to remain the primary unit in terms of Indian political purchase, much it would seem, will depend on how Indian relationships develop with the Democratic Party. Indian voters tend to vote for the Democratic Party, perhaps a reflection of the continuing dire circumstances in which so many of them live. In 2009 the median income of American Indian and Alaska Native households was only $37,348, 23.6 percent of all Indians were in poverty and 24.1 percent lacked health insurance cover. Thus Indian peoples came out strongly for John Kerry in the 2004 elections and were part of the Obama coalition along with the other larger minority groups. Sampling of counties with high Native American population percentages suggests that Native American support for Obama and other Democrats remained strong in 2010.[32] It is well known that a Democratic voter registration surge was key to President Obama's comfortable win in the 2008 campaign when he scored one of the widest popular vote victories in U.S. history. Prior to and since that win he has been careful to show continued empathy and concern about Indian country. When campaigning for the presidential primary he was adopted by the Crow in Montana and given the name "Barack Black Eagle."

Since becoming president President Obama has encouraged tribal leaders to interact with top administration officials and held a second and then third Native American conference at the White House in December, 2010 and 2011, welcoming leaders from the nation's 565 federally recognized tribes. The previous meeting in November 2009 was the first of its kind for 15 years. Other positive moves include a late 2010 settlement for certain Native American trust funds; the Indian Healthcare Act, passed as part of the sweeping health care law Congress adopted in March 2010; a landmark tribal justice measure giving Native Americans more power to police their reservations and prosecute criminals signed in July 2010; Obama's initiation of November as National American Indian and Alaskan Native Heritage Month and his call for all Americans to celebrate the day after Thanksgiving as National Native American Heritage Day. In late 2009 the Obama administration also agreed to a $3.4 billion settlement of a class action suit—the largest settlement American Indians have ever received from the U.S. government, in recompense for the loss of royalties for oil, mineral, and other leases promised to Indian peoples when Indian land was placed in trust by the government under the 1887 Dawes Act. The settlement means that every individual with a trust account is to receive $1000; $2 billion is earmarked for the government to buy back Indian land and $60 million is for scholarships for American Indian children. By now the reader will perhaps not be surprised to learn that, in light of confusion over records, it is not yet clear exactly how many people will be affected by the settlement—it may be up to 500,000.

Population figures matter in Native America, both on the ground and as indices of cultural politics as the above has shown. Census estimates suggest that by 2050 there will be 8.6 million American Indians and Alaska Natives, including those of more than one race, a real advance but still less than 2 percent of the population by then. Yet the power and impact of Indian identity has never directly or simply correlated with the number of Indian individuals enumerated. Today Indian sovereign, treaty, and humanitarian rights are also promoted within international frameworks such as the Organization of American States, the World Council of Indigenous Peoples and the United Nations' Working Group on Indigenous Populations. They are part of a chorus of transnational claims for indigenous rights, often linked to environmental movements, whose power continues to grow. At the recent White House Tribal Nations Conference (December 16, 2010), President Obama gave these organizations an unprecedented boost by agreeing to sign the United Nations Declaration on the Rights of Indigenous Peoples. Prior to this, the United States had been one of only three nations in the world not to have signed it. A president doing so represents a real step forward, even though it is not legally binding.

It remains to be seen whether the United States signing the declaration will serve to make Indian decisions to allow energy developments on their land more easily enforceable. Tex Hall, head of the Great Plains Tribal Chairman's Association and one of the twelve regional tribal leaders who was invited to the 2011 White House Tribal Nations Conference seems to think it might. "We should have the ability to take land into trust if it's within our exterior boundaries for any economic project, be it a refinery or be it a buffalo or wild horse sanctuary— whatever it is we want to do—without everybody saying, 'No, they can't' and the [interior] secretary listening to those public comments. If I want to develop it, I still have to wait for the Bureau of Indian Affairs."[33] Certainly the global race to use nuclear energy to provide more power is unlikely to abate. In the United States, where no new nuclear plant has come onstream since 1996, the future may see not only a number of traditional, billion-dollar reactors but also a great many smaller, scalable reactors, similar in design to those found on nuclear-powered ships and submarines. Whether Indian land will prove as attractive to the builders of these reactors as it has proven for the builders of their larger cousins remains to be seen.

Since the 1960s Indians may have begun to "appear" in unprecedented numbers but they have continued to "disappear" in other significant ways. At the risk of being macabre, it is revealing to take a close look at why today's Indian peoples die. Doing so reveals a set of propensities that are hard for the nonscientist not to link to colonialism and its legacy—that is, to the spiritual and psychological stresses of living surrounded by a dominant settler society. In comparison to other racial groups, American Indians or Alaskan Natives are much more likely to die from diabetes. It is the fourth most likely reason for their deaths unlike whites for whom it is the seventh. Like Asian and Pacific Islanders, for American Indians and Alaskan Natives suicide is the eighth most likely reason they would die, for whites it is the tenth. If, aside from the top big killers of all Americans (heart disease, cancerous malignancies etc.), an obesity-related disease or depression does not kill Indian people, then an alcohol-related disease will. Uniquely among U.S. racial groups, for American Indians and American Natives chronic liver disease and cirrhosis of the liver is the fifth most likely cause of death.[34]

Whether or not it results directly in death, contemporary violence against Native American peoples remains highly disproportionate and of profound concern. Although the gathered statistical sample sizes are inadequate, it is clear that American Indians and Alaskan Natives experience significantly higher rates of violent victimization than other groups (in 2010, 42.2 per 1,000 compared with 13.6 percent per 1,000).[35] Native Americans experience violent crime at more than twice the national average rate across all age groups, housing locations, and by gender. They are more likely to experience it at the hands of someone of a different race and the criminal victimizer is more likely to have consumed alcohol preceding the offense. According to National Crime Victimization Survey annual average percentages for 1992–2001, about 60 percent of American Indian victims of violence described the offender as white. Alcohol use by the offender is a factor in a high percentage of all violence carried out against Native Americans and it plays a special role in domestic violence. The rate of violent victimization among American Indian women was more than double that among all U.S. women and nearly 4 in 5 American Indian victims of rape/sexual assault across 1992–2001 described the offender as white. A large segment of reported violence against Indians from 2000 to 2002 seems to have happened away from Indian reservations or Indian lands.

Indian people are it seems, both sinned against and sinning. They make up a disproportionate number of those enjoying the hospitality of federal prisons with 16 percent of all U.S. Indian offenders entering prisons in 2001 doing so for violent crimes. From 1977 to 2002, 820 people were executed in prison, eight of them Indian—1 percent of those executed.[36] On January 1, 2010, 37 Native Americans were on state and federal death row, 1.1 percent of the death row population. The suicide rate for American Indians in jails is higher than for non-Indians.[37] The figures for Canada are equally disturbing. According to Prison Justice, a Canadian activist organization, during 2005–2006 Aboriginal people made up 4 percent of the Canadian population but 24 percent of admissions to provincial/territorial prison custody and 18 percent of admissions into federal custody.[38] Things are especially bad in Manitoba and Saskatchewan where Aboriginal peoples, some 16 percent of the population, make up 71 percent of the Manitoba prison population and 79 percent of that of Saskatchewan. Why? According to a 1991 report, the answer is not related solely to high Aboriginal crime rates. Instead, crucial and intertwined factors explain indigenous overrepresentation in Manitoba's jails that include "cultural oppression, social inequality, the loss of self-government and systematic discrimination."[39]

The discussion above has presented a multifaceted picture of the Indian presence across time that holds within it both promise and problems for the future. As this book concludes we look now in our final chapter explicitly toward the future and at how old and new thinking might figure in our response to unprecedented global environmental change. A fulcrum for the discussion will be the recent popular film *Into the Wild*.

CHAPTER 8

~

Future Directions Into and Out of the Wild

[The] earth has changed in profound ways, ways that have already taken us out of the sweet spot where humans so long thrived. We're every day less the oasis and more the desert. The world hasn't ended, but the world as we know it has—even if we don't quite know it yet. We imagine we still live back on that old planet, that the disturbances we see around us are the old random and freakish kind. But they're not. It's a different place. A different planet. It needs a new name. Eaarth. Or Monnde, or Tierrre, Errde. [ ] This is one of those rare moments, the start of a change far larger and more thoroughgoing than anything we can read in the records of man, on a par with the biggest dangers we can read in the records of rock and ice.

—Bill McKibben, *Eaarth: Making Life on a Tough Planet.*[1]

The fact that we are still connected with nature is precisely why we are not ready to take the ecological crisis seriously, because we still feel we are protected by the natural order. People can tell you it's the end of the world and then you go outside and my God, the trees are there, the sun is shining and so on. My point is we should not only denaturalise nature but ourselves.

—Slavoj Žižek, *Living in the End Times.*[2]

... the future of the species may depend upon whether there can ever be any contingencies of reinforcement, contrived or natural, that will induce us to act upon those predictions. We may "know" that certain things are going to happen, but knowing is

not enough; action is needed. Why should it occur? That is perhaps the most terrifying
question in the history of the human species.

—B. F. Skinner, "Why we are not acting to save the world."[3]

In the above quotations from the author Bill McKibben and from philosophers
Slavoj Žižek and B. F. Skinner consider perhaps the most important conundrum
now facing the world's populations-our curious ability to be aware of imminent
ecological catastrophe but simultaneously to discount that awareness when it
comes to the bulk of our day-to-day actions. We human beings find it hard to
believe deep down in the cataclysmic potential of climate change when superficially the natural world seems more or less has it always has. It seems we are pre-
disposed to discount scientific warnings when such warnings are seismically large
and when the predicted negative change is progressive rather than sudden.

Perhaps this is linked to the peculiar cognitive detachment that has too often
characterized the human herd within capitalism. Consider, for example, the fact
that most of us in the top-consuming nations are, at least on some level, aware
of that our overconsumption is predicated on significant underconsumption
among other populations elsewhere; however, we continue to overconsume any-
way. We are also aware, on some level, that our continued overconsumption is
what is causing most environmental stress. Little substantively in this regard has
changed for centuries. Voltaire was able to write in 1759 about the fictional character Candide's visit to Surinam with his servant Cacambo and their exposure by
the roadside to "a negro stretched out on the ground. He had only half his clothes
on him, in other words some blue linen shorts. The poor man was missing his left
leg, and his right hand." When they asked what had happened they were assured
that this was normal. "If we are working in the sugar-mill and get one of our fin-
gers caught in the grinding-wheel," the man explained, "they cut off our hand. If
we try to run away, they cut off a leg. I've been in both situations. That's the price
you pay for eating sugar in Europe."[4] While sugar remains an important nexus
within capitalism, today we might usefully substitute beef for sugar when we
think about the lack of synchronicity between consumption and awareness that
Voltaire put his finger on back in 1759. Many of us have read of what Norman
Myer in 1981 dubbed "the hamburger connection"—the way in which the rapid
growth of beef exports from Central America to fast-food chains in the United
States drives deforestation. That connection has become more acute since
the 1980s, in particular after Brazil sanctioned phenomenal growth in cattle numbers in its Amazon states in 1997. While the rate of deforestation has recently
slowed, Brazil's destruction of the world's lungs, the Amazonian rainforest, is still
directly connected to U.S. overconsumption of hamburger meat. And yet,
increasing public awareness of that fact has not seriously limited meat consumption in North America. In the United States obesity rates remain among the

highest in the world, a situation the fast-food industry, with hamburger sales at its heart, is strongly implicated in.[5]

How to make sense of this—our failure to act meaningfully to rectify a situation of overconsumption and associated environmental destruction that Western societies know has accelerated dangerously in recent decades? Are we like the greedy, cruel, pugnacious but gallant Old Norse gods of myth, who knew that their doom—Ragnorök—was foretold, but who just could not imagine a way to set about making their world secure? Or, are we as Rebecca West described—simply partly mad? She wrote depressingly in 1941:

> Only part of us is sane: only part of us loves pleasure and the longer day of happiness, wants to live to our nineties and die in peace, in a house that we built, that shall shelter those who come after us. The other half of us is nearly mad. It prefers the disagreeable to the agreeable, loves pain and its darker night despair, and wants to die in a catastrophe that will set back life to its beginnings and leave nothing of our house save its blackened foundations.[6]

If the poet W. H. Auden is to be believed, describing what he saw as *The Age of Anxiety* in 1948, we are as a race worse still. We cling fearfully to what we know until there is nothing left to cling to. As he put it, "We would rather be ruined than changed/We would rather die in our dread/Than climb the cross of the moment/And let our illusions die."[7]

Perhaps most worryingly of all, too little at the level of environmental awareness seems to be changing for the better. Some of the highest profile examples within Western culture of the young engaging meaningfully with environmental issues show all of the same symptoms of a mythologized, ahistorical, and unreflective relationship with nature that were isolated in our opening chapter. It seems that the impulse to connect with nature today is packaged in a way that denies colonialism, separates man as a species from nature, and reiterates all the tropes about the sublime that characterized the early American nineteenth century. A perfect example in this regard is the 2007 film *Into the Wild*, to which we now turn. It movingly told the story of a young man named Chris McCandless and his tragic quest for self-realization in America's great outdoors. In 1992 he gave his $24,000 college fund to charity and for the next two years roamed over the West—communing with nature, living among the poor, and studiously avoiding contact with his worried family back in upper middle-class Annandale, Virginia. He did, however, make meaningful contact with a series of surrogate family members, some of whom had also lost touch with their sons. Each of these admired him greatly and wished to mediate his ineluctable desire to lose (or find) himself through raw exposure to nature. McCandless died four months into his last wilderness experience north of Mt. McKinley in Alaska, and his emaciated corpse was found in an abandoned school bus not far from the boundaries of Denali National Park. His parents had resorted to using a private detective to try to find their son, but his determination to ensure meaningful solitude in the outdoors made him beyond contact.

The film tapped into a powerful and entirely understandable desire within the just-maturing young and others to transcend society and escape certain of its repressive urban and suburban mores. However, it also reinscribed most if not all of the old lies about "wild" America—especially the notion that it is devoid of human communities, especially the indigenous human presence, and that it is a suitable crucible wherein the lonely, justified Euro-American male may test himself so as to find the ultimate in value and meaning. In discussing *Into the Wild*, we confront the remarkable strength of the modern nostalgia for a fuller life. It is tied fast to a hoary set of clichés about "wild" nature that require that indigenous peoples and their abiding relationships to place be steadfastly ignored.

DISAPPEARING BACK INTO THE WILD

Chris McCandless's life story has exerted an intensely powerful pull on some of the United States' foremost male artistic talents. The book of Chris McCandless's life was written by Jon Krakhauer, a writer of cracklingly commercial non-fiction then known primarily as a mountaineer and journalist for *Outside* magazine. The film of Chris McCandless's life was directed by Sean Penn, one of the most talented actors and principled filmmakers of his generation. Penn is from an acting family and seems to have inherited independent thinking, his father the actor/director Leo Penn having been blacklisted during the McCarthy era for refusing to testify at anti-Communist hearings. Sean Penn invested a great deal into directing the film *Into the Wild* on several levels, spending almost a decade securing the rights to make it and taking great care to get the support, involvement, and sanction of the McCandless family. The award-winning soundtrack to the film was created by the revered alternative rock star Eddie Vedder, who promoted the work with his first solo tour. He is best known as the frontman for the phenomenally successful band, *Pearl Jam*, formed in 1990 in Seattle at the beginning of what became known as the grunge movement. The empathy each of the three artists felt for the young Chris McCandless combined to make his tragic story a critical and popular hit. Krakhauer's book is now required reading on a number of school and college courses;and as his parents testify in an introduction to the 2011 *Back to the Wild Book & DVD* containing Chris McCandless's photographs and writings, there is "a steadily growing international interest in Chris's story."[8] Like Leslie Marmon Silko, Krakhauer's work has attracted an American Academy of Arts and Letters award. Eddie Vedder's soundtrack was nominated for a Golden Globe and won a number of other awards while the *Into the Wild* film was nominated for a 2007 Academy Award and grossed over $55.5 million worldwide.

On some level, every artistic expression, whatever its ostensive subject, is a reflection of its author or authors. It would be simplistic to suggest that each of the artists who combined to so powerfully promote the Chris McCandless story did so because they saw something that links to their own personal history, but a plausible case for that can be made nonetheless. McCandless had nursed a smoldering resentment and anger against his father after learning after graduating from high school that his father had been a bigamist and kept it secret from his second family, within which Chris McCandless was the youngest son. His father kept the bigamy up after Chris was born. The McCandless family have also not hidden the fact the family was subject to domestic abuse and the film of Chris McCandless's life suggests that this abuse came from his father.[9] Vedder's songs tell an analogous story of his having been lied to as a young man. A key song in his repertoire is "Alive," written after he found out that the man he presumed to be his father was in fact his stepfather and that his biological father had by that stage died. Vedder then stopped using his stepfather's name. A number of Pearl Jam's songs reveal a keen understanding of child abuse, domestic violence, and injustice, and its frontman has stated between songs that helping others is the path to healing for those abused. Sean Penn, in contrast, makes clear publicly that his was an entirely positive upbringing but his problems containing his urges to violently attack paparazzi, the fact that his ex-wife charged him with domestic abuse battery, and an assault and battery charge on an extra on the set of the film *Colours* were all tabloid fodder in the 1980s. Like McCandless he has been fearless in expressing his independence of thought even when it has made him subject to ridicule.

The reader will by now perhaps be noting that the emphasis in the above is not on land at all, on nature, or the "wild" unless it is the wilderness of the human soul. This is because the central subject of neither the book nor the film *Into the Wild* is in fact wilderness. Instead their focus is on the awkward task of coming of age and the self-testing and risk-taking impulses that impel young males as they work out how to heal emotional wounds from the past. *Into the Wild* is not about engagement with land, nature, or landscape even on a reciprocal aesthetic level. It is about the emotional needs of a certain type of young American male, one who pays only limited attention to the specifics of place or to the histories, stories, wisdom and communities of those who for generations have lived in that place. To the extent that *Into the Wild* makes land into landscape, a passive backdrop for an emotional and spatial journey with a white American male at the center, it does both land, nature, and environmental justice a disservice. It perpetuates a centuries-old American narrative where land and nature are there to serve white male needs, not least the need to forge an "authentic" identity. Thus conveniently it is constructed as "empty" both of indigenous presence and of the intricate and messy realities of competing frontiers, post-colonial populations, and of meaningful "society" however defined.

Chris McCandless's story should be seen as a recent installment within a foundational genre in American writing about heroic souls who, like Huckleberry Finn, escape "smothery" civilization by "lighting out for the Territory." Escape into the trackless wild is in this sense key to the American myth of self, a myth that has been most powerfully articulated in terms of commercial exposure by real and fictional males, from Mark Twain's Huckleberry Finn, to John Dunbar, the hero of the film *Dances With Wolves* acted within and directed by Kevin Costner; to Holden Caulfield, hero of J. D. Salinger's *Catcher in the Rye* (who dreams of hitchhiking west "where it was very pretty and sunny and where nobody'd know me and I'd get a job"). These are comparatively recent examples, but the paradigm can be traced back as far the very earliest stories Americans told about themselves such as the Mary Rowlandson captivity narrative of 1682. Like Chris McCandless, Mary Rowlandson described a wilderness experience that was both physical and spiritual although her lessons for the "new world" told a Christian story of perseverance through suffering. The common theme for all of these figures is of maturing, a process that has always mapped directly onto America's vision of itself. As Jerry Griswold described this narrative arc with reference to America's children's fiction, America likes to imagine itself "as a young country, always making itself anew, rebelling against authority, coming into its own, and establishing its own identity."[10] In a broader analytical sense an analogous argument was made by Richard Slotkin in his trilogy of books about the American frontier. McCandless fits perfectly Slotkin's definition of what he calls the complete "American of the Myth"—"one who had defeated and freed himself from both the 'savage' of the Western wilderness and the metropolitan regime of authoritarian politics and class privilege."[11]

Ironically, if we follow Slotkin's powerful analyses, the *Into the Wild* phenomenon feeds directly into the same expansionist thinking that left-leaning activists such as Sean Penn speak so vociferously against within American foreign policy. During the George Bush Jr. years, Penn railed against the excesses of cowboy foreign policy within the White House, but in *Into the Wild* he reinvigorated the frontier myth that underpins the cowboy's continued cultural survival. Just as heroes do in the mythic patterns Slotkin describes, McCandless "regressed" to a primal state so as to purge himself of the false values of the metropolis. He may not have been able to return materially, but his ideas have done so through the *Into the Wild* book and film and they speak to the perennial desire to forge a renewed social contract in America. Penn and Krakhauer may have intended to use McCandless and the myth of the frontier in this instance as a means of promoting ecological awareness and emotional understanding, but given the deeply stained past of the myth reinscribed and both book and film's use of the environment as an "empty" but magisterial emotional backdrop, it is difficult to see how this could have been fully achieved.

In *Into the Wild* the myth of the American frontier, whilst it was never monolithic, is clearly showing its age. Unlike the heroes of the past, its hero is no longer capable of communing successfully with either Indians or the wilderness, neither can he physically reintegrate with society. Its story does little more than reiterate an old anxiety about the problematic nature of American virtue expressed in 1787 by Benjamin Franklin. Franklin wrote to James Madison that America could remain virtuous only "while there remain vacant lands in any part of America. When we get piled together upon one another in large cities, as in Europe, we shall ... go to eating one another, as they do there."[12] Chris McCandless knew this same anxiety but realizing that true wilderness, truly "vacant" land, was an impossibility, his only recourse was to impose it on his chosen lands by throwing away his topographical map, dismissing his timepiece and disassociating himself from all community.[13] In this sense he truly is the flawed and confused all-American hero of our times. While his violence is primarily emotional (against his family), his "creation" of uninhabited wilderness was as deliberate as the creation of "wilderness" lands devoid of Indians was at the beginning of the century.

Chris McCandless very deliberately created his wilderness challenges (taking limited food with him into Denali, only a low-caliber rifle, no GPS, no compass, no Geological Survey map, and no shelter), and he refused the counsel of elders and other males knowledgeable about the outdoors (who, for example, warned him about the dangers of traveling in the backcountry during the treacherous spring/summer snow melt). Having not learned to air-dry and so preserve the meat he needed to kill to survive, a skill a number of Alaskan indigenous and nonindigenous communities could have taught him, Chris McCandless suffered the distress of watching the moose he killed largely rot away. Thus despite comparisons repeatedly made in the popular press, his experience was in no way comparable to the ritual coming-of-age initiations practiced by a variety of indigenous communities. These are done *within* communities, rather than in rejection of them; and even if solitary in nature as with some Native American Indian vision quests, they are carried out under the guidance of tribal elders.[14] Alan Borass, Professor of Anthropology at Kenai Peninsula College, Soldotna, Alaska, wrote the following specifically for this volume to explain just how different Chris McCandless's experience was from Native American practices in Alaska:

> While there is great variation in the details of Native American vision quests, a common theme is to immerse oneself in a spiritually powerful liminal state seeking a purpose, not "different from" as in McCandless' case, but "convergent with" established roles in one's community. The quest is typically done in isolation, distant from a village, but not in wilderness. Wilderness is a foreign concept to most Native Americans and it certainly was to the Dena'ina and Koyukon in whose territory McCandless undertook his vision quest. To go "into the wild" is based on binary opposition of "civilization" and "wilderness." To the Nena'ina and Koyukon, and perhaps every other Native American culture, there is no such dichotomy; there is simply land and water and sky made

up of the tangible but populated with spirits of nature embedded in the place which gave it soul.

Over the millennia Native Americans learned that it is the soul of the place that will help one find purpose and meaning in life and it is their community in which one applies that purpose.[15]

In contrast, Chris McCandless's self-imposed quest was an attempt to achieve a new spiritual awareness through exclusion and isolation from any community, a strategy wholly at odds with the bulk of indigenous American practice.

Despite the toweringly beautiful scenery that reappears throughout the film of his life, McCandless had to work hard to generate the level of isolation and survival challenge he craved. Even then, he died only 30 miles from the George Parks Highway in that most suburban of vehicles, a school bus, symbolic in itself of how human the landscape was and remains. He died just 16 miles from a road patrolled by the National Park Service and unbeknown to him, four unoccupied cabins lay within a six-mile radius. Krakhauer also notes that there was at the time a hand-tram with which he might have been able to cross the Teklanika River had he been able to reach it. Furthermore, the fact that McCandless was not eaten by bears or wolves probably cannot be disassociated from the controversial attempts at predator control that have been carried out in the region.[16] In sum, McCandless took himself to lands that in their own way are as full of human politics and human influence as his Virginian suburban home.

Chris McCandless died from starvation and isolation but this does not mean that his survival achievements were paltry or that he was wholly unprepared. To the contrary, he survived over 113 days in extreme conditions and he made a preparatory attempt to understand how land-based survival could be achieved in the part of Alaska he was visiting. He bought an Indian book at the Fairbanks campus bookstore, the highly respected ethnobotanist Priscilla Russell Kari's study of how the Dena'ina Indians of Southcentral Alaska use plants. Accounts vary as to whether his misidentification of toxic seeds or mold growing on seeds he ate speeded his death, but if he was in fact poisoned by his own hand it is yet another tragic irony given that he wrote with glee inside the bus itself about concluding his "SPIRITUAL PILGRIMAGE." It continues, "NO LONGER TO BE POISONED BY CIVILIZATION HE FLEES, AND WALKS ALONE UPON THE LAND TO BECOME LOST IN THE WILD."[17]

Whilst publishing about the mysterious lives of lost visionaries in the American wild is a growing and lucrative field, with new books with major presses appearing as recently as 2011 on figures like Everett Ruess who went missing in Davis Gulch in Utah in 1934, the focus tends to be on those who wrote and described their thoughts for others.[18] It is significant that both Ruess and McCandless left written records of their thoughts and travels, allowing their tragedies a literary context. Furthermore both figures took books with them on their travels, invented their own alternative personas to suit the "wild" and gave those alter egos names. Given the general narrative arc of his publications overall, one could say that Krakhauer's forte is writing about and dramatizing extreme behavior. What was extreme about Chris McCandless was his response to key writers on nature such as Henry David Thoreau, Leo Tolstoy, Boris Pasternak, and Jack London. Oddly, he would often quote their work in his journal in between references to his own alter ego in the third person, evidence for many previous commentators that he was mentally unstable. Of course, if writing may be said to have killed Chris McCandless, then Jon Krakhauer's gripping and emotional prose is also what has ensured his enduring fame, a fame that in part supports a number of charitable organizations selected by his family.[19]

It seems that the literary dimension to the relationship with nature contemporary America is most comfortable with is strange. It reinscribes the old myth of man as being outside of nature and perpetuates the idea that somehow a virgin frontier *does* still exist somewhere in America (usually Alaska) that is capable of bestowing an impossibly exclusive spiritual awareness. As Randall Roorda has asked rhetorically, "What can it mean to turn away from other people, to evade all sign of them for purposes that exclude them by design, then turn back toward them in writing, reporting upon, accounting for, even recommending to them the conditions of their absence?"[20] Lawrence Buell has pondered the same theme, isolating an "aesthetics of relinquishment" within writing about nature, where material assets get given away and with them, albeit temporarily, the protagonist's very sense of a separate human self. As explained above, it is a myth of exile, immersion in Otherness, mastery of that Otherness, and return that is foundational to the stories Americans have always told about themselves in history essays such as Frederick Jackson Turner's 1893 *The Significance of the Frontier in American History*, in dime novels, in children's literature, great works of literature, cowboy films, and science fiction tales.[21]

In Jon Krakhauer's hands, Chris McCandless is a reincarnation of the frontier hero for our times. Like the best of the old-time cowboys, he is portrayed as powerfully attractive to women but chivalrous, even sexless; he has a special empathy with animals; and predictably, he might even be part Indian—his "dark and emotive" eyes "suggested a trace of exotic blood in his heritage—Greek, maybe, or Chippewa."[22] Like *Shane*, star of the foundational 1953 American western and like Christ, he deliberately goes among the poor, lending his skills to them rather than offering them to the highest bidder. Like the Western hero of old, it is as if he discovers pristine American landscape for the first time, something truly remarkable given how industrially developed modern Alaska now is.[23] He finds nature that, in Raymond Williams's terms, "contrasts with man, except presumably with the man looking at it."[24] He is, once again, the innocent New World American Adam R. W. B. Lewis described in 1955, reburnished by Krakhauer and Penn for Generation X and the Bush era. Chris McCandless is the new (and old) American Adam, "emancipated from history, happily bereft of ancestry, untouched and undefiled by the usual inheritances of family and race; an individual standing alone, self-reliant and self-propelling, ready to confront whatever awaited him with the aid of his own unique and inherent resources."[25]

While many of us can understand McCandless's craving to bring throbbing urgency, intensity, and richness to life and his insatiable desire for new experience, it is hard to see him as the pilgrim or monk Jon Krakhauer would like us to.[26] His communion with nature left him unable to map out any new spiritual terrain. It seems that today he is revered primarily for what he rejected, what offended him on multiple levels, rather than for what he achieved. The poignant 142 Fairbanks bus where he died has seen a great increase in visitors in particular since the release of the 2007 *Into the Wild* film and, sadly, someone has died trying to make the 40-mile round-trip hike to see it.[27] Given how agonizing and gruesome the main stages of his death are likely to have been before the stupor associated with the end stages of acute dehydration and starvation set in, it is highly regrettable that with the book, film, and soundtrack, Chris McCandless's life has been received by so many as a glamorous and positive portrayal of his choices. Rather than encourage its readers, viewers, and listeners toward a fuller appreciation of the history of American "wilderness" and of its indigenous and settler relationships, the *Into the Wild* phenomenon has reinscribed the oldest of American myths least suited to helping us all face the environmental, cultural, and resource problems of the future. It has fostered a blinkered and dangerous understanding of American land as vacant and "wild" and promoted a version of spirituality that is acutely individualistic. It has promoted a spirituality tied to imagery and fantasy rather than to actual lands, people, places, and relationships. Chris McCandless was, of course, absolutely right that nature is wonderful and capable of bestowing psychological healing and liberation. However, to use nature to orchestrate a self-challenging dance with death is a symptom of mental distress rather than an example to be followed.

The example of how a man might relate to the nature that Jon Krakhauer, Sean Penn, and Eddie Vedder package so attractively in the *Into the Wild* phenomenon is far from positive. As Krakhauer puts it in a cringe-inducing section of his book where he invokes his own prior "Alaskan adventure":

> I was stirred by the dark mystery of mortality. I couldn't resist stealing up to the edge of doom and peering over the brink. The hint of what was concealed in those shadows terrified me, but I caught sight of something in the glimpse, some forbidden and elemental riddle that was no less compelling than the sweet, hidden petals of a woman's sex.
>
> In my case—and, I believe, in the case of Chris McCandless—that was a very different thing from wanting to die.[28]

Of all the ways of relating to nature that powerful and influential males such as Krakhauer, Penn, and Vedder might have chosen to promote to young people and others, it is an odd choice at a time of global environmental crisis to emphasize the opportunities nature offers to explore the central mystery of death (or whatever riddle accompanies it). We live, after all, in a time when rather than individual self-challenge in isolation what is called for as never before is greater understanding of communal interests and understanding of how history and the flow of capital affects both the environment and multiple interlinked communities. As we search for a means to implement strategies in response to climate change, what is needed is greater connection to place *within* communities rather than the valorization of individual quests to find spiritual fullness in lands constructed as "empty." The *Into the Wild* phenomenon hymned the beauty of certain American landscapes, but did so in much the same way nineteenth-century Romantic painters like Frederick Church, Thomas Moran, and Albert Bierstadt did-by emphasizing their sublime power and agency as national symbols but largely ignoring their human inhabitants.

It is too often forgotten that Chris McCandless rejected societal isolation toward the end of his ordeal in Alaska. His S.O.S. note, to which he added his real name, was not shown in the *Into the Wild* film but it read: "I AM ALL *ALONE*. THIS IS *NO JOKE*. IN THE NAME OF GOD, PLEASE REMAIN TO SAVE ME." We can only hope that there will be no more Chris McCandlesses writing notes of this sort. His desire to learn from nature and to escape from what is stifling about Western society was incontrovertibly a wholesome impulse, but wholesale rejection of society and ill-prepared immersion in nature as a an acutely harsh self-imposed challenge is ultimately sterile and narcissistic folly. We cannot know how Chris McCandless approached death, but we can hope that somehow he found a sense of connection in that desolate place that had been lacking throughout his life. If we learn anything from the McCandless story it is perhaps that cultivating a sense of how we as humans are intimately bound to place is key to our survival as a species in the future. We need to reawaken our connection to specific places and specific lands so as to rekindle a sense of belonging that some indigenous communities, despite horrific odds, have never lost. We must dispense with an ahistorical nostalgia for what never was and instead engage with the urgent task of protecting who and what is living in the places we call home. As Chris McCandless sensed, this is as much a spiritual task as it is a political and economic one. It calls for a kindness and inclusiveness within our understanding of the spiritual landscape that has not always characterized mainstream religions. It is a kindness and inclusiveness that individuals need to apply to themselves as much as to others, as part of, rather than discrete from, the natural world.

These are issues the cultural anthropologist Richard Nelson of Sitka, Alaska, has described with particular eloquence. He wrote:

And what of rootedness in death among humans? I was raised to believe that the souls of people who have lived well are given the reward of heaven, far removed from the place that nurtured them in life, remote even from the earth itself. And those who commit evil are threatened with the punishment of hell—to spread eternity deep inside the body of the earth.

When I asked Koyukon people about death, they said a person's spirit is reluctant to leave the company of friends and family, so for a time it lingers near them. The spirits of virtuous people eventually wander along an easy trail to the afterlife, in a good place on the Koyukon homeland. Those who have lived badly follow a long trail of hardship and suffering, but they finally arrive among the others. The dead sustain themselves as hunters and mingle through the spirit world of nature, eternally rooted to their place on earth.[29]

OTHER FUTURES, NEW WAYS OF THINKING

Today, our relation to the natural world is under question as never before. Perversely at a time of extreme threat to the processes and entities that sustain ongoing life, for a number of our greatest thinkers the intellectual significance of nature is on the wane. The spectrum of debate is wide but nature as a factor in our global future is increasingly seen as secondary to man and his machines. Some argue for commendable reasons that we should recognize this is in fact mankind's era, that we, rather than nature, are the dominant force on earth. Others go even further, claiming that the human era is in itself over and that we live at the dawn of a "post-human" age when artificial intelligence will reign supreme. Notoriously in 1993, the retired San Diego State University professor and science fiction writer Vernor Vinge predicted that non-human sapience would be with us before 2030. Computers would "awake" with superhuman intelligence, a shift so singular and profound that if and when it happens it would be a truly transcendental event.[30]

The shift in thinking among geologists referred to above is at least comprehensible. Geologists today tell us that we live in the Anthropocene age, the age of man, an epoch when mankind's influence has so accelerated that it has changed a host of fundamental natural processes including the carbon cycle and the nitrogen cycle. Some estimate that 90 percent of the world's plant activity is now found in ecosystems where humans play a significant role. Our use in particular of artificial nitrogen fertilizer, as well as use of fossil fuels and scientific breeding methods, has made agriculture powerful as never before with 38 percent of the planet's ice-free land devoted to it. A limited and homogenous group of crops, livestock, and living things that manage to get on well with humans now dominate the world's ecosystems. The extinction rate for the rest is far higher than during any previous geological period. A fifth of birds are threatened with extinction, as are 40 percent of mammals and fish, a third of amphibians, and up to half of all plant species.[31] Some argue that up to one million species will be extinct or doomed to extinction by 2050.[32] The last five catastrophic mass extinctions of plants and animals in the past half billion years were caused by asteroid impacts and other natural events; now humans may be causing a sixth. The Harvard biologist E. O. Wilson has calculated that human biomass is already one hundred times larger than that of any other large animal species that has ever walked the earth.[33] We are at least seven billion souls, a human population that has doubled since 1950. Two billion more are expected by 2050. Of course, geological awareness that man has inaugurated a wholly new era within the earth's deep history is not new. As far back as 1870 Antonio Stoppani suggested the term "anthropozoic," but it was not taken seriously. However, since the Nobel scientist Paul Crutzen began popularizing the term "anthropocene" in 2002, the new term has gained acceptance. Crutzen hopes it will be a warning to the world.[34]

What is the likely impact of this cross-disciplinary intellectual placing of mankind's activities at the center of this epoch's history? Perhaps in ways contrary to Crutzen's intention, it may be used to justify large-scale tinkering with natural forces, particularly geoengineering, because of the new sense that humans are fully capable of fundamentally impacting on the world's essential processes. This has great potential but is also worrying given the enormous impact of the first big piece of deliberate geoengineering, the invention of the nitrogen-fixing Haber process in the late nineteenth century. This allowed the annual amount of nitrogen fixed on land to go up by more than 150 percent and human population levels to soar, causing a host of unanticipated ancillary problems that we are forced to grapple with now. Alternatively, it may simply lead to an emphasis on small and piecemeal changes in light of a new awareness that large-scale planetary change can be induced by just such seemingly limited actions. Some argue that the first option is more likely, however, because of the unprecedented energy that technology seems destined to unleash from solar and/or nuclear sources over the coming centuries. This is predicted to be the kind of power that could make it possible for man to alter all the truly big things currently limiting his reach—the hydrologic cycle by which water circulates on, above, and below the surface of the earth, the speed of the carbon cycle, and our (in)ability to recycle industrial metals. Because such changes may be ahead, it is argued that it is therefore better to involve ourselves directly in nature's fundamental processes than to try to put the genie back in the bottle and carve out a low-impact future. Any global drive to reinstate low-impact conditions is talked of negatively by such commentators because it is seen as necessitating selective repression of populations.[35]

Where does all of this leave indigenous thought and indigenous peoples? The immediate answer is that it and they are too often ignored, although there is hope. A wider set of changes within intellectual life are afoot including, to some extent, a rapprochement or at least a partial coming together, of the sciences and the humanities. The fact that the environment is now increasingly studied, thought about, and engaged with *in conjunction with* as opposed to separately from human communities is connected to a larger set of boundaries that are getting broken down. Part of what is getting broken down is a view of nature that suggests it is outside of culture, that it is a largely unchanging and passive entity against which cultures can define themselves and that historians can use as a backdrop for larger, human-focused narratives. In these older narratives, humankind *did things to* nature, rather than nature doing things to humankind. Today there is an increasing awareness that nature and culture are not in fact separate. There is increasingly pervasive recognition that humans are animal, a recognition spearheaded by Darwin's work in the early nineteenth century, which revolutionized dominant thinking by demonstrating that human culture is integral to nature and part of its changing character. Not only are we part of nature in this new way of thinking but nature itself is more protean and dynamic than had previously been thought. There is less discussion now of ecological equilibrium, of essential states of balance to which nature can be said to revert over time, and more of a sense of nature and especially of climate as inherently changeable, indeed subject to profound shifts sometimes over short timescales. This is change we now recognize that can be influenced pivotally and irrevocably by human behavior.

Some have suggested that it is appropriate to see these conceptual changes in the context of certain of the foundations of Enlightenment thinking being fundamentally recontextualized and in particular a new awareness developing of mystery and relativity across disciplines. Environmental historian Tom Griffiths argues that new thinking in the queen of sciences—mathematics, and in the humanities—is now becoming embedded, which "revives an animistic view of nature that existed in Europe before the scientific revolution, and which still remains in many parts of the world."[36] It recognizes conditionality, uncertainty, complexity, and interrelationship. Thus Griffiths quotes the mathematician and renowned historian of science Jacob Bronowski who described this emerging elusive and relational understanding of the world in the 1970s. Bronowski wrote, "The world is not a fixed, solid array of objects, out there, for it cannot be fully separated from our perception of it. It shifts under our gaze, it interacts with us, and the knowledge that it yields has to be interpreted by us. There is no way of exchanging information that does not demand an act of judgment."[37] Thus contemporary ecologists such as Timothy Morton urge us to dispense with or at least fundamentally deconstruct most of the language of ecology—including words and ideas such as "nature," deemed to be too Romantic and in binary relationship to other slippery terms like "culture." Perhaps unhelpfully, Morton does not advise us on what terms we *should* use to describe the all-too-real non-human world. Instead, he tells us to think generally in terms of universal interconnectedness, what he calls an infinite "mesh." Those familiar with Indian history and the intersubjectivity that characterizes many Indian traditions may raise a wry smile at the fact that a non-Indian philosopher via the most convoluted of routes is now advocating an idea basic to so many Indian lifeways. It brings to mind Ambrose Bierce's version of the passage from Ecclesiastes: "Truly there is nothing new under the sun but there are lots of old things we don't know."[38]

These ideas matter because of how they may influence our behavior in the future. As Al Gore put it in 2007, "[Our environmental crisis] is in part a spiritual crisis. It's a crisis of our own self-definition-who we are. Are we creatures destined to destroy our own species? Clearly not."[39] He repeated similar thinking in his 1992 book, *Earth in the Balance: Ecology and the Human Spirit*, earning himself the tag "the environmental Evangelicalist." Gore did not specify a particular religion, his concern was more to diagnose a global problem, and he became in the process one of the first high-profile figures to state expressly that the environmental crisis was, "for lack of a better word, spiritual."[40] Scientists themselves are increasingly aware that science and politics are unlikely to be enough to prompt global behavioral action in response to climate change. To mobilize large numbers of people for ecological change religion, spirituality, and ethics need to be brought to bear also. Thus in the 2004 anniversary edition of *Limits to Growth*, Donella Meadows, Dennis Meadows, and others admitted:

> In our search for ways to encourage the peaceful restructuring of a system that naturally resists its own transformation we have tried many tools. The obvious ones are—rational analysis, data systems thinking, computer modelling, and the clearest words we can find. Those are tools anyone trained in science and economics would automatically grasp. Like recycling, they are useful, necessary, and they are not enough.[41]

The Stanford biologist Paul Ehrlich has been even more explicit about the need to involve culturally specific mores and ethics in the quest to save the world from environmental disaster, stating, "[f]or the first time in human history, global civilization is threatened with collapse ... The world therefore needs an ongoing discussion of key ethical issues related to the human predicament in order to help generate the urgently required response."[42] It is to just such a discussion of ethics that this book contributes. It asks that we begin a fundamental reflection on how we think about land and spirit in the United States. It asks that we pay serious attention to the diversity of indigenous thinking on the topic and, just as importantly, that we reflect meaningfully on the reasons why such thinking has been so often silenced.

Notes

SERIES FOREWORD

1. Luther Standing Bear, *Land of the Spotted Eagle*, Boston: Houghton Mifflin, 1933, p. xix.

2. A detailed examination of this process can be found in Keller, Robert H. & Turek, Michael F., *American Indian & National Parks*, Tucson: The University of Arizona Press, 1998.

INTRODUCTION

1. Pinker has also been linked since June, 2011 to the new private organization the New College of the Humanities, London, U.K. Born in 1954, Pinker could arguably be described as Generation Jones, following Jonathan Pontell; however, he displays little of that generation's supposed lack of optimism or general cynicism.

2. John Gray, "Delusions of Peace," *Prospect* (September 21, 2011), Issue 187.

3. Pinker admits Hobbes and Rousseau were more sophisticated than the stereotypes he connects them to but connects them to them nonetheless so as to belittle more recent "romantic" and "politically correct" thinking (Pinker, *Better Angels*, 36). The best book to date giving proper context to the noble savage myth and the historical error of confusing Rousseau's work with primitivism is Terry Ellingson's *The Myth of the Noble Savage* (Berkeley, CA: University of California Press, 2001).

4. *Rousseau, Judge of Jean-Jacques: Dialogues*, III, quoted in Laurence Cooper, *Rousseau, Nature & the Problem of the Good Life* (University Park, PA: The Pennsylvania State University Press, 1999), 18. For more on Rousseau and ecological concerns, particularly his paradoxical ideas about the expanded self and the "good life," see Joseph H. Lane & Rebecca R. Clark, "The Solitary Walker in the Political World: The Paradoxes of Rousseau and Deep Ecology," *Political Theory* 34, no. 1 (Feb. 2006), 62–94.

5. Pinker, *Better Angels*, 44–45. Pinker's take on what anthropologists call "prestate societies" owes much to the work and sources of Tel Aviv University political scientist Azar Gat. See, for example, Azar Gat "The Pattern of Fighting in Simple, Small-Scale, Prestate Societies," *Journal of Anthropological Research* 55, no. 4 (Winter, 1999), 563–83. Pinker's sexually violent intertribal record is taken from work by the late Smithsonian scholar E. S. Burch. A more nuanced take on the period and peoples involved can be found in Ernest Burch's own "Traditional Eskimo Societies on Northwest Alaska," *SENRI Ethnological Studies* 4 (1980), 253–304.

6. See Konrad Lorenz, *On Aggression* (London: Methuen, 1966).

7. For example, Pinker's risible generalization, "Tribal people, anthropologists have shown, often single out despised in-laws for allegations of witchcraft, a convenient pretext to have them executed," 137. For more on the use of the ethnographic present tense and the denial of cultural and societal development coeval with Western development to indigenous peoples see Johannes Fabian, *Time and the Other: How Anthropology Makes its Object* (New York: Columbia University Press, 1983). A more thoughtful take on cannibalism can be found in Francis Barker, Peter Hulme & Margaret Iversen, *Cannibalism and the Colonial World* (Cambridge: Cambridge University Press, 1998) and chapter three of this volume.

8. Ironically, there is evidence that Voltaire named Dr. Pangloss, the scholar with the redoubtable faith that this was the best of all possible worlds, after Rousseau.

9. K. H. Redford, "The Ecologically Noble Savage," *Cultural Survival Quarterly* 15 (1): 46–48.

10. I am indebted to Professor Ray Hames of the University of Nebraska in constructing this synopsis of anthropological approaches to indigenous conservation. For further comment and discussion see Raymond Hames, "The Ecologically Noble Savage Debate," *Annual Review of Anthropology* 36 (2007), 177–90 and the references therein.

11. Pinker, *Better Angels*, 11.

12. Jon Butler, "Jack-in-the-Box Faith: The Religion Problem in Modern American History," *The Journal of American History* (March 2004), 1358.

13. See Terry Teachout, *The Skeptic: A Life of H. L. Mencken* (New York: Harper Collins, 2002).

14. See, for example, Perry Miller's *The New England Mind: The Seventeenth Century* (New York: Macmillan, 1939); Kenneth Murdock, *Literature and Theology in Colonial New England* (Cambridge, Mass.: Harvard University Press, 1949) and Susan L. Mizruchi, *The Science of Sacrifice: American Literature and Modern Social Theory* (Princeton, NJ: Princeton University Press, 1998).

15. See U.S. Census Bureau Facts for Features: American Indian & Alaskan National heritage Month November 2011, . . .www.census.gov/newsroom/. . ./facts_for_features _special_editions/ and http://www.census.gov/prod/cen2010/briefs/c2010br-02.pdf; accessed 8/28/2011. Interpreting U.S. Census data is complex, not least because Native Hawaiians and Other Pacific Islanders and American Indian and Alaskan Natives are more likely than other groups to report multiple racial heritage in census responses. See Harvard University Native American Program Native American Statistics Project, Table Table 6 http://hunapstatisticsproject.info/TribeCategory/AllAmericanIndianPopulation. htm and Joy Porter, "Population Matters in Native America" in *America's Americans: Population Issues in U.S. Society and Politics*, edited by Philip Davies & Iwan Morgan

(London: Institute for the Study of the Americas, University of London, School of Advanced Study, 2007).

16. These include the Inuit and Aleutians of the circumpolar region, the Saami of northern Europe, the Aborigines and Torres Strait Islanders of Australia, and the Maori of New Zealand. China and India together have more than 150 million indigenous and tribal people. Indigenous peoples represent perhaps over 6 percent of the world population. See Leaflet No. 1 Indigenous Peoples and the United Nations System: An Overview, United Nations Office at Geneva.

17. Here we may recall as a sample, the heartfelt hopes and dreams many interest groups expressed about the first female Prime Minister in the United Kingdom, Margaret Thatcher, elected in 1979 and in the run-up to his election in 2008, about the first African-American President of the United States Barack Obama.

18. Emile Durkheim, "L'Origine du marriage dans l'espèce humaine, d'apres Westermarck." *Revue philosophique* XL: 606–7 [article 606–23].

19. See "Science as Vocation 1918–1919" in *Max Weber: Essays in Society*, trans. and ed. by H. H. Gerth & C. Wright Mills (New York: Oxford University Press, 1964), 155.

20. Max Weber, *The Protestant Ethic.*

21. It is recognized that the term and movement known as environmentalism only fully cohered in the West in the 1950s. However, concern for man's environment in the broadest sense and a desire maintain its processes are as old as man himself. This book uses environment to invoke this broad-based concern across time.

22. Anthony Giddens, *The Politics of Climate Change* (2011), 55, 57.

23. See "Republican Base Heavily White, Conservative, Religious," June 1, 2009, GALLUP, accessed Nov. 11, 2011 http://www.Gallup.com/poll/118937/republican-base-heavily-white-conservative-religious.aspx and "Little Change in Opinions about Global Warming: Increasing Partisan Divide on Energy Policies," (Oct. 27, 2010), Pew Research Center for the People and the Press.

24. Paul Collier, *The Bottom Billion* (Oxford: Oxford University Press, 2007). Seventy percent of the bottom billion are in Africa and some live in Bolivia, Myanmar, Cambodia, Haiti, Laos, North Korea, and Yemen.

CHAPTER 1

1. Raymond Williams, "Ideas of Nature," in *Problems in Materialism and Culture* (London: Verso, 1980), 67.

2. Yvor Winters, *Forms of Discovery*, 2.

3. See Bernard Spilka, *Spirituality: Problems and directions in operationalizing a fuzzy concept.* Paper presented at the annual conference of the American Psychological Association, Toronto (August 23, 1993), 1.

4. An indigenous discussion of religion and the sacred is the subject of the initial chapter of Peggy Beck et al., *The Sacred*, 3–31.

5. A useful discussion of the fascinating but highly contingent concept "shamanism" is Ronald Hutton's *Shamans: Siberian Spirituality and the Western Imagination* (London: Hambledon, 2001).

6. Niels Nielsen, Jr. et al. *Religions of the World*, 2d ed. (New York: St. Martin's Press, 1988).

7. A book that makes exhaustive reference to the intermingling between natural philosophy and religion during the sixteenth and seventeenth centuries but, alas, never really details it across some 563 pages is Stephen Gaukroger's *The Emergence of Scientific Culture: Science and the Shaping of Modernity, 1210–1685* (New York: Clarendon Press of Oxford University Press, 2006).

8. Vine Deloria Jr., *The World We Used to Live In* (2006), 199. While it does not detract from Deloria's overall point he seems to confuse Francis and Roger Bacon here. Francis (1561–1626) rather than Roger Bacon (1214/20–1292) is usually credited with advocating prying nature's secrets from her and the idea is contextualized further later in this chapter. Roger Bacon does, however, occupy a key place in the story of how Western philosophy first came to envisage separate domains for material and spiritual being. See, for example, Thomas S. Maloney, "The Extreme Realism of Roger Bacon," *Review of Metaphysics*, 38 (June 1985), 807–37.

9. *Keywords* (1976), 268–69.

10. Marx, *"The Eighteenth Brumaire of Louis Bonaparte"* (1855), *Karl Marx and Frederick Engels, Selected Works* (New York: International Publishers, 1984), 97; Habermas, "A Review of Gadamer's *Truth and Method*," *Hermeneutics*, ed. Wachterhauser, 268, 270.

11. Krupat, *All That Remains*, xii.

12. Matt. 4:1–11, "Then Jesus was led up by the Spirit into the wilderness to be tempted by the devil." See also Kenneth R. Olwig, "Re-inventing Common Nature: Yosemite and Mount Rushmore—A Meandering Tale of a Double Nature," in *Uncommon Ground: Rethinking the Human Place in Nature*, ed. William Cronon (New York: W.W. Norton & Company, 1996, 1995), 399.

13. Donald Worster, *Nature's Economy: A History of Ecological Ideas* (Cambridge: Cambridge University Press, 1985 [1977]).

14. The Greek stoic Chrysippus (c. 280–206 BC) said "the world and all the things that it contains were made for the sake of gods and men" but Greek and Roman thought had a strong sense that man was capable of making a negative impact upon nature. Quoted in Coates, *Nature*, 27.

15. Genesis 1:28, King James version.

16. See Hessel, *After Nature's Revolt: Eco-Justice and Theology* (Philadelphia: Fortress Press 1992). *Theology for Earth Community: A Field Guide* (Maryknoll: Orbis Books, 1996).

17. See, for example, Peter Coates, *Nature*, 71.

18. In the novel *Wuthering Heights*, the character Catherine compares her love for another, Heathcliff, to the "eternal rocks" and tells her servant "I AM Heathcliff!" Muir's language about nature suggests the same elemental and complete identification with the object loved. Emily Bronte, *Wuthering Heights* (London: Thomas Cautley Newby, 1847), 66.

19. John Muir to Jeanne Carr (Fall, 1870), in Michael P. Cohen, *The Pathless Way: John Muir and American Wilderness* (1984), 122.

20. For more on Muir's relationships with native peoples see Richard F. Fleck, "John Muir's Evolving Attitudes Toward Native American Cultures," *American Indian Quarterly* 4, no. 1 (Feb. 1978), 19–31.

21. Exodus, 32:1–35; 14:3; Mark 1:12–13; Matthew 4:1–11; Luke 4:1–13, King James version.

22. Merchant, "Reinventing Eden: Western Culture as Recovery Narrative," in Cronon (1996), 136.

23. Bacon (1964), 93; Bacon (1870), Vol. 4, 115. For a comprehensive discussion of the point about Bacon and the violence or otherwise of his language, see Peter Pesic, "Wrestling with Proteus: Francis Bacon and the 'Torture' of Nature," *Isis* 90 (1999): 81–94. See also Nieves H. De Madariaga Mathews, *Francis Bacon: The History of a Character Assassination* (New Haven, Conn.: Yale University Press, 1996) and Alan Soble, "In Defence of Bacon," from Noretta Koertge, ed. *A House Built on Sand: Exposing Postmodernist Myths About Science* (Oxford: Oxford University Press, 1998), 195–215. For a persuasive and trenchant reply to FOBs (Friends of Bacon), see Carolyn Merchant, "The Scientific Revolution and *The Death of Nature*," *Isis* 97 (2006): 513–33. Here Merchant links Bacon to the experimental method that "arose out of techniques of human torture transferred onto nature," 532.

24. Richard Bernheimer, *Wild Men in the Middle Ages: A Study in Art, Sentiment, and Demonology* (Cambridge: Harvard University Press, 1952), 19–20.

25. Hayden White, "The Forms of Wildness: Archaeology of an Idea," in *The Wild Man Within: An Image in Western Thought from the Renaissance to Romanticism*, ed. Edward Dudley & Maximillian E. Novak (Pittsburgh: University of Pittsburgh Press, 1972), 3–38. Reference, 7.

26. Hayden White, *The Forms of Wildness*, 37.

27. Kenneth R. Olwig, "Re-inventing Common Nature: Yosemite and Mount Rushmore—A Meandering Tale of a Double Nature" in *Uncommon Ground: Rethinking the Human Place in Nature*, ed. William Cronon (New York: W.W. Norton & Company, 1996, 1995), 401–3.

28. A detailed examination of this process can be found in Robert H. Keller & Michael F. Turek, *American Indian & National Parks* (Tucson: The University of Arizona Press), 1998. See also Mark D. Spence, *Dispossessing the Wilderness: Indian Removal and the Making of National Parks* (New York: Oxford University Press), 1999.

29. Renato Rosaldo, *Culture and Truth: The Remaking of Social Analysis* (Boston: Beacon, 1989), 70

30. See Edmund Burke, *A Philosophical Enquiry into the Origin of Our Ideas of the Sublime and the Beautiful*, ed. James T. Boulton, 1958 (Notre Dame: University of Notre Dame Press, 1968); Immanuel Kant, *Observations on the Feeling of the Beautiful and Sublime*, 1764, trans. John T. Goldthwait (Berkeley: University of California Press, 1960); William Gilpin, *Three Essays: On Picturesque Beauty; on Picturesque Travel; and on Sketching Landscape* (London, 1803).

31. T. J. Jackson Lears, *No Place of Grace: Antimodernism and the Transformation of American Culture 1880–1920*, 1981, 58.

32. George Bancroft, *The History of the United States from the Discovery of Continent*, 10 vols.(Boston: Little, Brown & Co., 1834–75). See also Merrill Lewis, "Organic Metaphor and Edenic Myth in George Bancroft's History of the United States," *Journal of the History of Ideas* 26 (Oct.–Dec. 1965), 587–92. For a useful summary of work about how Indian peoples shaped their environments see Richard White and William Cronon, "Ecological Change and Indian-White Relations," in *History of Indian-White Relations*, ed. Wilcomb Washburn, Vol. 4 of *Handbook of North American Indians*, ed. William Sturtevant (Washington, DC: Smithsonian Institution, 1988), 417–29.

33. See Francis Jennings, *The Invasion of America: Indians, Colonialism and the Cant of Conquest* (New York: Norton, 1975), 81–82.

34. Margaret Sanborn, *Yosemite: Its Discovery, Its Wonders and Its People* (1981 [Random House], Yosemite National Park: Yosemite Association, 1989), 47, 17, 24–29, 238.

35. Tenaya cursed those who came to Yosemite and brutally killed his youngest son. According to Margaret Sanborn he said, "You may kill me … but I will follow in your footsteps; I will not leave my home, but be with the spirits among the rocks, the waterfalls, in the rivers and in the winds; wherever you go I will be with you. You will not see me, but you will feel the spirit of the old chief, and grow cold … " (Tenaya quoted in Sanborn, p. 52).

36. According to William Bright, however, Yosemite Valley is from the Southern Miwok /yohhe'meti "they are killers." Such negative place-name and community-name translations are a commonplace of military conquest, since settlers often enquired about a tribe's name from rival tribes with whom they were already able to communicate.

37. Sanborn, 54, 56.

38. Christopher Columbus, *The Four Voyages*, trans. and ed. Walter Cohen (New York: Penguin Books, 1969), 56.

39. William Apess, *A Son of the Forest*, 1829, 7.

40. Thomas King, *Green Grass, Running Water*, 1993, 41.

41. See William Bright, *Native American Placenames of the United States* (Norman: University of Oklahoma Press, 2004), 9

42. Keith H. Basso, *Wisdom Sits in Places: Landscape and Language among the Western Apache* (Albuquerque: University of New Mexico Press, 1996); Steven Feld & Keith H. Basso (eds.), *Senses of Place* (Sch. Am. Res. Adv. Sem. Ser.), xii (Santa Fe: School of American Research Press, 1996).

43. Martin Heidegger, *Building Dwelling Thinking.* In *Martin Heidegger: Basic Writings*, D. Krell, ed., 319–39 (New York: Harper & Row, 1977).

44. Keith H. Basso, *Wisdom Sits in Places*, 66, 73, xv, 13.

45. See Sanborn, 8.

46. Ngũgĩ wa Thiong'o, *Decolonizing the Mind: The Politics of Language in African Literature* (London: James Curry, 1986).

47. Yi-Fu Tuan, "Rootedness versus sense of place." *Landscape*, 24 (1980), 6 [article, 3–8].

48. Mary Louise Pratt, *Imperial Eyes: Travel Writing and Transculturation* (London & New York: Routledge, 1992), 4, 7.

49. See Kevin McCardle, "What Makes a Vista Scenic?," *History, Architecture and Landscape* 1, no. 1 (Winter 2011): 12–13, and Paul Rogers, "New Plan to Preserve the views in Yosemite begins with 'timber'!," Mercurynews.com, 07/23/2011; accessed 1/08/2011 http://www.mercurynews.com/science/ci-18539564.

50. William Cronon, ed. *Uncommon Ground: Rethinking the Human Place in Nature* (New York: W.W. Norton & Company, 1996), 85.

51. Wendell Berry, *Home Economics* (San Francisco: North Point, 1987), 143.

52. Michael Pollan, *Second Nature: A Gardener's Education* (New York: Atlantic Monthly Press, 1991), 188.

53. Thom Kuehls, *Beyond Sovereign Territory: The Space of Ecopolitics* (Minneapolis: University of Minnesota Press, 1996).

54. Leslie Marmon Silko, "Landscape, History, and the Pueblo Imagination," *Antaeus* 57 (Autumn, 1986), 83–94, emphasis in original, quotation, 90.

55. Leslie Marmon Silko, *Yellow Woman and a Beauty of the Spirit: Essays on Native American Life Today* (New York: Simon, 1997), 94–95.

CHAPTER 2

1. See Paul S. Sutter's *Driven Wild: How the Fight Against the Automobile Launched the Modern Wilderness Movement* (Seattle: University of Washington Press, 2002) for a broader critique of Cronon's idea of wilderness.

2. As Gary Snyder puts it in his withering critique of writers like Cronon et al., whom he accuses of "moral and political shallowness": "So we understand the point about nature being in one sense a cultural construct, and what isn't?" He has a point, but some things such as gravity and splitting the atom are less amenable to cultural interpretation than others. Gary Snyder, "Nature as Seen from Kitkitdizzie Is No 'Social Construction,'" *Wild Earth* 6, no. 4 (Winter, 1996/7), 1–4.

3. *The Middle Ground* (Cambridge: Cambridge University Press), 1991, xv.

4. Stanley Diamond, *In Search of the Primitive: A Critique of Civilization* (New Brunswick: Transaction Publishers, 1974), 39.

5. In Roger Shattuck, *Marcel Proust* (Princeton, NJ: Princeton Paperbacks, 1974), 131.

6. See in the British context Richard Drayton, *Nature's Government: Science, Imperial Britain, and the 'Improvement' of the World* (New Haven: Yale University Press, 2000) and the work of Lucile H. Brockway in, for example "Science and Colonial Expansion: The Role of British Royal Botanic Gardens," *American Ethnologist*, 6, no. 3 (Aug. 1979), 449–65.

7. Michael Pollan, *Second Nature: A Gardener's Education* (New York: Atlantic Monthly Press, 1991), 133.

8. Jamaica Kincaid, *My Garden (Book)* (New York: Farrar, Strauss and Giroux, 1999), 123.

9. Paul Robbins and Julie T. Sharp, "Producing and Consuming Chemicals: The Moral Economy of the American Lawn," *Economic Geography* 79, no. 4 (October 2003), 432, 438.

10. See Allen W. Johnson & Timothy Earle, *The Evolution of Human Societies: From Foraging Group to Agrarian State*, 2nd ed. (Stanford, CA: Stanford University Press, 2000), 136–40. See also Melvin Ember, "Statistical Evidence for an Ecological Explanation of Warfare," *American Anthropologist* 84, (Sept. 3, 1982), 645–49.

11. Kenneth R. Olwig, "Reinventing Common Nature: Yosemite and Mount Rushmore—A Meandering Tale of a Double Nature," in Cronon, *Uncommon Ground*, 384.

12. Muir quoted in Kenneth R. Olwig, ibid., 384.

13. Keller & Turek, *American Indians and National Parks*, 20.

14. See Elizabeth Godfrey, *Yosemite Indians*, revised by James Snyder (Yosemite National Park: Yosemite Natural History Association, 1973). Robert F. Heizer, *The Eighteen Unratified Treaties of 1851–1852 Between the California Indians and the United States Government* (Berkeley: University of California Archaeological Research Facility, 1972).

15. Edward D. Castillo, ed., "Petition to Congress on Behalf of the Yosemite Indians," *Journal of California Anthropology* 5:2 (1979), 271–77.

16. Keller & Turek, xiii; 233.

17. George Catlin, *North American Indians* (1832). Ed. Peter Matthiessen (New York: Penguin, 2004).

18. Karen R. Jones & John Wills, *The Invention of the Park: From the Garden of Eden To Disney's Magic Kingdom* (Cambridge: Polity, 2005).

19. Giovanni da Verrazzano to King Francis 1, July 8, 1524, quoted in Antonelli Gerbi, *Nature in the New World*, 114.

20. Thomas R. DeGregori, *The Environment, Our Natural Resources, and Modern Technology* (Ames, Iowa: Iowa State Press, 2002), 33–38.

21. Roosevelt quoted in Jones & Wills, 67.

22. John Muir, *Our National Parks* (Madison: University of Wisconsin Press, [1901], 1981), 1.

23. John Muir, *The Yosemite* (New York: Doubleday, [1912], 1962), 197.

24. Cronon, *Uncommon Ground*, 458.

25. Luther Standing Bear, *Land of the Spotted Eagle* (Boston: Houghton Mifflin, 1933), xix. The best recent discussion of Standing Bear and his relationship to the environment is Lee Schweninger's "Between the People and the Land" in *Listening to the Land* (Athens: University of Georgia Press, 2008), 57–75.

26. Linda Tuhiwai Smith, *Decolonizing Methodologies: Research and Indigenous Peoples* (New York: Zed Books, 1999), 50–53.

27. Luther Standing Bear, *Land of the Spotted Eagle* (Boston: Houghton Mifflin, 1933), 248.

28. Clara Sue Kidwell & Alan Velie, *Native American Studies* (Edinburgh: Edinburgh University Press, 2005), 22.

29. For an exception, see Anita Endrezze in *Here First: Autobiographical Essays by Native American Writers*, eds., Arnold Krupat and Brian Swann (New York: The Modern Library, 2000: 134); A. A. Hedge Coke in *Speaking for the Generations*, ed. Simon J. Ortiz (Tucson: The University of Arizona Press, 1998), 104.

30. Jeannette C. Armstrong in *Speaking for the Generations*, ed. Simon J. Ortiz (Tucson: The University of Arizona Press, 1998), 175, 183.

31. Simon Ortiz in *Speaking for the Generations*, ed. Simon J. Ortiz (Tucson: The University of Arizona Press, 1998, xiii); Leslie Marmon Silko in *Speaking for the Generations*, ed. Simon J. Ortiz (Tucson: The University of Arizona Press, 1998), 15.

32. Vine Deloria Jr., *God is Red* (New York: Grossett and Dunlap, 1973), 76, 73, 74.

33. Peter Coates, *Nature: Western Attitudes Since Ancient Times* (Cambridge: Polity Press, 1998), 4.

34. Calvin Martin, *Keepers of the Game: Indian-Animal Relationships and the Fur Trade* (Berkeley: University of California Press, 1978), 157.

35. Peter Coates, *Nature: Western Attitudes Since Ancient Times* (Cambridge: Polity Press, 1998), 87.

36. Ted Perry quoted in Malcolm Jones, "Just Too Good Too Be True: Another Reason to Beware of False Eco Prophets," *Newsweek* (May 4, 1992), 68. See also "Remembering Chief Seattle: Reversing Cultural Studies of a Vanishing Native American Author(s)," Crusca Bierwert, *American Indian Quarterly* 22, no. 3 (Summer, 1998), 280–304. Inexplicably, Bierwert's article refers to a "Ted Parry."

37. Christopher Vecsey and Robert W. Venables, eds. *American Indian Environments: Ecological Issues in Native American Indian History* (Syracuse NY: Syracuse University Press, 1980).

38. Bruce Johansen and Donald Grinde in *Ecocide of Native America: Environmental Destruction of Indian Lands and Peoples* (Santa Fe, NM: Clearlight Publications, 1995).

39. Paul Leicester Ford, *The Writings of Thomas Jefferson*, 10 vols. (New York: G. P. Putnam & Sons, 1892–99), 441.

40. Bruce Johansen and Donald Grinde in *Ecocide of Native America: Environmental Destruction of Indian Lands and Peoples* (Santa Fe, NM: Clearlight Publications, 1995), 52.

41. James Treat, "Participating with Nature," *Muscogee Nation News*, August 2011.

42. Excerpted from Editors, *A Basic Call to Consciousness, Akwesasne Notes* (New York: Mohawk Nation via Rooseveltown, 1978) and quoted in Johansen & Grinde, *Ecocide*, 267.

43. Luther Standing Bear, *Land of the Spotted Eagle* (Boston: Houghton Mifflin, 1933), 97.

44. C. S. Lewis, "Nature" in *Studies In Words* (Cambridge University Press, Cambridge, 1960), 45–46.

45. Marjorie Hope Nicolson, *Mountain Gloom and Mountain Glory: The Development of the Aesthetics of the Infinite* (New York: W.W. Norton, 1959), 1.

46. Peter Coates, *Salmon* (Chicago: University of Chicago Press, 2006); *American Perceptions of Immigrant and Invasive Species: Strangers on the Land* (Berkeley: University of California Press, 2006).

47. Lineu Castello, *Rethinking the Meaning of Place; Conceiving Place in Architecture-Urbanism* (Surrey: Ashgate, 2010), xiv.

48. David Abram, *The Spell of the Sensuous*, 183–84.

CHAPTER 3

1. Rabindranath Tagore, *Sādhanā: The Realisation of Life* (New York: MacMillan, 1913), 43.

2. From Rabindranath Tagore's speech entitled "Civilisation's Crisis," delivered 7 May 1941 at Santiniken, India.

3. Catherine L. Albanese, *Reconsidering Nature Religion* (Harrisburg, Penn.: Trinity Press International, 2002), 4.

4. Leslie Marmon Silko, *Ceremony* (New York: Viking, 1977), 1.

5. Christopher Columbus, *The Voyages of Christopher Columbus*, ed. Cecil Jane (London: Hakluyt Society, 1930), 148–49.

6. Christopher Columbus, *The Voyages of Christopher Columbus*, 236, 238.

7. Cecil Jane translation revised by L. A. Vigneras, *The Journal of Christopher Columbus* (London: Hakluyt Society, 1960), 200.

8. E. P. Goldsmidt, "Not in Harrisse," *Essays Honoring Lawrence C. Wroth* (Portland, Maine: Anthoensen Press, 1940), 140; quoted in Stanley L. Robe in *The Wild Man Within*, eds. Dudley & Novak, 44.

9. Christopher Columbus, *The Voyages of Christopher Columbus*, 236, 238.

10. Jane & Vigneras, *The Journal of Christopher Columbus*, 194–200.

11. See Johann Bachofen, *Das Mutterrecht* (1861); John McLennan, *Primitive Marriage* (1865) and in the American context, the influential Lewis Henry Morgan, *Ancient Society* (1877). For incisive discussion of the "promiscuous horde" idea see Adam Kuper, *The Reinvention of Primitive Society* (2005).

12. Author's italics. *Mundus Novus Albericus Vespuccius Laurentio Petri de Medicis salute plurimam dicit* appear as *Vespucci Reprints, Texts, and Studies*, vol. 5, trans. Geroge T. Northrup (Princeton: Princeton University Press, 1916).

13. Jack Forbes, *Columbus and Other Cannibals* (1992 ed.), 33, 98.

14. Quoted in W. Arens, *The Man Eating Myth*, 10.

15. bell hooks, in *Black Looks* (1992), 21–39; Dean MacCannell, in *Empty Meeting Grounds* (1992), 17–23; Deborah Root, *Cannibal Culture* (1996).

16. See Bruce Johansen & Robert Maestas, *Wasi'chu: The Continuing Indian Wars*.

17. See C. Richard King, "The (Mis)uses of Cannibalism in Contemporary Cultural Critique," *Diacritics*30, no. 1 (Spring 2000), 106–23.

18. Bronislaw Malinowski, Introduction to Julian Lips, *The Savage Hits Back*, trans. Julius E. Lips, vii.

19. For more on Jung, see his biography by Wehr (1987).

20. David Fontana, *Psychology, Religion and Spirituality, Oxford: Blackwell* (2003), 102.

21. Max Horkheimer & Theodor Adorno, *Dialectic of Enlightenment* (1944), (New York: Continuum, 1993), 7, 9.

22. Charles Taylor, *The Secular Age* (2007), 25, 5.

23. Hume, *History of Great Britain*, quoted in John Greville Agard Pocock, *Barbarism and Religion. Volume II. Narratives of Civil Government* (Cambridge: Cambridge University Press, 1999), 203; Charles Taylor, *The Secular Age* (2007), 239.

24. Charles Taylor, *The Secular Age* (2007), 239.

25. Keith Thomas, *Religion and the Decline of Magic* (New York: Charles Scribner's Sons, 1971), 267, 643.

26. Max Weber, *From Max Weber* (1946), 265, 155.

27. Paul Shepard, *Nature and Madness* (Athens: University of Georgia Press, 1982); see also Paul Shepard, *Coming Home to the Pleistocene* (Washington, DC: Island Press, 1998); James Serpell, *In the Company of Animals* (Oxford: Blackwell, 1986).

28. Boyce Rensberger, *The Cult of the Wild* (New York: Doubleday, 1977), 17–18.

29. Henry Sharp, "Dry Meat and Gender: the Absence of Chipewyan Ritual for the Regulation of Hunting and Animal Numbers" in *Hunter-Gatherers: Property, Power and Ideology*, Tim Ingold, David Riches, and James Woodburn (eds.) (New York: St Martin's Press, 1988), 183–91, quotation, 186.

30. There are aspects of *Maps and Dreams* that are reminiscent of Carlos Castaneda's books on Don Juan. At the very least, Joseph Patash is made to stand for all his people as, for example, when Brody writes of him "But his composure and eloquence were not those of an old man; they expressed the completeness and distinctiveness of a culture." Hugh Brody, *Maps and Dreams: Indians and the British Columbia Frontier* (London: Faber & Faber, 2002), 6, 134.

31. Hugh Brody, *Maps and Dreams: Indians and the British Columbia Frontier* (London: Faber & Faber, 1981), 213, 178, 281, 37, 40, 43, 267.

32. See Paul Ricoeur, *Symbolism of Evil*, trans. by Emerson Buchanan (New York: Harper & Row, 1967).

33. See Donald R. Lach, *Asia in the Making of Europe: The Century of Discovery* (Chicago: University of Chicago Press, 1965), vol. 1, book 1, 4.

34. Unnamed tribesman quoted in Robert F. Berkhofer, Jr., *The White Man's Indian: Images of the American Indian From Columbus to the Present* (New York: Vintage Books, 1978), 4.

35. Ray A. Young Bear, *Remnants of the First Earth* (New York: Grove Press, 1996), xii.

36. Ray A. Young Bear, *Remnants of the First Earth* (New York: Grove Press, 1996), 250.

37. See G. Deleuze and F. Guattari, *A Thousand Plateaus: Capitalism and Schizophrenia*, trans. B. Massumi (London: Continuum, 2004 [first published as *Mille Plateaux*, vol. 2 of *Capitalisme et Schizophrénie*, Paris: Minuit, 1980.]).

38. Tim Ingold, *Being Alive: Essays on Movement, Knowledge and Description* (London: Routledge, 2011), 168, 174, 175.

39. K. Johnson, "An Open Letter to the Public from the President of the Makah Whaling Commission." 8/6/98. Accessed 11/11/2011 http://NCSEonline.org/nae/docs/makaheditorial.html.

CHAPTER 4

1. Hayden White, in *The Wild Man Within*, 33

2. See Antonello Gerbi, *Nature in the New World: From Christopher Columbus to Gonzalo Fernández de* Oviedo (Pittsburgh, PA: University of Pittsburgh Press, 1985), 42.

3. David Hume, "Of National Characters," *The Philosophical Works*, ed. Thomas Hill Green & Thomas Hodge Grose, 4 vols. (Darmstadt, 1964), 3: 252 n. 1; Gates's emphasis in Henry Louis Gates, Jr., *"Race," Writing, and Difference*, 10.

4. Quoted in Achebe, 1978: 74 and recapitulated by H. Trevor-Roper, 1969, 6.

5. See for example, James Adair, *History of the American Indians*, 4; Hugh Jones, *Present State of Virginia*, 56, 57.

6. [Italics not in original.] Quoted in ed. Charles Gibson, *The Spanish Tradition in America* (New York: Harper & Row, 1968), 59–60.

7. Quoted in John L. Myres, "The Influence of Anthropology on the Course of Political Science," *University of California Publications in History* 4, no. 1 (Berkeley, 1916), 29n.

8. Edmund Berkeley & Dorothy Smith Berkeley, *The Correspondence of John Bartram, 1734–1777*, 400.

9. Paul A. W. Wallace, *Conrad Weiser: Friend of Colonist and Mohawk*, 403.

10. *Della moneta* quoted in Anonello Gerbi, *Nature in the New World*, 63.

11. Abram, *The Spell of the Sensuous*, 254.

12. Abram, "On the Ecological Consequences of Alphabetic Literacy: Reflections in the Shadow of Plato's PHAEDRUS," Aisling Magazine 32, accessible at http://www.aislingmagazine.com/aislingmagazine/articles/TAM32/ethical/davidabram.html, p. 5.

13. Abram writes with power and a romance that cannot fail to inspire. The hope is that drawing our attention to nature will foster an awareness of "the speech of the things themselves." Such a hope is part of a transcendental vision with a long history in the United States but, as was the case in the past, it lacks a delineated political, cultural, and most importantly spiritual dynamic so as to foster action. Abram's solution: "Finding phrases that lace us in contact with the trembling neck-muscles of a deer holding its antlers high as it swims toward the mainland" is, alas, not enough. It is also language too easily assimilated by a literary market intent on selling the idea of nature while taking attention away from the grittier processes whereby individuals and communities ensure nature remains respected and lived with sustainably. Abram, *The Spell of the Sensuous*, 274.

14. Johnson quoted in Jack M. Sosin, *Whitehall and the Wilderness: The Middle West in British Colonial Policy, 1760–1775*, 365.

15. Checochinican quoted in David L. Preston, *The Texture of Contact*, 128; Teedyuscung quoted in David L. Preston, *The Texture of Contact*, 127; Conrad Weiser quoted in David L. Preston, *The Texture of Contact* 158; William M. Darlington, *Christopher Gist's Journals*, 47.

16. Michael Leroy Oberg, *Dominion and Civility: English Imperialism and Native America, 1585–1685* (Ithaca: Cornell University Press, 1999), 124.

17. Lahontan, *New Voyages to North-America*, 1, 36.

18. Quoted in David L. Preston, *The Texture of Contact*, 47.

19. Robert Gray, "A Good Speed to Virginia" (1609), in Kate Aughterson, *The English Renaissance* (London: Routledge, 1998), 531–32.

20. *A True Declaration of the State of the Colonie in Virginia . . . (London, 1610)*, in Peter Force, comp., *Tracts and Other Papers, Relating Principally to the Origin, Settlement, and Progress of the Colonies in North America . . .* (Washington, DC, 1836–1846), III, no. 1, 6. *Hakluytus Posthumus, or Purchas His Pilgrimes . . .* (Glasgow, 1905–07), XIX, 232. Quoted in Gary B. Nash, *The Wild Man Within*, Dudley & Novak, eds., 64.

21. Antonello Gerbi, *Nature in the New World: From Christopher Columbus to Gonzalo Fernández de Oviedo* (Pittsburgh, PA: University of Pittsburgh Press, 1985), 81.

22. Dante Aligheri, *Paradiso*, XIX, 70–78, tr. Dorothy L. Sayers.

23. Joy Harjo in Laura Coltelli, *Winged Words: American Indian Writers Speak*, 64.

24. Silko quoted in Joni Adamson, *American Indian Literature, Environmental Justice and Ecocriticism* (Tucson: University of Arizona, 2001), 164.

25. Lee Schweninger, *Listening to the Land: Native American Literary Responses to the Landscape* (Athens: University of Georgia Press, 2008), 15.

26. Timothy Egan, "An Indian without Reservations." *New York Times Magazine* (18 January 1998), 16–19.

27. Winona LaDuke, *All Our Relations: Native Struggles for Land and Life* (Cambridge, MA: South End Press, 1999), 1.

28. Paula Gunn Allen, "Iyani: It Goes This Way," *The Remembered Earth: An Anthology of Contemporary American Indian Literature*, ed. Geary Hobson (Albuquerque: University of New Mexico Press, 1980), 191–93.

29. Robert M. Nelson, *Place and Vision: The Function of Landscape in Native American Fiction* (New York: Peter Lang AG, 1993), 7, 1.

30. See Yi-Fu Tuan, *Space and Place: The Perspective of Experience* (Minneapolis: University of Minneapolis, 1977), 47.

31. "Where I ought to be: a writer's sense of place," in *Louise Erdrich's* Love Medicine: *a Casebook*, ed. Hertha D. Sweet Wong (Oxford University Press, 2000), 44, 48.

32. Arnold Krupat, *The Turn to the Native: Studies in Criticism and Culture* (Lincoln: University of Nebraska Press, 1996), 39.

33. "Where I ought to be: a writer's sense of place," in *Louise Erdrich's* Love Medicine: *a Casebook*, ed. Hertha D. Sweet Wong (Oxford University Press, 2000), 49.

34. William Bevis, "Native American Novels: Homing In," in *Recovering the Word: Essays on Native American Literature*, Brian Swann and Arnold Krupat, eds. (Berkeley, CA: University of California Press, 1987), 602.

CHAPTER 5

1. Shaw quoted in Michael Holroyd, *Bernard Shaw: The Lure of Fantasy*, Vol. 3 (New York: Random House, 1991), 400.

2. In *Critique of Judgement*, Kant distinguished the critical faculty of judgment from theoretical and practical knowledge. Immanuel Kant, *Critique of Judgement*

(trans. J. Creed Meredith), [1790] (Oxford: Oxford University Press, 1978). See also M. H. Abrams, "Art-as Such: The Sociology of Modern Aesthetics," *Bulletin of the American Academy of Arts and Sciences* 38, 6: 8–33.

3. Simon J. Ortiz, *Woven Stone* (Tucson: University of Arizona Press, 1992), 7.

4. Here I am indebted to Janet C. Berlo & Ruth B. Phillips, *Native North American Art* (Oxford: Oxford University Press, 1998), 138.

5. Father Morice, quoted in Judy Thompson, "No Little Variety of Ornament: Northern Athapaskan Artistic Traditions," in Julia D. Harrison et al., *The Spirit Sings: Artistic Traditions of Canada's First Peoples* (Toronto: McClelland & Stewart, 1987), 140.

6. Quoted in Bill Holm, *Northwest Coast Indian Art*, 5–7.

7. Thomas Kuhn, *The Structure of Scientific Revolutions* (Chicago: University of Chicago Press, 1970), 161.

8. For more on the archaeological and ethnological record supporting this approach see Janet C. Berlo & Ruth B. Phillips, *Native North American Art* (Oxford: Oxford University Press, 1998), 28–29.

9. T. J. Jackson Lears, *No Place of Grace: Antimodernism and the Transformation of American Culture, 1880–1920* (Chicago: University of Chicago Press, 1981), xvii.

10. Elizabeth Hutchinson, *The Indian Craze: Primitivism, Modernism, and Transculturation in American Art, 1890–1915* (Durham: Duke University Press), 2009.

11. Quoted in T. J. Jackson Lears, *No Place of Grace*, 41, from *Nachgelassene Werke, Nietzsches Werke*, ed. Elisabeth Förster-Nietzsche (Leipzig, 1903), 13: 316–17.

12. Perhaps, however, we should see the American fondness for Nietzsche and the sovereignty of the self he espoused but claimed was impossible to grasp as simply yet another antimodern impulse. One that in the end simply helps us rail against a set of processes almost impossible for either individuals or groups to elude. For more on Nietzsche and the complexities of the American desire to praise his iconoclasm, see Jennifer Ratner-Rosenhagen, "Conventional Iconoclasm: The Cultural Work of the Nietzche Image in Twentieth-Century America," 93 (3) (2006), 728–54.

13. Angel DeCora, "Native Indian Art," in Report of the Executive on the Proceedings of the First Annual Conference of the Society of American Indians Held at the University of Ohio, Columbus, Ohio (October 12–17, 1911), 1: 82–87. Washington, DC: Society of American Indians (1912), quotation, 87.

14. John Ruskin, *Sesame and Lilies: Two Lectures Delivered at Manchester in 1864* (London: Smith, Elder, 1865), 148.

15. It is an irony that Indian corners had associations within the non-Indian world with what were considered masculine virtues given that most of what was displayed was the work of Indian women.

16. Edward Cornplanter to Joseph Keppler (July 19, 1901), in Joseph Keppler Jr. Iroquois Papers, Division of Rare and Manuscript Collections, Cornell University Library.

17. Udo Keppler was adopted by the Seneca in 1899 and given the honorary name Gy-ant-wa-ka.

18. William A. Jones, *Annual Report of the Commissioner of Indian Affairs to the Secretary of the Interior* (Washington, DC: Government Printing Office, 1900), 23.

19. *Indian Industries League Annual Report for 1900*, 5, quoted in Erek Krenzen Trump, "The Indian Industries League and Its Support of American Indian Arts, 1893–1922:

A Study of Changing Attitudes toward Indian Women and Assimilationist Policy," PhD dissertation (Boston University, 1996), 260.

20. Stella K. Tillyard, *The Impact of Modernism, 1900–1920: Early Modernism and the Arts & Crafts Movement in Edwardian England* (New York: Routledge, 1988).

21. Warren Susman, *Culture as History: The Transformation of American Society in the Twentieth Century* (New York: Pantheon, 1984), 153–154.

22. Advertisement, inside front cover, *Indian School Journal* (January 1905). Quoted in Hutchinson, *The Indian Craze*, 75.

23. This Native arts program was supported by the Hudson Bay Company, the Canadian Handicrafts Guild and the Canadian Government.

24. James Houston, "Contemporary Art of the Eskimo," *The Studio* 147 (February 1954), 44. James Houston quoted in Kristin K. Potter, "James Houston, Armchair Tourism, and the Marketing of Inuit Art" in *Native American Art in the Twentieth Century*, edited by W. Jackson Rushing III (New York: Routledge, 1999), 47.

25. James Houston, "Contemporary Art of the Eskimo," *The Studio* 147 (February 1954), 44.

26. Lisa K. Neuman, "Painting Culture: Art and Ethnography at a School for Native Americans," Ethnology, 45, no. 3 (Summer 2006), 182.

27. Beatrice Levin quoted in Neuman, ibid., 183.

28. Arthur C. Parker, "Museum Motives Behind the New York Arts Project," *Indians at Work* 2, no. 15 (June 1935), 11.

29. Arthur C. Parker to President Jones, November 21, 1935, Arthur Caswell Parker Papers, 1860–1952 (Rush Rhees Library, University of Rochester New York).

30. For further detail on the Morgan collection and the circumstances of its production, see Richard Rose, "The Lewis Henry Morgan Collection at the Rochester Museum," in *Iroquois Studies: A Guide to Documentary and Ethnographic Resources from Western New York and the Genesee Valley*, edited by Russell A. Judkins (Department of Anthropology, State University of New York and Geneseo Foundation, 1987). See also Joy Porter, chapter seven of *To Be Indian: The Life of Iroquois-Seneca Arthur Caswell Parker* (Norman: University of Oklahoma Press, 2001).

31. Shelly Errington, "What Became of Authentic Primitive Art?," *Cultural Anthropology* 9, no. 2 (May 1994), 201, 204, 207.

32. The Greek and Latin terms for art, for example, referred to much that we would call craft or science. See M. Staniszewski, *Believing Is Seeing: Creating the Culture of Art* (New York: Penguin, 1995).

33. Rina Swentzell, original manuscript version of "In and Out of the Swirl: A Conversation on Community, Art and Life," by Lucy R. Lippard and Rina Swentzell in *Parallaxis* (Santa Fe, NM: Western States Arts Federation, 1996), 14.

34. See, for example, Joyce Szabo's discussion of the importance of individuality with Plains Indian imagery. Joyce Szabo, "Individuality and Cultural History: The Question of Artistic Representation Imagery," *American Indian Art* Magazine 23, no. 4 (1998), 80–90.

35. Marianna Torgovnick makes the interesting point in "Making Primitive Art High Art," *Poetics Today* 10, no. 2, Art and Literature II (Summer 1989), 299–328 on 302 that primitive art became high art in England at about the same time that Virginia Woolf felt that human character changed—in December, 1910. Woolf's comment was prompted by a visit to the famous exhibition "Manet and the Post-Impressionists" mounted by Roger

Fry in London. See Virginia Woolf "Mr Bennet and Mrs Brown," in *Collected Essays*, 1, 319–37 (New York: Harcourt, Brace & World), 1925, 320.

36. Norman Bryson, *Vision and Painting: the Logic of the Gaze* (New York: Cambridge University Press, 1983).

37. Brian O'Doherty, *White Cube: The Ideology of the Gallery Space* (San Francisco: Lapis Press, 1986), 79.

38. Frederick E. Hoxie, "Ethnohistory for a Tribal World," *Ethnohistory* 44, no. 4 (Autumn 1997), 599–600 [article: 595–615].

39. William J. Hapiuk, Jr., "Of Kitsch and Kachinas: A Critical Analysis of the *Indian Arts & Crafts Act of 1990*," *Stanford Law Review* 53, no. 4 (April 2001), 1009–75.

40. From a letter from Jimmie Durham to the curators of "Land, Spirit, Power: First Nations at the National Gallery of Canada" (March 1992). Quoted in Charlotte Townsend-Gault, "Hot Dogs, a Ball Gown, Adobe and Words: The Modes and Materials of Identity," in *Native American Art in the Twentieth Century*, ed. W. Jackson Rushing III (London: Routledge, 1999), 127.

41. Quoted in Connie Lauerman, "What Do They Have to Prove? Native American Artists Grapple with Questions of Culture, identity and Seeing Beyond Stereotypes," *Chicago Tribune*, Dec. 24, 1995, 7, quoted in Hapiuk, ibid., 1036.

42. Henry Louis Gates, Jr. "Authenticity or the Lesson of Little Tree," *New York Times*, November 24, 1991, 7.

43. Richard White, quoted in Hapiuk, ibid., 1023.

44. Richard Shiff, "The Necessity of Jimmie Durham's Jokes," *Art Journal* 51, no. 3 (Autumn 1992), 74 [article 74–80].

45. Russell Lynes, *The Tastemakers* (New York: Grosset & Dunlap, 1949), 7.

46. David Harvey, *The Condition of Postmodernity: An Enquiry into The Origins of Cultural Change* (Oxford: Basil Blackwell, 1989).

47. Jimmie Durham in conversation with Jeannette Ingberman; see Jeannette Ingberman et al., *Jimmie Durham: The Bishop's Moose and the Pinkerton Men* (New York: EXIT Art, 1989), 31.

48. See, for example, the Indian artists Phoebe Dufrene's argument that "Artists of Native American ancestry are in a 'no-man's land.' Because we are neither white nor descendants of Europeans, our art is not 'American'." Dufrene resents the exclusion of Native American Indian art from the category "Western art." See Phoebe Dufrene, "A Response to Mary Erikson: It is Time to Redefine 'Western' and 'Non-Western' Art or When Did Egypt Geographically Shift to Europe and Native Americans Become Non-Western," *Studies in Art Education* 35, no. 4 (Summer 1994), 252–53. Quotation 253.

49. Leroy N. Meyer, "In Search of Native American Aesthetics," *Journal of Aesthetic Education* 35, no. 4 (Winter 2001), 26.

50. Hartley Burr Alexander, *L'Art et la Philosophie des Indiens de L'Amerique du Nord* (Paris: Éditions Ernest Lerous, 1926), 12, quoted in Meyer, 28.

51. William Powers, "Oglala Song Terminology," in *Sacred Language: The Nature of Supernatural Discourse in Lakota* (Norman: University of Oklahoma Press, 1986), quoted I. Meyer, 33.

52. James Clifford, *The Predicament of Culture: Twentieth-Century Ethnography, Literature, and Art* (Cambridge: Harvard University Press, 1988), 95.

53. Bruce Bernstein, "The Indian Art World in the 1960s and 1970s" in *Native American Art in the Twentieth Century*, edited by W. Jackson Rushing III (New York: Routledge, 1999), 68.

54. Theresa S. Smith with Blake Debassige, Shirley Cheecho, James Simon Mishibinjima, and Leland Bell, "Beyond the Woodlands, Four Manitoulin Painters Speak Their Minds," *American Indian Quarterly* 18, no. 1 (Winter–Spring, January 1, 1994), 22.

55. Rebecca Belmore quoted in Charlotte Townsend-Gault, "Hot Dogs, a Ball Gown, Adobe and Words: The Modes and Materials of Identity," in *Native American Art in the Twentieth Century*, ed. W. Jackson Rushing III (London: Routledge, 1999), 119; Susan Stewart in *I Stand In the Centre of the Good: Interviews with Contemporary Native American Artists* (Lincoln: University of Nebraska Press, 1994), 235.

56. George Longfish in Lawrence Abbott, *I Stand in the Centre of the Good: Interviews with Contemporary Native American Artists* (Lincoln: University of Nebraska Press, 1994), 167; Jane Quick-to-See Smith, ibid., 226.

57. Luna, however, is clear that his primary audience is in fact Indian. "I make work for Indian people first, because I believe that's my audience. Even though I may have a show where very few Indians come, if any Indians come at all, because that's not something the community does on a frequent basis, but I make it in a kind of way that's very simple and direct." See *Tribal Identity: An Installation by James Luna* (Hood Museum of Art, Dartmouth College, 1995), 5. Installation displayed October 11–December 24, 1995.

58. In the last ten years or so James Luna has often worked with a backing band. This has served to greatly up the entertainment level of his performances and to make the wait between his worthy conceptual arguments and the next laugh less awkward. Luna, whose work commands a high fee, likes to film his audiences whose confused responses to his challenges often speak directly to the yawning gulf between well-intentioned liberal understandings and Indian concerns. The author thanks James Luna for his good humor and for providing her with a number of examples of his work over the years.

59. James Luna quoted by Kelly Swanson in the publicity material for "Petroglyphs in Motion" (October 19–November 12, 2005), imagineNATIVE film + media arts festival. Toronto Arts Council.

60. Rick Hill in Lawrence Abbott, *I Stand in the Centre of the Good: Interviews with Contemporary Native American Artists* (Lincoln: University of Nebraska Press 1994), 76; G. Peter Jemison, ibid., 97.

61. Carl Beam quoted in Ian McLachlan, "Making *Mizzins*—Remaking History: The Columbus Project of Carl Beam," *Artscraft* 2, no. 2 (Summer 1990), 11.

62. See Arnold Krupat, *All That Remains: Varieties of Indigenous Expression* (Lincoln: University of Nebraska Press, 2009).

CHAPTER 6

1. Steven Feld, "Voices of the Rainforest," *Public Culture* 4, no. 1 (1991), 139.

2. See Michael Parenti, *Democracy for the Few*, 6th ed. (New York: St. Martin's Press. 1995), 7–14.

3. See E. N. Wolff, "Recent Trends in household wealth in the United States: Rising Debt and the Middle-class Squeeze—an update to 2007" (2010) and "Recent Trends in household wealth in the United States: Rising Debt and the Middle-class Squeeze" (2007).

4. See Stewart Lansley, *The Cost of Inequality: Three Decades of the Super-Rich and the Economy*, 2011.

5. On the perception of wealth inequality see Michael I. Norton & Dan Ariely, "Building a Better America—One Wealth Quintile at a Time," *Perspectives on Psychological Science* (2010). On social mobility see L. A. Keister, *Getting Rich* (2005).

6. Recently high profile economists have started seriously considering what respected historians of the Great Depression, notably Robert S. McElvaine in 1984 in *The Great Depression: America, 1929–1941*, have suggested for decades—that profound maldistribution of wealth leads to debt bubbles, a Ponzi economy, and economic depression. On the economists' side, see the work of Steve Keen of the University of Western Sydney, Emmanuel Saez at UC Berkeley, Thomas Piketty at the Paris School of Economics, and Robert B. Reich also at UC Berkley, in particular his book, *Aftershock: The Next Economy and America's Future* (New York: Knopf, 2010). Worryingly, given the obvious parallels with today, only global war finally "solved" the economic woes of the first modern Western depression era.

7. On environmental racism see Irwin Weintraub, "Fighting Environmental Racism: A Selected Annotated Bibliography," *Electronic Green Journal*, Issue 1 (June 1994). Accessed on 22/11/2010 at http://www.mapcruzin.com/El/ejigc.html.

8. See U.S. General Accounting Office, *Siting of Hazardous Waste Landfills and Their Correlation with Racial and Economic Status of Surrounding Communities* (Washington, DC: U.S. Government Printing Office, 1983).

9. Al Gedicks, *The New Resource Wars: Native and Environmental Struggles against Multinational Corporations* (Boston: South End Press, 1993); Noah Sachs, "The Mescalero Apache Indians and Monitored Retrievable Storage of Spent Nuclear Fuel: A Study in Environmental Ethics," *Natural Resources Journal* 36 (1996), 881–912; Gail Small, "War Stories: Environmental Justice in Indian Country," *The Amicus Journal* 16 (1994): 38–41.

10. Little about gaining power from coal can properly be called clean. Mountaintop blasting and removal is profoundly destructive on multiple levels and smokestack emissions result in around 24,000 human deaths a year in the United States. For more, see one of the very few academic books on the phenomenon, the well-written *Bringing Down the Mountains: The Impact of Mountaintop Removal Surface Coal Mining on Southern West Virginia Communities, 1970–2004 (West Virginia and Appalachia)* by Shirley Steward Burns (Chicago, IL: West Virginia Press), 2007.

11. Office of the Inspector General, Evaluation Report, *Tribal Superfund Program Needs Clear Direction and Actions to Improve the Tribal Superfund Program* (Report No. 2004-P-0035, Sept. 30, 2004) at 2, available at www.epa.gov/oig/reports/2004/20040930-2004-P-00035.pdf.

12. An example is Chemical Waste Management, a Delaware Corporation with its principal place of business in Oak Brook, Illinois. See United States Reports Vol. 504 Cases Adjudged in The Supreme Court at October Term, 1991, Washington: U.S. Government Printing Office, 1996, 334–970.

13. An example of one of the many scholars who are happy to transpose the word genocide from the Jewish experience to that of Native Americans, see Daniel Brook, "Environmental Genocide: Native Americans and Toxic Waste," *American Journal of Economics and Sociology* 57, no. 1 (Jan., 1998): 105–13.

14. VX is a tasteless and odorless nerve agent that paralyzes the muscles and is highly persistent in the environment. Only the United States and Russia are known to possess it.

15. Leon Bear quoted in "High Level Atomic Waste Dump Targeted at Skull Valley Goshute Indian Reservation in Utah," Nuclear Information and Resource Service, prepared Feb. 15, 2001 by Kevin Kamps. Accessed 14/12/2010 at http://www.nirs.org/factsheets/pfsejfactsheet.htm.

16. See also *The United States v The Northern Paiute Nation et al.* Appeal No. 3-66, United States Court of Claims, April 19, 1968.

17. Catherine Fowler, unpublished paper on Timbisha Shoshone ethnoecology presented at a panel on Timbisha Land Restoration, Timbisha tribal village, Death Valley, California, May 26, 1996. Quoted in Kuletz, *Tainted Deserts*, 211.

18. Orbin Harney quoted in Kuletz, *The Tainted Desert*, 217.

19. See Marjane Ambler, "On Reservations: No Haste, No Waste," *Planning* 57 (11) (Nov. 1991), 26–29.

20. See Teresa Williams, "Pollution and Hazardous Waste on Indian Lands: Do Federal Laws Apply and Who May Enforce Them?," *American Indian Law Review* 17 (1992), 282.

21. Jerome D. Frank & Jon C. Rivard, "Antinuclear Admirals—An Interview Study," *Political Psychology* 7, no. 1 (1986), 28, 42.

22. See Robert Vandenbosch and Susanne E. Vandenbosch, *Nuclear Waste Stalemate* (Salt Lake City: University of Utah Press, 2007), 248.

23. Draft Report to the Secretary of Energy of the Blue Ribbon Commission on America's Nuclear Future (July 29, 2011) at www.brc.gov. accessed 10/7/2011.

24. Valerie L Kuletz, *The Tainted Desert: Environmental and Social Ruin in the American West* (New York: Routledge, 1998), 47. Kuletz's is an extremely valuable and heartfelt book by an exceptional writer but like most ground-breaking books, it is not without flaws. Some assertions and quotations are under-referenced or asserted without necessary reference to the larger debate (e.g., statements on the level of radiation that is deemed lethal). It is also problematic but by no means disruptive of its key arguments that the book makes repeated reference to the now discredited work of Ward Churchill, the former chair of the ethnic studies department at the University of Colorado whose employment was discontinued because of academic misconduct in 2007.

25. National Academy of Sciences/ National Academy of Engineering. "Rehabilitation Potential of Western Coal Lands," *Report to the Energy Policy Project of the Ford Foundation*, draft document. Washington DC: Ford Foundation, 1973.

26. Valerie L Kuletz, *The Tainted Desert: Environmental and Social Ruin in the American West* (New York: Routledge, 1998), 10, 37. Other significant uranium reserves in the United States are on Navajo, Laguna Pueblo, Havasupai, and Colville Confederated Tribal Lands; at pre-1948 Hispanic Land Grants at Cebolleta and San Mateo Springs; at the Sioux Lands in the Black Hills of Dakota and at the Spokane Reservation in the state of Washington (30 miles upstream from the Yakima Reservation).

27. Nassim Nicholas Taleb, "The Fourth Quadrant: A Map of the Limits of Statistics," September 15, 2008. An edge Original Essay, http://www.edge.org/3rd_culture/taleb08_index.html, accessed November 1, 2011. See also Nassim Nicholas Taleb, "Errors, Robustness and the Fourth Quadrant," *International Journal of Forecasting* 25, no. 4, (February 14, 2009), available at www.edge.org/3rd_culture/taleb08/taleb08_index.html.

28. For more on the complexities of evaluating risk see Inge F. Goldstein & Martin Goldstein, *How Much Risk? A Guide to Understanding Environmental Health Hazards* (Oxford: Oxford University Press, 2002).

29. My sincere thanks to Brian Wynne for his communications on risk as science. See B. Wynne, "Public Understanding and Communication of Science and Risk: what do we know?," *Journal of NIH Research* 15 (1991), 341–49; B. Wynne, "Risk and Environment as Legitimatory Discourses of Technology: Reflexivity Inside-Out," *Current Sociology* 20 (2002), 459–77; Wynne, B., *Rationality and Ritual: Participation and Exclusion in Nuclear Decisions* (London and Washington DC: Earthscan, 2010).

30. Charles C. Reith & Bruce M. Thomson, *Deserts as Dumps? The Disposal of Hazardous Materials in Arid Ecosystems* (Albuquerque: University of New Mexico Press, 1992), 231; 321. The scientific method is in this sense discrete from science per se. The former properly adhered to is perhaps man's best hope for the future while the latter is as subject to human influence as any other human activity.

31. Hal Rothman, *On Rims and Ridges: The Los Alamos Area Since 1880* (Lincoln: University of Oklahoma Press, 1992), 208.

32. Grace Thorpe, "Radioactive Racism? Native Americans and the Nuclear Waste Legacy?," *Indian Country Today*, 1995. Grace Thorpe founded the National Environmental Coalition of Native Americans in 1993.

33. For more on a Kafkaesque situation where the federal government has attempted to force Shoshone peoples to accept funds in compensation see Noriko Ishiyama, "Nevada Test Site and Yucca Mountain: The Construction of Nuclear Space and Racism," *The American Review*, Issue 42 (2008), 57–76 (in Japanese).

34. See Valerie Taliman, "The Untold Story: Native American Nuclear Guinea pigs" News From Indian Country, 31 January 1994 http://www.highbeam.com/doc/1P1-2229822.html—with same access date as original.

35. See Advisory Committee on Human Radiation Experiments "Final Report," Washington, DC.: Government Printing Office (October, 1995). Report no. 061-000-00-848-9, 255–531.

36. See "Nuclear waste: pretreatment modifications at DOE Hanford's B Plant should be stopped." Report to the chairman, Environment, Energy and Natural Resources Subcommittee, Committee on Government Operations, House of Representatives/United States General Accounting Office, 1991, Washington, DC. See also R. E. Gephart and R. E. Lundgren, *Hanford Tank Clean-up: A Guide to Understanding the Technical Issues* (Columbus Ohio: Battelle Press, 1998) and Laura A. Hanson, "Radioactive Waste Contamination of Soil and Groundwater at the Hanford Site," *Principles of Environmental Toxicology* (Nov. 2000), available at www.agls.uidaho.edu/etox/resources/case_studies/HANFORD.PDF.

37. Amchitka is 900 miles from the Russian coast.

38. Jerome D. Frank & Jon C. Rivard, "Antinuclear Admirals—An Interview Study," *Political Psychology* 7, no. 1 (1986), 41.

39. See Jeffrey St Clair, "30 Years After: the Legacy of America's Largest Nuclear Test," *In These Times*, www.inthesetimes.com/projectcensored/stclair2317.html.

40. See Norm Buske & Pamela Miller, Nuclear Flashback: The Threat of the U.S. Nuclear Complex (February 1998); http://www.akaction.org/Publications/Military_Waste_in_Alaska/Nuclear_Flashback_Part_Two_1998.pdf.

41. See Lorna Arnold and Katherine Pyne, *Britain and the H Bomb* (London: Palgrave Macmillan, 2001).

42. Thomas Princen, *Treading Softly: Paths to Ecological Order* (Michigan: The MIT Press, 2010), 76.

43. Proverbs 21:3, American King James Version of the Bible.

44. Hosea 6:4–6, American King James Version of the Bible.

45. Matthew 5:23–24, American King James Version of the Bible.

46. For the rejection of Girard's universal theory of sacrifice see C. Bell, *Ritual Theory, Ritual Practice* (Oxford: Oxford University Press, 1992), 174–5.

47. Dennis King Keenan, *The Question of Sacrifice* (Bloomington & Indianapolis: Indiana University Press, 2005), 1.

48. Susan L. Mizruchi, *The Science of Sacrifice: American Literature and Modern Social Theory* (Princeton, NJ: Princeton University Press, 1998), 2, 369.

49. See H. Hubert & M. Mauss, *Sacrifice: Its Nature & Function* [1899], 1964; E. E. Evans-Pritchard, *Nuer Religion* (Oxford: Clarendon Press, 1956); Victor Turner, "Sacrifice as Quintessential Process: Prophylaxis or Abandonment?," *History of Religion* 16: 3 (1977), 189–215.

50. Albert Smith quoted in Paul Rosier, *Serving their Country*, 87.

51. Marilou Awiakta, *Selu: Seeking the Corn-Mother's Wisdom* (Golden, Colorado: Fulcrum Publishing, 1993), 185–86.

52. R. J. Lifton and E. Olson, "The Nuclear Age," in E. S. Shneidman (ed.), *Death: Current Perspectives* (Palo Alto, California: Mayfield, 1976), 102.

53. See Henry Shue, "Subsistence Emissions and Luxury Emissions," *Law and Policy* 15 (1993), 39–59.

54. Charles Bowden, "Native Lands," *National Geographic* 218, no. 2 (August 2010), 80–97.

55. Grant Meyer quoted in Pete Spotts, "Los Alamos Fire could become the largest in New Mexico History," *The Christian Science Monitor* (June 30, 2011).

56. Marian Naranjo quoted in "Las Conchas Fire Woke Us Up: Let Us Now Stop The Plutonium Bomb Factory" by Subhankar Banerjee, July 1, 2010, Climate storytellers.org www.climatestorytellers.org/storytellers/subhankar-banerjee/, accessed 09/30/2011.

57. Mission Mountains Tribal Wilderness A Case Study, Native Lands and Wilderness Council, Pablo, MT, 2005, 10.

58. Mission Mountains Tribal Wilderness A Case Study, Native Lands and Wilderness Council, Pablo, MT, 2005, 12.

59. Mission Mountains Tribal Wilderness A Case Study, Native Lands and Wilderness Council, Pablo, MT, 2005, 28.

60. See Pacific Northwest Electric Power Planning and Conservation Act, 16 U.S.C. 839 *et seq.* Section 4 (h)(10)(A).

61. See Charles Brill, *Red Lake Nation: Portraits of Ojibway Life* (1992).

62. At present no policy exists regulating the extraction of peat within Ontario. See "Background Information for the Development of a Fisheries Management Plan in Fisheries Management Zone 4," June 2010, Ontario Ministry of Natural Resources.

CHAPTER 7

1. See William Denevan, "The Caribbean, Central America, and Yucatán: Introduction," in *The Native Population of the Americas in 1492*, W. M. Denevan (ed.) (Madison: University of Wisconsin Press), 35–41.

2. For more, see Joy Porter, "Population Matters in Native America," in *America's Americans: Population Issues in U.S. Society and Politics*, Philip Davies & Iwan Morgan, eds. (London: Institute for the Study of the Americas), 31–50.

3. James Mooney, *The Aboriginal Population of America North of Mexico*, Smithsonian Miscellaneous Collections 80, no. 7 (Washington, DC: Smithsonian Institution, 1928).

4. Alfred Kroeber, "Native American Population," *American Anthropologist* 36, no. 1 (1934): 1–25; *Cultural and Natural Areas of Native North America* (Berkeley: University of California Press, 1939); A. Rosenblat, "El desarrollo de la población indígena de América," *Tierra Frime*1, no. 1 (1935): 115–33; 1, no. 2, 117–48; 1, no. 3, 109–41; Julian H. Steward, "The Native Population of South America," in *Handbook of South American Indians*, J. H. Steward (ed.), Bureau of American Ethnology Bulletin 5, no. 143 (Washington DC: Smithsonian Institution, 1949), 655–68.

5. See Henry F. Dobyns, "Estimating Aboriginal American Population: An Appraisal of Techniques with a New Hemispheric Estimate," *Current Anthropology* 7 (1966), 395–416; and *Their Number Became Thinned* (Knoxville: University of Tennessee Press, 1983).

6. David E. Stannard, *American Holocaust: The Conquest of the New World* (Oxford: Oxford University Press, 1993), p. 151.

7. See Niall Ferguson, *Empire: The Rise and Demise of the British World Order and Lessons for Global Power* (New York: Basic Books, 2003) and *Colossus: The Rise and Fall of the American Empire* (London: Penguin Books, 2004). Ferguson is a right-leaning historian and his description of America as empire had considerable impact. However, many on the left had been analyzing United States imperialism in-depth for decades prior to his publications. As David Harvey put it ably with reference to the empire trend in 2003, "What, if anything, is new about all this?" (*The New Imperialism*, 6, 7). Highly able discussions of the United States as an empire prior to Ferguson include Walter A. McDougall, *Promised Land, Crusader State: The American Encounter with the World Since 1776* (Boston: Houghton Mifflin, 1997) and A. J. Bacevich, *American Empire: The Realities and Consequences of U.S. Diplomacy* (Cambridge: Cambridge University Press, 2002).

8. Here I am thinking of a dear colleague Richard J. Cawardine who in 2004 won the Gettysburg College and Gilder Lehrman Institute of American History Lincoln Prize for *Lincoln* (London: Longman, 2003), a fine book, which, despite its emphasis on Lincoln's moral and spiritual life, made almost no analytical reference to the profoundly negative effects of Lincoln and his administration on Indian peoples.

9. Graham Greene, quoted in Richard Drinnon, *Facing West: The Metaphysics of Indian Hating and Empire Building* (New York: Meridian, 1980).

10. A sample of criticism of Dobyns's work includes Donald Joralemon, "New World Depopulation and the Case of Disease," *Journal of Anthropological Research* 38 (1982), 108–27; and Ann F. Ramenofsky, *Vectors of Death: The Archaeology of European Contact* (Albuquerque, NM: University of New Mexico Press, 1989). For an extended list, see Joy Porter, "Population Matters in Native America," in *America's Americans: Population Issues in U.S. Society and Politics*, Philip Davies & Iwan Morgan, eds. (London: Institute for the Study of the Americas), 31–50.

11. Russell Thornton, *American Indian Holocaust and Survival: A Population History Since 1492* (Norman: University of Oklahoma Press, 1987).

12. Douglas H. Ubelaker, "North American Indian Population Size, A.D. 1500 to 1985," *American Journal of Physical Anthropology* 45 (1988), 661–66; William Denevan, *The Native Population of the Americas in 1492* (Madison: University of Wisconsin Press, 1992); A. J. Jaffe, *The First Immigrants from Asia: A Population History of the North American Indians* (New York: Plenum Press, 1992); Kirkpatrick Sale, *The Conquest of Paradise: Christopher Columbus and the Columbian Legacy* (New York: Plume, 1990).

13. David Henige, *Numbers from Nowhere: The American Indian Contact Population Debate* (Norman: University of Oklahoma Press, 1998), 6, 8, 9, 79.

14. There was also strategic use of pathogens as part of germ warfare against Indian peoples, in particular by the British; but the suggestion of the use of smallpox-infested blankets was made repeatedly by a number of commentators in eighteenth-century America and justified by the Indians' supposed animal nature. The instance of smallpox-infested blankets and handkerchiefs being used to deplete Chief Pontiac's forces during a siege of Fort Pitt, Pittsburgh during the summer of 1763 is well documented. For more, see Ann F. Ramenofsky, *Vectors of Death* (1989), esp. 148 and Robert L. O'Connell, *Of Arms & Men: A History of War, Weapons and Aggression* (New York: Oxford University Press, 1989), esp. 171.

15. Thornton et al. (1991), 39.

16. Thornton, "Aboriginal North American Population and Rates of Decline, ca. AD 1500–1900," (1997), 311.

17. Nov. 1, 2010 facts for Features: American Indian and Alaska National Heritage Month November, 2011. . . .www.census.gov/newsroom/. . ./facts_for_features_special _editions/.

18. See C. M. Snipp, *American Indians* (1989) and J. Matthew Shumway and Richard H. Jackson, "Native American Population Patterns," *Geographical Review* 85, no. 2 (April 1995), 186.

19. See Margo Brownell, "Who is an Indian? Searching for an Answer to the Question at the Core of Federal Indian Law," *University of Michigan Journal of Law Reform* 34 (2000): 273–320.

20. See Vine Deloria Jr., *Behind the Trail of Broken Treaties: An Indian Declaration of Independence* (Austin: University of Texas Press, 1974).

21. Leonard Peltier, quoted in Jack Utter, *American Indians: Answers to Today's Questions* (Norman: University of Oklahoma, 2001), 65.

22. Richard H. Pratt, *Official Report of the Nineteenth Annual Conference of Charities and Correction* (1892), 46–59. Reprinted in Richard H. Pratt, "The Advantages of Mingling Indians with Whites," *Americanizing the American Indians: Writings by the "Friends of the Indian" 1880–1900* (Cambridge, Mass.: Harvard University Press, 1973), 260.

23. Tiffany Waters, "Biometrics in Indian Country: The Bloody Fight for Authenticity," *Fourth World Journal: A Publication of the Center for World Indigenous Studies* 6, no. 1 (2005).

24. M. Annette Jaimes, "Federal Indian Identification Policy: A Usurpation of Indigenous Sovereignty in North America," *The State of Native America: Genocide, Colonization, and Resistance*, ed. M. Annette Jaimes (Boston: South End Press, 1992), 129 [chapter 123–138].

25. Ted Means, statement to the South Dakota Indian Education Association, Pierre, SD, 16 November 1975; quoted in M. Annette Jaimes, "Federal Indian Identification

Policy: A Usurpation of Indigenous Sovereignty in North America," *The State of Native America: Genocide, Colonization, and Resistance*, ed. M. Annette Jaimes (Boston: South End Press, 1992), 131.

26. Hilary N. Weaver, "Indigenous Identity: What Is It and Who Really Has It?", *American Indian Quarterly* 25, no. 2 (Spring 2001), 249–50. On Lumbee identity see also Karen I. Blu, *The Lumbee Problem: The Making of an American Indian People* (Lincoln: University of Nebraska Press, 2001).

27. Chadwick Allen, *Blood Narrative: Indigenous Identity in American Indian and Maori Literary and Activist Texts* (Durham: Duke University Press), 2002.

28. Eva Marie Garroute, *Real Indians: Identity and the Survival of Native America* (Berkeley: University of California Press, 2003), 125–27.

29. Russell Thornton, "Population History of Native North Americans," in *A Population History of North America*, Michael R. Haines and Richard H. Steckel, eds. (Cambridge: Cambridge University Press, 2000), 41.

30. Here Shoemaker echoes conclusions also drawn previously by Stephen Cornell in *The Return of the Native: American Indian Political Resurgence* (New York: Oxford University Press, 1988). Nancy Shoemaker, *American Indian Population Recovery in the Twentieth Century* (Albuquerque: University of New Mexico Press, 1999), 101, 103.

31. See J. C. Day, "Population Projections of the United States by Age, Sex, Race and Hispanic Origin: 1993–2050," *Current Population Report* (Washington, DC: U.S. Bureau of the Census, 1993), 25–110.

32. I am indebted to the nonpartisan election analyst and colleague Dr. Rhodes Cook for information on Indian voting patterns. See Rhodes Cook, *Mapping the Political Landscape* (Washington DC: Pew Research Center, 2005), 149. Dr. Cook provided a sample showing strong Democratic support in the following counties with a high Native American population level: Shannon Co., SC, Todd Co., SD, Sioux County, ND, Buffalo County, SD, Apache Co, AZ.

33. Tex Hall quoted in ArgusLeader.com, Dec. 17, 2010. Accessed 17/12/10, http://www.argusleader.com/article/20101217/NEWS/12170319/1001/news.

34. Melonie Heron, National Vital Statistics Reports 59, no. 8 (Aug. 26, 2001): 11–12. An analysis of statistics from 2007 that acknowledge understatement in Native American Indians numbers because of misclassification on death certificates.

35. Jennifer L. Truman, National Crime Victimization Survey Criminal Victimization, 2010, U.S. Department of Justice (September, 2011), NCJ 235508, Bureau of Justice Statistics.

36. Steven W. Perry, U.S. Department of Justice, Bureau of Justice Statistics, A BJS Statistical Profile, 1992–2002, "American Indians and Crime," (December 2004), NCJ 203097.

37. S. Perry, "American Indians and Crime: A BJS Statistical Profile, 1992–2002," U.S. Department of Justice, Bureau of Justice Statistics, 2004.

38. Prison Justice, "Prison Facts and Statistics," http://www.prisonjustice.ca/politics/facts_stats.html.

39. See chapter 4 of "The Justice System and Aboriginal People," the Aboriginal Justice Implementation Commission, 1991. See Manitoba Government Home page: http://www.ajic.mb.ca/index.html; accessed 19th September 2011.

CHAPTER 8

1. Bill McKibben, *Eaarth: Making Life on a Tough Planet* (New York: Times Books), 6.

2. Slavoj Žižek, *Living in the End Times* (London: Verso, 2010), 364. It is worth noting that Professor Žižek is a philosopher whose work is comic and performative. Only sometimes does he say something worth repeating, as in this case where he simply calls for the world to move on from denial and to begin to comprehend something hitherto beyond our collective experience—imminent ecological catastrophe. The above description does him no disservice since, with considerable charm, as he has pointed out of himself, "A lot of what I write is blah, blah, bullshit, a diversion from the 700-page book on Hegel I should be writing." Žižek, quoted in "A Life in Writing: Slavoj Žižek" by Stuart Jeffries, *Saturday Guardian*, 16/07/11, 12–13.

3. In B. F. Skinner, ed. *Recent Issues in the Analysis of Behaviour* (Columbus, OH: Merrill, 1988), 113–20. Quotation, 8.

4. Voltaire, *Candide or Optimism*, translated from the German of Dr. Ralph (Geneva: Cramer, 1759), chapter 19, 89. On sugar, see Sidney Mintz's uneven but intriguing study, *Sweetness and Power: The Place of Sugar in Modern History* (New York: Viking, 1985).

5. See Norman Myers, "The Hamburger Connection: How Central America's Forests Became North America's Hamburgers," *Ambio* 10: 3–8; and L. E. Andersen, C. W. J. Granger, E. J. Reis, D. Weinhold, and S. Wunder, *The Dynamic of Deforestation and Economic Growth in the Brazilian Amazon* (Cambridge: Cambridge University Press, 2002). A bedrock for understanding the malign influence of fast food on America is Eric Schlosser's *Fast Food Nation: The Dark Side of the All-American Meal* (Orlando, FL.: Harcourt Mifflin Harcourt, 2001).

6. Rebecca West, *Black Lamb & Grey Falcon: A Journey Through Yugoslavia* (London: Penguin, 1944 (1941)), 1102.

7. W. H. Auden, *The Age of Anxiety: A Baroque Eclogue* (London: Faber & Faber, 1948).

8. See *Back to the Wild Book & DVD*, available from the Christopher Johnson McCandless Memorial Foundation. Christopher McCandless, *Back to the Wild*, n.a. (Twin Star Press, 2011).

9. The film makes use of the Sharon Olds poem "Go Back to May 1937." In this poem Olds, the daughter of an alcoholic father, writes poignantly of the dilemma of the child whose parents "do bad things to children." Perhaps the clearest evidence of how wronged Chris McCandless felt by his parents is the degree of calculation that went into his rejection of them—he was careful not to accept gifts from them, it should be remembered, "because they will think they have bought my respect" (Krakhauer, *Into the Wild*, 21).

10. Jerry Griswold, *Audacious Kids: Coming of Age in America's Classic Children's Books* (Oxford: Oxford University Press, 1992).

11. Richard Slotkin, *Regeneration through Violence: The Mythology of the American Frontier, 1600–1860* (Middletown: Wesleyan University Press, 1973); *Fatal Environment: The Myth of the Frontier in the Age of Industrialization, 1800–1890* (New York: Atheneum, 1985); *Gunfighter Nation: The Myth of the Frontier in Twentieth-Century America* (New York: Atheneum, 1992), 11. See also the seminal and courageous work by Henry Nash Smith, *Virgin Land: The American West as Symbol and Myth* (Cambridge: Cambridge University Press, 1978), and for a grittier and more complex approach to the West, Patricia Nelson Limerick's equally groundbreaking *The Legacy of Conquest: the Unbroken Past of the American West* (New York: W.W. Norton & Co., 1987). A more recent analysis

of the phenomenon of regeneration through exile can be found in John P. O'Grady's *Pilgrims to the Wild: Everett Ruess, Henry David Thoreau, John Muir, Clarence King, Mary Austin* (Salt Lake City: University of Utah Press, 1993).

12. Thomas Jefferson to James Madison, Dec. 20, 1787, in *The Life and Selected Writings of Thomas Jefferson*, Adrienne Koch and William Peden eds. (New York: Random House, 1944), 440–41.

13. A decidedly post-60s hero, McCandless echoes the outsider ethos of Peter Fonda in the 1969 film *Easy Rider* by ridding himself of his watch. Fonda, in an iconic scene, throws away his watch as he sets off to find himself in an odyssey by motorcycle that in comparison is humorous rather than tragic. It seems that McCandless did have a basic road map since this is listed by the Alaska Coroner's Office among his returned items to the McCandless family, but it was not detailed enough to allow him to hike to safety in time. For more on the issue of why McCandless did not hike to safety and a suggestion that Krakhauer and Penn constructed the idea that McCandless had no map, ID, or money, see Ron Lamothe's *Call of the Wild*, TerrIncognita Films, http://www.terraincognitafilms.com/wild/call_debunked.htm, accessed 8/25/2011.

14. Perhaps counterintuitively, a useful place to start in exploring Native American Indian vision quest traditions is Calvin Martin's 1987 edited collection, *The American Indian and the Problem of History* (Oxford: Oxford University Press). See also David Martinez, "The Soul of the Indian: Lakota Philosophy and the Vision Quest," *Wicazo Sa Review* 19, no. 2 (Fall, 2004).

15. Letter to author, 8/26/2011.

16. See Timothy Rawson, *Changing Tracks: Predators and Politics in Mt. McKinley National Park* (Fairbanks: University of Alaska Press, 2001).

17. Alexander Supertramp a.k.a. Christopher McCandless quoted in Jon Krakhauer, *Into the Wild* (New York: Pan Books, 1998), 162. McCandless's capitals in original. As Krakhauer's book explains, when they were helicoptered in to look at the bus where their son died, McCandless's parents gathered a bouquet of wildflowers and left them there in memory of their son. The bouquet contained the perennial monkshood or wolfsbane, one of the most deadly toxins known to man. Professor Alan Borass, of Kenai Peninsula College, Alaska uses this fact to illustrate how a lack of awareness of nature and place characterized both parents and son. This is perhaps asking too much of the McCandlesses who were, after all, only making the briefest of visits under conditions of extreme stress. In any case, monkshood needs to be ingested to begin to have effects similar to strychnine; skin contact with the plant's petals brings only irritation, dizziness, and nausea. Alan Borass, "Never Underestimate Flower Power," *Anchorage Daily News*, April 3, 2002.

18. Philip L. Fradkin, *Everett Ruess: His Short Life, Mysterious Death and Astonishing Afterlife* (Berkeley: University of California Press, 2011). It is now thought that Ruess was murdered by Ute Indians.

19. Like McCandless, Krakhauer also seems to have entirely misread Thoreau. Krakhauer claims that because of Thoreau's essay "On the Duty of Civil Disobedience," McCandless "considered it his responsibility to flout the laws of the state" (Krakhauer, *Into the Wild*, 28). Very significantly, however, Thoreau *did not* espouse a duty to seek out the state for confrontation, rather he argued that a man's duty was to correct any injustice he directly causes and to not cooperate with other injustices. This is very far from advocating a duty to flout all laws.

20. Randall Roorda, *Dramas of Solitude: Narratives of Retreat in American Nature Writing* (Albany: SUNY Press, 1998), xiii.

21. Frederick Jackson Turner, "The Significance of the Frontier in American History," *Report of the American Historical Association* (1893), 199–227.

22. Jon Krakhauer, *Into the Wild* (New York: Pan Books, 1998), 16.

23. See Lawrence Buell, *The Environmental Imagination: Thoreau, Nature Writing and the Formation of American Culture* (Cambridge, MA: Harvard University Press, 1995), 67–75. John Muir also traveled in Alaska and dismissed the indigenous presence there and indigenous knowledge of the land, even though he had a number of Tlingit guides making his trip possible—Kadechan Toyette, John Stickeen, and Charlie Sitka. See Susan Kollin, "The Wild, Wild North: Nature Writing, Nationalist Ecologies and Alaska," American *Literary* History 12, no. 1/2 (Spring–Summer, 2000), 48.

24. Raymond Williams, *Problems in Materialism and Culture: Selected Essays* (London: Verso, 1980), 77.

25. R. W. B. Lewis, *The American Adam: Innocence, Tragedy, and Tradition in the Nineteenth Century* (Chicago: University of Chicago Press, 1955), 5.

26. Jon Krakhauer, *Into the Wild* (New York: Pan Books, 1998), 85, 198.

27. Claire Jane Ackerman, 29, from Switzerland died while attempting to cross the Teklanika River so as to reach the bus. Fatally, she was attempting to use being tied to a rope as an aid. Her male companion survived and claimed they had been "just hiking." See report by Carolyn Kellogg, " 'Into the Wild' fan dies trying to reach McCandless' bus," *Los Angeles Times*, August 17, 2010. Refer also to the song, "The Last Steps (of Claire Jane Ackerman)" by Alaskan band The Council of Smokers and Drinkers.

28. Jon Krakhauer, *Into the Wild*, 154–55.

29. Richard Nelson, "The Forest of Eyes" in *Alaska: Reflections on Land and Spirit*, edited by Robert Hedin and Gary Holthaus (Tucson: The University of Arizona Press, 1989), 56–57.

30. Vernor Vinge, "What is the Singularity?" Presented at the VISION-21 Symposium sponsored by NASA Lewis Research Center and the Ohio Aerospace Institute, March 30–31, 1993.

31. While these figures are generally held to be accurate or conservative, the reader will appreciate that it is notoriously difficult to estimate the true number of species worldwide.

32. J. A. Pounds and R. Puschendorf, "Ecology: Clouded Futures," *Nature* (Jan. 8, 2004): 427 (6970), 145–8.

33. See E. O. Wilson, *The Future of Life* (New York: Vintage, 2002).

34. Paul Crutzen, quoted in "Enter the Anthropocene Age of Man" by Elizabeth Kolbert, *National Geographic* 219, no. 3 (March 2011), 60–86; quotation 77.

35. *Revolutions that Made the Earth*, Tim Lenton & Andrew Watson (Oxford: University of Oxford Press, 2011).

36. Tom Griffiths, "The Humanities and an Environmentally Sustainable Australia," *Australian Humanities Review*, Issue 43 (December 2007), 2.

37. Jacob Bronowksi quoted in Griffiths, ibid., 2. See also Jacob Bronowski, *The Ascent of Man* (Boston: Little, Brown & Co, 1973), 364.

38. Ambrose Bierce, *The Devil's Dictionary* (New York: Neale, 1911).

39. Al Gore, "Growing beyond Green," *San Antonio Express*: speech delivered at the 2007 National Convention for the American Institute of Architects, San Antonio, Texas, May 5, 2007.

40. Al Gore, *Earth in the Balance: Ecology and the Human Spirit* (Boston: Rodale Books, 1992), 204–5.

41. Donella H. Meadows, Dennis Meadows & Jørgen Randers, *Limits to Growth: The 30 Year Update* (Post Mills, VT: Chelsea Green Publishing, 2004), 269.

42. See Paul Ehrlich & Donald Kennedy, "Millennium Assessment of Human Behavior," *Science* 309, no. 5734 (July 22, 2005), 562–563.

Bibliography

~

Abram, David. *The Spell of the Sensuous: Perception and Language in a More-than-Human World*. New York: Vintage, 1996.

Abram, David. "On the Ecological Consequences of Alphabetic Literacy: Reflections in the Shadow of Plato's PHAEDRUS." Aisling Magazine 32, accessible at http://www .aislingmagazine.com/aislingmagazine/articles/TAM32/ethical/davidabram.html.

Abrams, M. H. "Art-as Such: The Sociology of Modern Aesthetics." *Bulletin of the American Academy of Arts and Sciences* 38, 6: 8–33.

Achebe, C. "The Role of the Writer in a New Nation." In *African Writers on African Writing*, Ed. G. D. Killam. London: Heinemann, 1978.

Adair, James. *The History of the American Indians*. London: Edward & Charles Dilly, 1775.

Adamson, Joni. *American Indian Literature, Environmental Justice and Ecocriticism*. Tucson: University of Arizona, 2001.

Albanese, Catherine L. *Reconsidering Nature Religion*. Harrisburg, Pennsylvania: Trinity Press International, 2002.

Allen, Chadwick. *Blood Narrative: Indigenous Identity in American Indian and Maori Literary and Activist Texts*. Durham: Duke University Press, 2002.

Ambler, Marjane. "On Reservations: No Haste, No Waste." *Planning* 57, no. 11 (Nov. 1991): 26–29.

Andersen, L. E., C. W. J. Granger, E. J. Reis, D. Weinhold, and S. Wunder. *The Dynamic of Deforestation and Economic Growth in the Brazilian Amazon*. Cambridge: Cambridge University Press, 2002.

Apess, William. *A Son of the Forest: The Experience of William Apes, A Native of the Forest, Comprising a Notice of the Pequod Tribe of Indians, Written by Himself*. New York: By the author. 1829. Revised as *A Son of the Forest: the Experience of William Apess, A Native of the Forest*. New York: By the author, G. F. Bunce, Printer, 1831.

Arens, W. *The Man Eating Myth: Anthropology and Anthropophagy*. Oxford: Oxford University Press, 1979.

Auden, W. H. *The Age of Anxiety: A Baroque Eclogue*. London: Faber & Faber, 1948.

Aughterson, Kate. *The English Renaissance*. London: Routledge, 1998.

Awiakta, Marilou. *Selu: Seeking the Corn-Mother's Wisdom*. Golden, Colorado: Fulcrum Publishing, 1993.

Bacevich, A. J. *American Empire: The Realities and Consequences of U.S. Diplomacy*. Cambridge: Cambridge University Press, 2002.

Bachofen, Johann Jakob. 1997 (original 1861). *Das Mutterrecht*. Suhrkamp. *Mother Right: A Study of the Religious and Juridicial Aspects of Gynecocracy in the Ancient World*. Lampeter: Edwin Mellen Press, 2006.

Bacon, Francis. *Works*. Ed. James Spedding, Robert L. Ellis, Douglas D. Heath. 14 vols. London: Longmans Green, 1870.

Bacon, Francis. *The Philosophy of Francis Bacon*. Ed. and trans. Benjamin Farrington. Liverpool: Liverpool University Press, 1964.

Bancroft, George. *The History of the United States from the Discovery of Continent*, 10 vols. Boston: Little, Brown & Co., 1834–75.

Barker, Francis, Peter Hulme, and Margaret Iversen. *Cannibalism and the Colonial World*. Cambridge: Cambridge University Press, 1998.

Basso, Keith H. *Wisdom Sits in Places: Landscape and Language among the Western Apache*. Albuquerque: University of New Mexico Press, 1996.

Beck, Peggy V., Anna Lee Walters, and Nia Franscisco. *The Sacred: Ways of Knowledge, Sources of Life*. Tsaile, Arizona: Navajo Community College Press, 1992.

Bell, C. *Ritual Theory, Ritual Practice*. Oxford: Oxford University Press, 1992.

Berry, Wendell. *Home Economics*. San Francisco: North Point, 1987.

Berkeley, Edmund and Dorothy Smith Berkeley. *The Correspondence of John Bartram, 1734–1777*. Gainsville: University Press of Florida, 1992.

Berkhofer, Robert F. Jr. *The White Man's Indian: Images of the American Indian From Columbus to the Present*. New York: Vintage Books, 1979.

Berlo, Janet C. and Ruth B. Phillips. *Native North American Art*. Oxford: Oxford University Press, 1998.

Bernheimer, Richard. *Wild Men in the Middle Ages: A Study in Art, Sentiment, and Demonology*. Cambridge: Harvard University Press, 1952.

Berry, Wendell. *Home Economics*. San Francisco: North Point, 1987.

Bierce, Ambrose. *The Devil's Dictionary*. New York: Neale, 1911.

Bierwert, Crusca. "Remembering Chief Seattle: Reversing Cultural Studies of a Vanishing Native American Author(s)." *American Indian Quarterly* 22, no. 3 (Summer 1998): 280–304.

Blu, Karen I. *The Lumbee Problem: The Making of an American Indian People*. Lincoln: University of Nebraska Press, 2001.

Bright, William. *Native American Placenames of the United States*. Norman: University of Oklahoma Press, 2004.

Brockway, Lucile H. "Science and Colonial Expansion: The Role of British Royal Botanic Gardens." *American Ethnologist* 6, no. 3 (Aug. 1979): 449–65.

Brody, Hugh. *Maps and Dreams: Indians and the British Columbia Frontier*. London: Faber & Faber, 1981.

Brody, J. J. *Indian Painters and White Patrons*. Albuquerque, NM: University of New Mexico Press, 1971.

Bronowski, Jacob. *The Ascent of Man*. Boston: Little, Brown & Co., 1973.

Bronte, Emily. *Wuthering Heights*. London: Thomas Cautley Newby, 1847.

Brook, Daniel. "Environmental Genocide: Native Americans and Toxic Waste." *American Journal of Economics and Sociology* 57, no. 1 (Jan. 1998): 105–13.

Bryson, Norman. *Vision and Painting: the Logic of the Gaze*. New York: Cambridge University Press, 1983.

Buell, Lawrence. *The Environmental Imagination: Thoreau, Nature Writing and the Formation of American Culture*. Cambridge, MA: Harvard University Press, 1995.

Bullard, Robert D. *Dumping in Dixie; Race, Class and Environmental Quality*. Boulder, CO: Westview Press, 1990.

Burch, Ernest. "Traditional Eskimo Societies on Northwest Alaska." *SENRI Ethnological Studies* 4 (1980): 253–304.

Burke, Edmund. *A Philosophical Enquiry into the Origin of Our Ideas of the Sublime and the Beautiful*. Ed. James T. Boulton, 1958. Notre Dame: University of Notre Dame Press, 1968.

Burns, Shirley Steward. *Bringing Down the Mountains: The Impact of Mountaintop Removal Surface Coal Mining on Southern West Virginia Communities, 1970–2004 (West Virginia and Appalachia)*. Chicago, IL: West Virginia Press, 2007.

Butler, Jon. "Jack-in-the-Box Faith: The Religion Problem in Modern American History." *The Journal of American History* (March 2004): 1357–78.

Castello, Lineu. *Rethinking the Meaning of Place; Conceiving Place in Architecture-Urbanism*. Surrey: Ashgate, 2010.

Castillo, Edward D., ed. "Petition to Congress on Behalf of the Yosemite Indians." *Journal of California Anthropology* 5, no. 2 (1979): 271–77.

Catlin, George. *North American Indians* (1832). Ed. Peter Matthiessen. New York: Penguin, 2004.

Cawardine, Richard J. *Lincoln*. London: Longman, 2003.

Clifford, James. *The Predicament of Culture: Twentieth-Century Ethnography, Literature, and Art*. Cambridge: Harvard University Press, 1988.

Coates, Peter. *Nature: Western Attitudes Since Ancient Times*. Cambridge: Polity Press, 1998.

Coates, Peter. *Salmon*. Chicago: University of Chicago Press, 2006.

Coates, Peter. *American Perceptions of Immigrant and Invasive Species: Strangers on the Land*. Berkeley: University of California Press, 2006.

Cohen, Michael P. *The Pathless Way: John Muir and American Wilderness*. Madison: University of Wisconsin Press, 1984.

Collier, Paul. *The Bottom Billion*. Oxford: Oxford University Press, 2007.

Coltelli, Laura. *Winged Words: American Indian Writers Speak*. Lincoln: University of Nebraska Press, 1990.

Columbus, Christopher. *The Four Voyages*. Trans. and ed. Walter Cohen. New York: Penguin Books, 1969.

Columbus, Christopher. *The Voyages of Christopher Columbus*. Ed. Cecil Jane. London: Hakluyt Society, 1930.

Cooper, Laurence. *Rousseau, Nature & the Problem of the Good Life*. University Park, PA: The Pennsylvania State University Press, 1999.

Cornell, Stephen. *The Return of the Native: American Indian Political Resurgence*. New York: Oxford University Press, 1988.

Cronon, William, ed. *Uncommon Ground: Rethinking the Human Place in Nature*. New York: W.W. Norton & Company, 1996, 1995.

Darlington, William M., ed. *Christopher Gist's Journals*. New York: Argonaut Press, 1966.

Davies, Philip and Iwan Morgan, eds. *America's Americans: Population Issues in U.S. Society and Politics*. London: Institute for the Study of the Americas, 2007.

Day, J. C. "Population Projections of the United States by Age, Sex, Race and Hispanic Origin: 1993–2050." *Current Population Report*. Washington, DC: U.S. Bureau of the Census (1993): 25–110.

DeCora, Angel. "Native Indian Art." In Report of the Executive on the Proceedings of the First Annual Conference of the Society of American Indians Held at the University of Ohio, Columbus, Ohio—October 12–17, 1911, 1: 82–87. Washington, DC: Society of American Indians, 1912.

DeGregori, Thomas R. *The Environment, Our Natural Resources, and Modern Technology*. Ames, Iowa: Iowa State Press, 2002.

Deleuze, G. and F. Guattari. *A Thousand Plateaus: Capitalism and Schizophrenia*. Trans. B. Massumi. London: Continuum, 2004 [first published as *Mille Plateaux*, vol. 2 of *Capitalisme et Schizophrénie*, Paris: Minuit, 1980].

Deloria, Vine, Jr. *Custer Died for Your Sins: An Indian Manifesto*. Macmillan, 1969.

Deloria, Vine, Jr. *The World We Used to Live In: Remembering the Powers of the Medicine Men*. Golden, CO: Fulcrum Publishing, 2006.

De Madariaga Mathews, Nieves H. *Francis Bacon: The History of a Character Assassination*. New Haven, CT: Yale University Press, 1996.

Denevan, William M., ed. *The Native Population of the Americas in 1492*. Madison: University of Wisconsin Press, 1976.

Diamond, Jared. *Collapse: How Societies Choose to Succeed or Fail*. New York: Viking, 2003.

Diamond, Stanley. *In Search of the Primitive: A Critique of Civilization*. New Brunswick: Transaction Publishers, 1974.

Dippie, Brian W. *The Vanishing American: White Attitudes and U.S. Indian Policy*. Middletown, CT: Wesleyan University Press, 1982.

Dobyns, Henry F. "Estimating Aboriginal American Population: An Appraisal of Techniques with a New Hemispheric Estimate." *Current Anthropology*, 7 (1966): 395–416.

Dobyns, Henry F. *Their Number Became Thinned: Native American Population Dynamics in Eastern North America*. Knoxville: University of Tennessee Press, 1983.

Drayton, Richard. *Nature's Government: Science, Imperial Britain, and the 'Improvement' of the World*. New Haven: Yale University Press, 2000.

Drinnon, Richard. *Facing West: The Metaphysics of Indian Hating and Empire Building*. New York: Meridian, 1980.

Dudley, Edward and Maximillian E. Novak, eds. *The Wild Man Within: An Image in Western Thought from the Renaissance to Romanticism*. Pittsburgh: University of Pittsburgh Press, 1972.

Dufrene, Phoebe "A Response to Mary Erikson: It is Time to Redefine 'Western' and 'Non-Western' Art or When Did Egypt Geographically Shift to Europe and Native Americans Become Non-Western." *Studies in Art Education* 35, no. 4 (Summer 1994).

Durkheim, Emile. "L'Origine du marriage dans l'espèce humanine, d'apres Westermarck." *Revue Philosophique* XL: 606–23.

Editors. *A Basic Call to Consciousness, Akwesasne Notes*. New York: Mohawk Nation via Rooseveltown, 1978.

Ehrlich, Paul and Donald Kennedy. "Millennium Assessment of Human Behavior." *Science* 309, no. 5734 (July 22, 2005): 562–63.

Ellingson, Terry. *The Myth of the Noble Savage*. Berkeley, CA: University of California Press, 2001.

Ember, Melvin. "Statistical Evidence for an Ecological Explanation of Warfare." *American Anthropologist*, 84 (Sept. 3, 1982): 645–49.

Errington, Shelly. "What Became of Authentic Primitive Art?" *Cultural Anthropology* 9, no. 2 (May 1994): 201–26.

Essays Honoring Lawrence C. Wroth. Portland, Maine: Anthoensen Press, 1940.

Evans-Pritchard, E. E. *Nuer Religion*. Oxford: Clarendon Press, 1956.

Fabian, Johannes. *Time and the Other: How Anthropology Makes its Object*. New York: Columbia University Press, 1983.

Feld, Steven. "Voices of the Rainforest." *Public Culture*, 4, no. 1 (1991).

Feld, Steven and Keith H. Basso, eds. *Senses of Place* (Sch. Am. Res. Adv. Sem. Ser.), xii. Santa Fe: School of American Research Press, 1996.

Ferguson, Niall. *Colossus: The Rise and Fall of the American Empire*. London: Penguin Books, 2004.

Ferguson, Niall. *Empire: The Rise and Demise of the British World Order and Lessons for Global Power*. New York: Basic Books, 2003.

Fleck, Richard F. "John Muir's Evolving Attitudes Toward Native American Cultures." *American Indian Quarterly* 4, no. 1 (Feb. 1978): 19–31.

Fontana, David. *Psychology, Religion, and Spirituality*. Oxford: Blackwell, 2003.

Forbes, Jack. *Columbus and Other Cannibals: The Wétiko Disease of Exploitation, Imperialism and Terrorism*. New York: Autonomedia, 1992.

Force, Peter. Tracts and Other Papers, Relating Principally to the Origin, Settlement and Progress of the Colonies in North America, From the Discovery of the Country to the Year 1776. 4 vols. Washington, DC: P. Force, 1836–46.

Ford, Paul Leicester. *The Writings of Thomas Jefferson*, 10 vols. New York: G. P. Putnam & Sons 1892–99.

Förster-Nietzsche, Elisabeth. *Nachgelassene Werke, Nietzsches Werke*, ed. Leipzig, 1903.

Fradkin, Philip L. *Everett Ruess: His Short Life, Mysterious Death and Astonishing Afterlife*. Berkeley: University of California Press, 2011.

Frank, Jerome D. and Jon C. Rivard. "Antinuclear Admirals—An Interview Study." *Political Psychology* 7, no. 1 (1986): 23–52.

Freud, Sigmund. (1927). *Future of an Illusion*. London: Hogarth Press (in vol. 19 of the Collected Works).

Garroute, Eva Marie. *Real Indians: Identity and the Survival of Native America*. Berkeley: University of California Press, 2003.

Gat, Azar. "The Pattern of Fighting in Simple, Small-Scale, Prestate Societies." *Journal of Anthropological Research* 55, no. 4 (Winter, 1999): 563–83.

Gatta, John. *Making Nature Sacred: Literature, Religion and Environment in America from the Puritans to the Present*. Oxford: Oxford University Press, 2004.

Gaukroger, Stephen. *The Emergence of Scientific Culture: Science and the Shaping of Modernity, 1210–1685.* New York: Clarendon Press of Oxford University Press, 2006.

Gedicks, Al. *The New Resource Wars: Native and Environmental Struggles against Multinational Corporations.* Boston: South End Press, 1993.

Gephart, R. E. and R. E. Lundgren. *Hanford Tank Clean-up: A Guide to Understanding the Technical Issues.* Columbus, OH: Battelle Press, 1998.

Gerbi, Antonello. *Nature in the New World: From Christopher Columbus to Gonzalo Fernández de Oviedo.* Pittsburgh, PA: University of Pittsburgh Press, 1985.

Gibson, Charles, ed. *The Spanish Tradition in America.* New York: Harper & Row, 1968.

Giddens, Anthony. *The Politics of Climate Change*, 2nd ed. [2009]. London: Polity, 2011.

Gill, Sam. *Mother Earth: An American Story.* Chicago: University of Chicago Press, 1991.

Gilpin, William. *Three Essays: On Picturesque Beauty; on Picturesque Travel; and on Sketching Landscape.* London, 1803.

Goldstein, Inge F. and Martin Goldstein. *How Much Risk? A Guide to Understanding Environmental Health Hazards.* Oxford: Oxford University Press, 2002.

Gore, Al. *Earth in the Balance: Ecology and the Human Spirit.* Boston: Rodale Books, 1992.

Green, Thomas Hill and Thomas Hodge Grose, eds. *David Hume, The Philosophical Works.* Vol. 3. Darmstadt, Germany: Scientia Verlag Aalen, 1964.

Griffiths, Tom."The Humanities and an Environmentally Sustainable Australia," *Australian Humanities Review*, Issue 43 (December 2007): 1–10. http://www.australian humanitiesreview.org/archive/Issue-December-2007/EcoHumanities/EcoGriffiths.html (accessed October 6, 2010).

Griswold, Jerry. *Audacious Kids: Coming of Age in America's Classic Children's Books.* Oxford: Oxford University Press, 1992.

Habermas, Jürgen. "A review of Gadamer's Truth and Method." In *Hermeneutics and Modern Philosophy*. Brice R. Wachterhauser, ed. (F. Dallmayr and T. McCarthy, trans.). Albany: State University of New York Press, 1986.

Haines, Michael R. and Richard H. Steckel, eds. *A Population History of North America.* Cambridge: Cambridge University Press, 2000.

Hapiuk, William J. Jr. "Of Kitsch and Kachinas: A Critical Analysis of the *Indian Arts & Crafts Act of 1990.*" *Stanford Law Review* 53, no. 4 (April 2001): 1009–75.

Hames, Raymond. "The Ecologically Noble Savage Debate." *Annual Review of Anthropology* 36 (2007): 177–90.

Harrison Julia D., Ruth Holmes Whitehead, Ruth B. Phillips, Ted J. Brasser, Judy Thompson, Bernadette Driscoll, and Martine J. Reid. *The Spirit Sings: Artistic Traditions of Canada's First Peoples.* Toronto: McClelland & Stewart, 1987.

Harvey, David. *The Condition of Postmodernity: An Enquiry into the Origins of Cultural Change.* Oxford: Basil Blackwell, 1989.

Harvey, David. *The New Imperialism.* Oxford: Oxford University Press, 2003.

Hedin, Robert and Gary Holthaus, eds. *Alaska: Reflections on Land and Spirit.* Tucson: The University of Arizona Press, 1989.

Heidegger, Martin. *Building Dwelling Thinking.* In *Martin Heidegger: Basic Writings*, D. F. Krell, ed. 319–39. New York: Harper & Row, 1977.

Heidegger, Martin. *Letter on Humanism.* In *Martin Heidegger: Basic Writings*, ed., D. F. Krell, 319–39. New York: Harper & Row, 1977, 193–242.

Hessel, Dieter. *After Nature's Revolt: Eco-Justice and Theology*. Philadelphia: Fortress Press, 1992.

Hessel, Dieter. *Theology for Earth Community: A Field Guide*. Maryknoll: Orbis Books, 1996.

Hobson, Geary, ed. *The Remembered Earth: An Anthology of Contemporary American Indian Literature*. Albuquerque: University of New Mexico Press, 1980.

Holm, Bill. *Northwest Coast Indian Art*. Washington: University of Washington Press, 1965.

Holroyd, Michael *Bernard Shaw: The Lure of Fantasy*, vol. 3. New York: Random House, 1991.

hooks, bell. *Black Looks: Race and Representations*. Boston: South End, 1992.

Horkheimer, Max and Theodor Adorno, *Dialectic of Enlightenment*, 1944. New York: Continuum, 1993.

Houston, James. "Contemporary Art of the Eskimo." *The Studio* 147 (February 1954).

Hoxie, Frederick E. "Ethnohistory for a Tribal World." *Ethnohistory* 44, no. 4 (Autumn, 1997): 599–600 [article: 595–615].

Hubert H. and M. Mauss. *Sacrifice: Its Nature & Function* [1899], 1964.

Hutchinson, Elizabeth. *The Indian Craze: Primitivism, Modernism, and Transculturation in American Art, 1890–1915*. Durham: Duke University Press, 2009.

Hutton, Ronald. *Shamans: Siberian Spirituality and the Western Imagination*. London: Hambledon, 2001.

Ingberman, Jeannette et al. *Jimmie Durham: The Bishop's Moose and the Pinkerton Men*. New York: EXIT Art, 1989.

Ingold, Tim. *Being Alive: Essays on Movement, Knowledge and Description*. London: Routledge, 2011.

Ingold, Tim, David Riches, and James Woodburn eds. *Hunter-Gatherers: Property, Power and Ideology*. New York: St Martin's Press, 1988.

Ishiyama, Noriko. "Nevada Test Site and Yucca Mountain: The Construction of Nuclear Space and Racism." *The American Review* Issue 42 (2008): 57–76 (published in Japanese).

Jaimes, M. Annette, ed. *The State of Native America: Genocide, Colonization, and Resistance*. Boston: South End Press, 1992.

Jennings, Francis. *The Invasion of America: Indians, Colonialism and the Cant of Conquest*. New York: Norton, 1975.

Johansen, Bruce E. *The Dirty Dozen: Toxic Chemicals and the Earth's Future*. Westport, CN: Praeger, 2003.

Johansen, Bruce E. "The High Cost of Uranium Mining on Navajoland." (Spring, 1997), 2, 2 *Akwesasne Notes New Series*, 10–12.

Johansen, Bruce E. and Donald Grinde. *Ecocide of Native America: Environmental Destruction of Indian Lands and Peoples*. Santa Fe, NM: Clear Light Publishers, 1995.

Johnson, Allen W. and Timothy Earle. *The Evolution of Human Societies: From Forgaing Group to Agrarian State*, 2nd ed. Stanford, CA: Stanford University Press, 2000.

Jones, Hugh. *The Present State of Virginia*. ed. Richard L. Morton, 1724; rpt. Chapel Hill, NC, 1956.

Jones, Karen R. and John Wills. *The Invention of the Park: From the Garden of Eden To Disney's Magic Kingdom*. Cambridge: Polity, 2005.

Jones, William A. *Annual Report of the Commissioner of Indian Affairs to the Secretary of the Interior*. Washington, DC: Government Printing Office, 1900.

Joralemon, Donald. "New World Depopulation and the Case of Disease." *Journal of Anthropological Research* 38 (1982): 108–27.

Judkins, Russell A., ed. *Iroquois Studies: A Guide to Documentary and Ethnographic Resources from Western New York and the Genesee Valley*. Department of Anthropology, State University of New York and Geneseo Foundation, 1987.

Jung, Kant, Immanuel. *Observations on the Feeling of the Beautiful and Sublime*. 1764, trans. John T. Goldthwait. Berkeley: University of California Press, 1960.

Kamps, Kevin. "High Level Atomic Waste Dump Targeted at Skull Valley Goshute Indian Reservation in Utah." Nuclear Information and Resource Service, prepared Feb. 15, 2001. Accessed 14/12/2010 at http://www.nirs.org/factsheets/pfsejfactsheet.htm.

Kant, Immanuel. *Critique of Judgement*. Trans. J. Creed Meredith [1790]. Oxford: Oxford University Press, 1978.

Keenan, Dennis King. *The Question of Sacrifice*. Bloomington & Indianapolis: Indiana University Press, 2005.

Keister, L. A. *Getting Rich: America's New Rich and How They Got That Way*. Cambridge: Cambridge University Press, 2005.

Keller, Robert and Michael Turek. *American Indians and National Parks*. Tucson: University of Arizona Press, 1998.

Kincaid, Jamaica. *My Garden (Book)*. New York: Farrar, Strauss and Giroux, 1999.

King, C. Richard. "The (Mis)uses of Cannibalism in Contemporary Cultural Critique." *Diacritics* 30, no. 1 (Spring, 2000): 106–23.

King, Thomas. *Green Grass, Running Water*. Boston: Houghton Mifflin, 1993.

Koch, Adrienne and William Peden, eds. *The Life and Selected Writings of Thomas Jefferson*. New York: Random House, 1944.

Koertge, Noretta, ed. *A House Built on Sand: Exposing Postmodernist Myths About Science*. Oxford: Oxford University Press, 1998.

Kohlhoff, Dean. *Amchitka and the Bomb: Nuclear Testing in Alaska*. Washington: University of Washington Press, 2003

Kollin, Susan. "The Wild, Wild North: Nature Writing, Nationalist Ecologies and Alaska." *American Literary History* 12, no. 1/2 (Spring-Summer, 2000): 41–78.

Krakhauer, Jon. *Into the Wild*. New York: Pan Books, 1998.

Krech, Shepard. *The Ecological Indian: Myth and History*. New York: Norton, 1999.

Krell, David Farrell. *Martin Heidegger: Basic Writings*. New York: Harper & Row, 1977.

Kroeber, Alfred L. *Cultural and Natural Areas of Native North America*. Berkeley: University of California Press, 1939.

Kroeber, Alfred L. "Native American Population." *American Anthropologist* 36, no.1 (1934): 1–25.

Krupat, Arnold. *The Turn to the Native: Studies in Criticism and Culture*. Lincoln: University of Nebraska Press, 1996.

Krupat, Arnold. *All That Remains: Varieties of Indigenous Expression*. Lincoln: University of Nebraska Press, 2009.

Kuehls, Thom. *Beyond Sovereign Territory: The Space of Ecopolitics*. Minneapolis: University of Minnesota Press, 1996.

Kuhn, Thomas. *The Structure of Scientific Revolutions*. Chicago: University of Chicago Press, 1970.

Kuletz, Valerie L. *The Tainted Desert: Environmental and Social Ruin in the American West.* New York: Routledge, 1998.

Kuper, Adam. *The Reinvention of Primitive Society.* London: Routledge, 2005.

Lach, Donald R. *Asia in the Making of Europe: The Century of Discovery.* Chicago: University of Chicago Press, vol. 1, book 1, 1965.

LaDuke, Winona. *All Our Relations: Native Struggles for Land and Life.* Cambridge, MA: South End Press, 1999.

Lahontan, Louis Armand de Lom d'Arce, Baron de. *New Voyages to North-America.* 2 vols. Ed. Reuben Gold Thwaites. Chicago: A. C. McClurg, 1905.

Lane, Joseph H. and Rebecca R. Clark. "The Solitary Walker in the Political World: The Paradoxes of Rousseau and Deep Ecology." *Political Theory* 34, no. 1 (Feb. 2006): 62–94.

Lears, T. J. Jackson. *No Place of Grace: Antimodernism and the Transformation of American Culture 1880–1920.* New York: Pantheon Books, 1981.

Lenton, Tim and Andrew Watson. *Revolutions that Made the Earth.* Oxford: University of Oxford Press, 2011.

Lewis, C. S. *Studies In Words.* Cambridge: Cambridge University Press, 1960.

Lewis, Merrill. "Organic Metaphor and Edenic Myth in George Bancroft's History of the United States." *Journal of the History of Ideas* 26 (Oct.–Dec. 1965): 587–92.

Lewis, R. W. B. *The American Adam: Innocence, Tragedy, and Tradition in the Nineteenth Century.* Chicago: University of Chicago Press, 1955.

Limerick, Patricia Nelson. *The Legacy of Conquest: the Unbroken Past of the American West.* New York: W.W. Norton & Co., 1987.

Lips, Julius E. *The Savage Hits Back or the White Man through Native Eyes.* Introduction by Bronislaw Malinowski. Translated from the German (by Vincent Benson). New Haven: Yale University Press, 1937.

Lippard, Lucy R. and Rina Swentzell. "In and Out of the Swirl: A Conversation on Community, Art and Life." *Parallaxis.* Santa Fe, NM: Western States Arts Federation, 1996.

Locke, John. *The Second Treatise on Government,* 1690. In *Two Treatises of Government by John Locke,* edited by Peter Laslett. Cambridge: Cambridge University Press, 2005.

Lorenz, Konrad. *On Aggression.* London: Methuen, 1966.

Lynes, Russell. *The Tastemakers.* New York: Grosset & Dunlap, 1949.

MacCannell, Dean. *Empty Meeting Grounds: The Tourist Papers.* New York: Routledge, 1992.

McKibben, Bill. *Eaarth: Making Life on a Tough Planet.* New York: Times Books, 2011.

Maloney, Thomas S. "The Extreme Realism of Roger Bacon." *Review of Metaphysics* 38 (June 1985): 807–37.

Martin, Calvin. *Keepers of the Game: Indian-Animal Relationships and the Fur Trade.* Berkeley: University of California Press, 1978.

Martin, Calvin. *The American Indian and the Problem of History.* Oxford: Oxford University Press, 1987.

Martinez, David. "The Soul of the Indian: Lakota Philosophy and the Vision Quest." *Wicazo Sa Review* 19, no. 2 (Fall, 2004).

Marx, Karl. *Karl Marx and Frederick Engels, Selected Works.* New York: International Publishers, 1984.

Meadows, Donella H., Dennis Meadows, and Jørgen Randers. *Limits to Growth: The 30 Year Update*. Post Mills, VT: Chelsea Green Publishing, 2004.

Merchant, Carolyn. "The Scientific Revolution and *The Death of Nature*." *Isis* 97 (2006): 513–33.

Meyer, Leroy N. "In Search of Native American Aesthetics." *Journal of Aesthetic Education* 35, no. 4 (Winter 2001): 25–46.

McCandless, Christopher. *Back to the Wild*, n.a.: Twin Star Press, 2011.

McCardle, Kevin. "What Makes a Vista Scenic?" *History, Architecture and Landscape* 1, no. 1 (Winter 2011): 12–13.

McDougall, W. *An Introduction to Social Psychology*. London: Methuen, 30th ed., 1950.

McDougall, Walter A. *Promised Land, Crusader State: The American Encounter with the World Since 1776*. Boston: Houghton Mifflin, 1997.

McElvaine, Robert S. *The Great Depression: America 1929–1941*. New York: Times Books, 1984.

McLachlan, Ian. "Making *Mizzins*—Remaking History: The Columbus Project of Carl Beam." *Artscraft* 2, no. 2 (Summer, 1990): 10–12.

McLennan, John. *Primitive Marriage*. Chicago: University of Chicago Press (1865), 1970.

Mintz, Sidney. *Sweetness and Power: The Place of Sugar in Modern History*. New York: Viking, 1985.

Mizruchi, Susan L. *The Science of Sacrifice: American Literature and Modern Social Theory*. Princeton, NJ: Princeton University Press, 1998.

Mooney, James. *The Aboriginal Population of America North of Mexico*. Smithsonian Miscellaneous Collections 80, no. 7. Washington, DC: Smithsonian Institution, 1928.

Morgan, Lewis Henry. *Ancient Society or Researches on the Lines of Human Progress from Savagery through Barbarism to Civilization*. London: MacMillan & Co., 1877.

Muir, John. *Our National Parks*. Madison: University of Wisconsin Press [1901], 1981.

Myers, Norman. "The Hamburger Connection: How Central America's Forests Became North America's Hamburgers." *Ambio* 10: 3–8, 1981.

Myres, John L. "The Influence of Anthropology on the Course of Political Science," *University of California Publications in History*. Berkeley, vol. 4, no. 1, 1916.

National Academy of Sciences/National Academy of Engineering. "Rehabilitation Potential of Western Coal Lands." *Report to the Energy Policy Project of the Ford Foundation*, draft document. Washington DC: Ford Foundation, 1973.

Nelson, Robert M. *Place and Vision: The Function of Landscape in Native American Fiction*. New York: Peter Lang AG, 1993.

Neuman, Lisa K. "Painting Culture: Art and Ethnography at a School for Native Americans." *Ethnology* 45, no. 3 (Summer, 2006): 173–92.

Ngũgĩ wa Thiong'o. *Decolonizing the Mind: The Politics of Language in African Literature*. London: James Curry, 1986.

Nicolson, Marjorie Hope. *Mountain Gloom and Mountain Glory: The Development of the Aesthetics of the Infinite*. New York: W.W. Norton, 1959.

Nielsen, N. C., N. Hein, F. E. Reynolds, A. L. Miller, S. E. Karff, A. C. Cowan, P. McLean, and T. P. Erdel, *Religions of the World*. New York: St. Martin's Press, 2nd ed., 1988.

Norton, Michael I. and Dan Ariely. "Building a Better America—One Wealth Quintile at a Time." *Perspectives on Psychological Science*, 2010. Accessed on 22/11/2010 at http://www.people.hbs.edu/mnorton/norton%20ariely%20in%20press.pdf.

Oberg, Michael Leroy. *Dominion and Civility: English Imperialism and Native America, 1585–1685*. Ithaca: Cornell University Press, 1999.

O'Connell, Robert L. *Of Arms & Men: A History of War, Weapons and Aggression*. New York: Oxford University Press, 1989.

O'Doherty, Brian. *White Cube: The Ideology of the Gallery Space*. San Francisco: Lapis Press, 1986.

Office of the Inspector General, Evaluation Report. *Tribal Superfund Program Needs Clear Direction and Actions to Improve the Tribal Superfund Program* (Report No. 2004-P-0035, Sept. 30, 2004) at 2, available at www.epa.gov/oig/reports/2004/20040930 -2004-P-00035.pdf.

O'Grady, John P. *Pilgrims to the Wild: Everett Ruess, Henry David Thoreau, John Muir, Clarence King, Mary Austin*. Salt Lake City: University of Utah Press, 1993.

Ortiz, Simon J. *Woven Stone*. Tucson: University of Arizona Press, 1992.

Parenti, Michael. *Democracy for the Few*, 6th ed. New York: St. Martin's Press, 1995.

Parker, Arthur C. "Museum Motives Behind the New York Arts Project." *Indians at Work* 2, no. 15 (June1935): 11–12.

Pesic, Peter. "Wrestling with Proteus: Francis Bacon and the 'Torture' of Nature." *Isis* 90 (1999): 81–94.

Pinker, Steven. *The Better Angels of Our Nature: the Decline of Violence in History and Its Causes*. London: Allen Lane, 2011.

Pocock, John Greville Agard. *Barbarism and Religion. Volume II. Narratives of Civil Government*. Cambridge: Cambridge University Press, 1999.

Pollan, Michael. *Second Nature: A Gardener's Education*. New York: Atlantic Monthly Press, 1991.

Porter, Joy. "Population Matters in Native America." In *America's Americans: Population Issues in U.S. Society and Politics*, Philip Davies & Iwan Morgan, eds. London: Institute for the Study of the Americas, University of London, School of Advanced Study, 2007.

Pratt, Mary Louise. *Imperial Eyes: Travel Writing and Transculturation*. London & New York: Routledge, 1992.

Pratt, Richard H. *Official Report of the Nineteenth Annual Conference of Charities and Correction* (1892), 46–59. Reprinted in Richard H. Pratt, "The Advantages of Mingling Indians with Whites," *Americanizing the American Indians: Writings by the "Friends of the Indian" 1880–1900*. Cambridge, MA: Harvard University Press, 1973, 260–71.

Preston, David L. *The Texture of Contact: European and Indian Settler Communities on the Frontiers of Iroquoia, 1667–1783*. Lincoln: University of Nebraska Press, 2009.

Princen, Thomas. *Treading Softly: Paths to Ecological Order*. Michigan: The MIT Press, 2010.

Purchas, Samuel. *Hakluytus Posthumus or Purchas his Pilgrimes: A History of the World in Sea Voyages . . .* , 20 vols. Glasgow, 1905–7.

Putnam, Robert. *Bowling Alone*. New York: Simon & Schuster, 2000.

Ramenofsky, Ann F. *Vectors of Death: The Archaeology of European Contact*. Albuquerque, NM: University of New Mexico Press, 1989.

Ratner-Rosenhagen, Jennifer. "Conventional Iconoclasm: The Cultural Work of the Nietzche Image in Twentieth-Century America." 93, no. 3 (2006): 728–54.

Rawson, Timothy. *Changing Tracks: Predators and Politics in Mt. McKinley National Park*. Fairbanks: University of Alaska Press, 2001.

Redford, K. H. "The Ecologically Noble Savage." *Cultural Survival Quarterly* 15, no. 1: 46–48, 1991.

Reich, Robert B. *Aftershock: The Next Economy and America's Future*. New York: Knopf, 2010.

Reith, Charles C. and Bruce M. Thomson. *Deserts as Dumps? The Disposal of Hazardous Materials in Arid Ecosystems*. Albuquerque: University of New Mexico Press, 1992.

Rensberger, Boyce. *The Cult of the Wild*. New York: Doubleday, 1977.

Robbins, Paul and Julie T. Sharp. "Producing and Consuming Chemicals: The Moral Economy of the American Lawn." *Economic Geography* 79, no. 4 (October, 2003): 425–51.

Roorda, Randall. *Dramas of Solitude: Narratives of Retreat in American Nature Writing*. Albany: SUNY Press, 1998.

Root, Deborah. *Cannibal Culture: Art, Appropriation, and the Commodification of Difference*. Boulder: Westview, 1996.

Rosenblat, Ángel. "El desarrollo de la población indígena de América." *Tierra Frime*. (1935), 1, no.1, 115–33; 1, no. 2, 117–48; 1, no. 3, 109–41.

Rosier, Paul C. *Serving Their Country: American Indian Politics and Patriotism in the Twentieth Century*. Cambridge, MA: Harvard University Press, 2009.

Rothman, Hal. *On Rims and Ridges: The Los Alamos Area Since 1880*. Lincoln: University of Oklahoma Press, 1992.

Rushing, W. Jackson III, ed. *Native American Art in the Twentieth Century*. New York: Routledge 1999.

Ruskin, John. *Sesame and Lilies: Two Lectures Delivered at Manchester in 1864*. London: Smith, Elder, 1865.

Sachs, Noah. "The Mescalero Apache Indians and Monitored Retrievable Storage of Spent Nuclear Fuel: A Study in Environmental Ethics." *Natural Resources Journal* 36 (1996): 881–912.

Sanborn, Margaret. *Yosemite: Its Discovery, Its Wonders and Its People*. Yosemite Association: Yosemite National Park, 1989.

Schlosser, Eric. *Fast Food Nation: The Dark Side of the All-American Meal*. Orlando, FL: Harcourt Mifflin Harcourt, 2001.

Schweninger, Lee. *Listening to the Land: Native American Literary Responses to the Landscape*. Athens: University of Georgia Press, 2008.

Serpell, James. *In the Company of Animals*. Oxford: Blackwell, 1986.

Shattuck, Roger. *Marcel Proust*. Princeton, NJ: Princeton Paperbacks, 1974.

Shepard, Paul. *Coming Home to the Pleistocene*. Washington, DC: Island Press, 1998.

Shepard, Paul. *Nature and Madness*. Athens: University of Georgia Press, 1982.

Shneidman, E. S., ed. *Death: Current Perspectives*. Palo Alto, California: Mayfield, 1976.

Shoemaker, Nancy. *American Indian Population Recovery in the Twentieth Century*. Albuquerque: University of New Mexico Press, 1999.

Shue, Henry. "Subsistence Emissions and Luxury Emissions." *Law and Policy* 15 (1993): 39–59.

Silko, Leslie Marmon. "Landscape, History, and the Pueblo Imagination." *Antaeus* 57 (Autumn, 1986): 83–94.

Silko, Leslie Marmon. *Yellow Woman and a Beauty of the Spirit: Essays on Native American Life Today*. New York: Simon, 1997.

Siting of Hazardous Waste Landfills and Their Correlation with Racial and Economic Status of Surrounding Communities. Washington, DC: U.S. Government Printing Office, 1983.

Skinner, B. F. ed. *Recent Issues in the Analysis of Behaviour.* Columbus, OH: Merrill, 1988.

Small, Gail. "War Stories: Environmental Justice in Indian Country." *The Amicus Journal* 16 (1994): 38–41.

Smith, Henry Nash. *Virgin Land: The American West as Symbol and Myth.* Cambridge: Cambridge University Press, 1978.

Smith, Theresa S. with Blake Debassige, Shirley Cheecho, James Simon Mishibinjima, and Leland Bell. "Beyond the Woodlands, Four Manitoulin Painters Speak Their Minds," *American Indian Quarterly* 18, no. 1 (Winter–Spring, January 1, 1994): 1–24.

Snyder, Gary. "Nature as Seen from Kitkitdizzie Is No 'Social Construction,'" *Wild Earth* 6, no. 4 (Winter, 1996/7): 1–4.

Sosin, Jack M. *Whitehall and the Wilderness: The Middle West in British Colonial Policy, 1760–1775.* Lincoln: University of Nebraska Press, 1961.

Spence, Mark D. *Dispossessing the Wilderness: Indian Removal and the Making of National Parks.* New York: Oxford University Press, 1999.

Speth, James. *The Bridge at the Edge of the World: Capitalism, the Environment, and Crossing from Crisis to Sustainability.* New Haven: Yale University Press, 2008.

Spilka, Bernard. "Spirituality: Problems and directions in operationalizing a fuzzy concept." Paper presented at the annual conference of the American Psychological Association, Toronto, Canada, August 23, 1993.

Staniszewski, M. *Believing Is Seeing: Creating the Culture of Art.* New York: Penguin, 1995.

Stannard, David E. *American Holocaust: The Conquest of the New World.* Oxford: Oxford University Press, 1993.

Steward, Julian H., ed. *Handbook of South American Indians,* vol. 5. Bureau of American Ethnology Bulletin no. 143. Washington, DC: Smithsonian Institution, 1949, 655–68.

Susman, Warren. *Culture as History: The Transformation of American Society in the Twentieth Century.* New York: Pantheon, 1984.

Sutter, Paul S. *Driven Wild: How the Fight Against the Automobile Launched the Modern Wilderness Movement.* Seattle: University of Washington Press, 2002.

Swann, Brian and Arnold Krupat, eds. *Recovering the Word: Essays on Native American Literature.* Berkeley, CA: University of California Press, 1987.

Sweet Wong, Hertha D., ed. *Louise Erdrich's* Love Medicine: *a Casebook.* Oxford: Oxford University Press, 2000.

Szabo, Joyce. "Individuality and Cultural History: The Question of Artistic Representation Imagery." *American Indian Art* Magazine 23, no. 4 (1998): 80–90.

Tagore, Rabindranath. *Sādhanā: The Realisation of Life.* New York: MacMillan, 1913.

Taleb, Nassim Nicholas. "Errors, Robustness and the Fourth Quadrant." *International Journal of Forecasting* 25, no. 4, 14 (February, 2009), available at SSRN: http://ssrn.com/abstract=1343042.

Taylor, Charles. *A Secular Age.* Cambridge: The Belknap Press of Harvard University, 2007.

Teachout, Terry. *The Skeptic: A Life of H. L. Mencken.* New York: Harper Collins, 2002.

Thomas, Keith. *Religion and the Decline of Magic.* New York: Charles Scribner's Sons, 1971.

Thornton, Russell. "Aboriginal North American Population and Rates of Decline, ca. AD 1500–1900." *Current Anthropology* 38, no. 2 (April 1997).

Thornton, Russell, Tim Miller, and Jonathan Warren. "American Indian Population Recovery Following Smallpox Epidemics." *American Anthropologist*, New Series 93, no. 1 (March 1991): 28–41.

Tillyard, Stella K. *The Impact of Modernism, 1900–1920: Early Modernism and the Arts & Crafts Movement in Edwardian England.* New York: Routledge, 1988.

Torgovnick, Marianna. "Making Primitive Art High Art." *Poetics Today* 10, no. 2, Art and Literature II (Summer, 1989): 299–328.

Trevor-Roper, Hugh. "The Past and Present: History and Sociology." *Past and Present* 42 (1969): 3–17.

Trump, Erek Krenzen. "The Indian Industries League and Its Support of American Indian Arts, 1893–1922: A Study of Changing Attitudes toward Indian Women and Assimilationist Policy." PhD dissertation, Boston University, 1996.

Tuan, Yi-Fu. *Space and Place: The Perspective of Experience.* Minneapolis: University of Minnesota, 1977.

Turner, Frederick Jackson. "The Significance of the Frontier in American History." *Report of the American Historical Association* (1893): 199–227.

Turner, Victor. "Sacrifice as Quintessential Process: Prophylaxis or Abandonment?" *History of Religion* 16: 3 (1977): 189–215.

Vandenbosch, Robert and Susanne E. Vandenbosch. *Nuclear Waste Stalemate.* Salt Lake City: University of Utah Press, 2007.

Vecsey, Christopher and Robert W. Venables, eds. *American Indian Environments: Ecological Issues in Native American Indian History.* Syracuse, NY: Syracuse University Press, 1980.

Vespucci Reprints, Texts, and Studies, vol. 5. Trans. George T. Northrup. Princeton: Princeton University Press, 1916.

Vigneras, L. A. Revision of translation by Cecil Jane. *The Journal of Christopher Columbus.* London: Hakluyt Society, 1960.

Voltaire. *Candide or Optimism.* Translated from the German of Dr. Ralph. Geneva: Cramer, 1759.

Wallace, Paul A. W. *Conrad Weiser: Friend of Colonist and Mohawk.* Philadelphia: University of Pennsylvania Press, 1945.

Waters, Tiffany. "Biometrics in Indian Country: The Bloody Fight for Authenticity." *Fourth World Journal: A Publication of the Center for World Indigenous Studies* 6, no. 1 (2005).

Weaver, Hilary N. "Indigenous Identity: What Is It and Who Really Has It?" *American Indian Quarterly* 25, no. 2 (Spring 2001): 240–55.

Weber, Max. *Max Weber: Essays in Society.* Trans. and ed. by H. H. Gerth & C. Wright Mills. New York: Oxford University Press, 1964.

Wehr, G. *Jung: A Biography.* Boston: Shambhala, 1987.

Weintraub, Irwin. "Fighting Environmental Racism: A Selected Annotated Bibliography." *Electronic Green Journal*, Issue 1 (June 1994). Accessed on 22/11/2010 at http://escholarship.org/uc/item/1qx663rf#page-1.

White, Lyn. Jr. (1968). "The Historical Roots of Our Ecologic Crisis." In L. T. White, *Machina Ex Deo: Essays in the Dynamism of Western Culture.* Cambridge, MA: MIT, 57–74.

West, Rebecca. *Black Lamb & Grey Falcon: A Journey Through Yugoslavia.* London: Penguin, 1944 (1941).

White, Richard. *The Middle Ground: Indians, Empires, and Republics in the Great Lakes Region, 1650–1815*. Cambridge: Cambridge University Press, 1991.

White, Richard and William Cronon. "Ecological Change and Indian-White Relations." In *History of Indian-White Relations*, ed. Wilcomb Washburn, 4 of *Handbook of North American Indians*, ed. William Sturtevant, Washington, DC: Smithsonian Institution, 1988, 417–29.

Williams, Raymond. *Keywords: A Vocabulary of Culture and Society*. Oxford: Oxford University Press, 1976.

Williams, Raymond. *Problems in Materialism and Culture*. London: Verso, 1980.

Williams, Teresa. "Pollution and Hazardous Waste on Indian Lands: Do Federal Laws Apply and Who May Enforce Them?" *American Indian Law Review* 17 (1992): 269–290.

Wilson, E. O. *The Future of Life*. New York: Vintage, 2002.

Winters, Yvor. *Forms of Discovery: Critical and Historical Essays on the Forms of the Short Poem in English*. Athens, Ohio: University of Ohio Press, 1967.

Wolff, E. N. "Recent trends in household wealth in the United States: Rising debt and the middle-class squeeze." *Working Paper No. 502*. Annandale-on-Hudson, NY: The Levy Economics Institute of Bard College.

Wolff, E. N. "Recent trends in household wealth in the United States: Rising debt and the middle-class squeeze—an update to 2007." *Working Paper No. 589*. Annandale-on-Hudson, NY: The Levy Economics Institute of Bard College.

Woolf, Virginia. "Mr Bennet and Mrs Brown." In *Collected Essays* 1 (New York: Harcourt, Brace & World, 1925), 319–37.

Worster, Donald. *Nature's Economy: A History of Ecological Ideas*. Cambridge: Cambridge University Press, 1985 [1977].

Wynne, B. *Rationality and Ritual: Participation and Exclusion in Nuclear Decisions*. London and Washington DC: Earthscan, 2010.

Wynne, B. "Risk and Environment as Legitimatory Discourses of Technology: Reflexivity Inside-Out." *Current Sociology* 20 (2002): 459–77.

Wynne, B. "Public Understanding and Communication of Science and Risk: What Do We Know?" *Journal of NIH Research* 15 (1991): 341–49.

Young Bear, Ray A. *Remnants of the First Earth*. New York: Grove Press, 1996.

Žižek, Slavoj. *Living in the End Times*. London: Verso, 2010.

Index

〜

Index

203

Wolff, Edward N., 92–93
Women and sexual relationships, 41–43
World resources, 91
Worster, Donald, 5
Writers of color, 110
Wynne, Brian, 102

Yakama Nation, 105
Yellowstone National Park, 12, 26
Yosemite National Park, 7, 12, 25–26;
former Indian country, 11; naming, 13,
14, 135 n.36; Olmsted designing, 11,
13–14, 29–30; Scenic Vista
Management Plan, 17; stories about
discovery, 17
Young Bear, Ray A., 51
Yowell, Raymond D., 105
Yucca Mountain, Nevada, 97–99,
100, 103

Žižek, Slavoj, 131, 170 n.2
Zuni peoples, 26

About the Author

JOY PORTER is Senior Lecturer & Associate Dean of the Faculty of Arts & Humanities at The University of Swansea, Wales, UK, author of *Native American Freemasonry: Associationalism and Performance in America* (University of Nebraska Press, 2011) and of *To Be Indian: The Life of Seneca-Iroquois Arthur Caswell Parker, 1881–1955* (University of Oklahoma Press, 2002), co-editor with Professor Kenneth Roemer (University of Texas, Arlington) of *The Cambridge Companion to Native American Literature* (University of Cambridge Press, 2005), editor of *Place and Indian History, Literature & Culture* for Peter Lang (2007), and co-author of *Competing Voices in Native America* (2009).